Confessions
of
a war bride

By Doris J. Paterson

Order this book online at www.trafford.com
or email orders@trafford.com

Most Trafford titles are also available at major online book retailers.

Printed in the United States of America.

ISBN: 978-1-4269-8958-2 (sc)

Library of Congress Control Number: 2011913920

Trafford rev. 08/10/2011

 www.trafford.com

North America & International
toll-free: 1 888 232 4444 (USA & Canada)
phone: 250 383 6864 ♦ fax: 812 355 4082

Dedicated to my angels,
who helped me on my jounrey

Front cover
Landed Immigrant, 1994
From *The Life Series*, acrylic and collage on paper
30 x 22 inches / 76.2 x 55.9 cm

Original owned by Yvonne Bonner & Greg Knowles
who are delighted with this choice for the cover

Landed Immigrant

The pull of what's safe, known
    and loved
    against the magnet
    of the new and possible.

Instead of my roles in theatre,
    our home will be my new stage.

My man waits for me.
    He is the gateway
    to new experience.

For now, doubts
    must stay quiet — I go
    through the doorway
    to new beginnings.

Doris Paterson, 1994

1:

My childhood in England

I was born on the 9th July 1924, in Gosport, near Portsmouth in England. A wrinkled, yellow-with-jaundice baby who was not pretty at all. When my father saw me, he said to my mother, "Surely she doesn't belong to us!"

My parents already had a little girl before I came on board. Her name was Peggy and she was born in Germany while my father Ernest, was in the English army and stationed in Germany. He was there in the army of occupation after World War I.

My mother, Kate, was a chef at a mansion owned by a German baroness and my father met her when the English soldiers requisitioned the mansion. My father was only twenty-one when they married, so, as the British army didn't give marriage allowances to soldiers until they were twenty-four years of age, their money was below subsistence level.

He was what we called a "scallywag," always making jokes and playing around and enjoying life to the full. My father was only seventeen when he joined the army. He came from a family who didn't attend church. During his registration as a soldier, he found himself in a long line-up of men who were approaching an officer sitting at a desk. The officer mumbled something which didn't make any sense to my father but as every man before him had replied "C of E, Sir", Dad did likewise.

When he was through, he asked another lad what "C of E" meant and was told Church of England. The officer had been asking what religion they belonged to. Because of that reply, our family became, and remained, members of the Church of England.

Ernest was sent back to England and Kate arrived a few months later in Gosport where they were married again but in a church. Kate gave her surname at the time as Parsons. We have no idea why, because her family name was Hampe. It must have been because anyone with a German name would be ostracized.

They were to stay for a while with my father's parents who lived in Sussex in a cold, field-stone house. Grandma was kind to Kate in spite of her nationality. But Kate found the house increased her sense of alienation. Often the wind howled like the howling of wolves around those walls till Kate thought she was going mad. She was pregnant with me.

One night she was sitting up late, unable to sleep with the noise of the wind. She looked up to see a face pressed to the window and she screamed and screamed; she thought it was a ghost but it was only my father, who had returned sooner than expected and was always joking around.

As soon as possible they moved to rent one room in a house in Gosport where I was born. The room had a fireplace and a shared bathroom down the hall. Peggy slept in a makeshift cot and I slept in a dresser drawer. The room was usually cold and father would walk down the rail-way tracks to find lumps of coal which had escaped from loaded railway wagons. They couldn't afford to buy any.

Ernest made up his mind to get out of poverty and become an engineer so he could earn a better salary. As he only had a grade five education and nowhere to study but in that small room, it meant my mother had to go for many walks with the children and constantly "shushed" us to stop crying or to keep quiet. She prayed for deliverance from such claustrophobic life.

He did it ! He got his engineer's papers and later, when he reached twenty-four years of age, the forces' marriage allowance came. They could now move into married quarters in Gosport.

I had the whooping cough when only three months old and my father gave me some porter (a strong beer) by tablespoons to calm the coughing. I nearly died — I went into convulsions and they had to send for the doctor who gave Dad a severe telling-off. No one sent for doctors in those days unless it was a matter of life and death. My father had no idea what he'd done until the doctor explained the peril he had put me under. The doctor stayed with me until I had passed the danger line and I slept for hours afterwards. My mother was often dismayed when my father took it upon himself to rectify a situation, thinking he knew the answer to everything. He took risks while she approached matters in a more mature way.

At four years of age, I was playing near a house when a piece of slate fell off the roof and as I looked up at the noise it made as it rattled down, it hit me on my right cheek and cut a gouge three inches long. I ran home, blood streaming down my face and my dress. My father picked me up, put me on the crossbar of his bike and rode me to the doctor's place.

"Don't cry now; be brave," he kept saying.

It took seven stitches to sew it together and I still have the scar. My father bought me some candy because I hadn't cried. I'm glad in a way that I have this scar because everyone was always saying: "It's all right for you because you're beautiful." I could say in return: "I'm not perfect because I have this scar right across my face."

I was four-and-a half when I went to first grade at school. I had blond hair in a pudding-bowl haircut and still wasn't pretty. Every morning the army lorry (truck) would stop outside the married quarters and I'd be helped to climb in the back with my sister Peggy to sit on wooden benches. The teacher was harsh and I was young to be in grade one, so when the teacher shouted, I wet my pants. Mother never shouted like that. It was horrendous to stand in the aisle and feel hot urine run down my legs to form a puddle on the floor. But in the future, I would recover from embarrassing situations because I now knew it wasn't the end of the world when this sort of thing happened..

Dad had a vegetable garden and when I went with him one day, he handed me what looked like a block of earth. "Here Doris," he said "you can grow your own mushrooms." And it was a miracle day when I saw lots of small white buttons appear on that block. I was so proud to take some home to Mother.

Daffodils in England are planted randomly to simulate natural settings. Adults know this but little girls don't. I picked an armful for Mother not knowing they were from the commanding officer's lawn.

"Where did you get them?" Mother asked with a worried look on her face and she sighed when I told her the area. I was taken upstairs, scrubbed clean and dressed in my blue Sunday dress then marched to the door of the commanding officer's house carrying the ill-gotten daffodils.

The colonel's wife was kindly when I handed over the golden bunch.

"Tell the lady you're sorry and you'll never do that again," Mother said

I cried because I had loved seeing those symbols of spring but it had turned out all wrong. I didn't think I should be sorry because the daffodils weren't fenced in and they were almost asking little girls to pick them.

Mother took Peggy and me to have tea with a Mrs.Staid. Mrs.Staid was the only person who talked with Mother. The lingering hatred of Germans simmered in English people and Mother was never free of it.

While they talked together, Mrs.Staid sensed Peggy and I were bored and told us to play in her daughter's room.

I can see them now, two very large china dolls about twenty inches high. One was white, dressed in a pale blue dress with white smocking and the other was black, wearing a pinafore dress printed with tiny flowers. I'd never seen a black doll and was enthralled with it. I gathered it into my arms and took her out to the garden. The garden path was made with flag-stones and I stumbled and fell.

It was with utter horror I stood looking at the shattered remains of the wonderful doll, the disconnected glass eyes stared up at me.

Peggy, Mrs.Staid and Mother came rushing to see what had happened. The daffodils I had picked would live again but the doll was gone forever. Worse for me was the look of despair on my mother's face: How could I have made Mother feel bad again because of something I had done?

South of Ireland (1929)

I was five years old when Dad was posted to the south of Ireland, close to Cork. I don't know why he was sent there, it could have had something to do with defences. The Irish hated the way the English had treated them on their own land throughout history and I never found out why we were tolerated in this outpost. We sailed from Wales on a boat which smelled of animals; the seas were choppy and I was sick.

When we arrived at the posting, we saw an old stone fort, looking like the illustrations of King Arthur's time. It was hugging the edge of a cliff, overlooking the sea. Dad took us close there sometimes. Weasels scurried amongst the stones and waves crashed against the rocks with a force to make us cower in fear. The passageways were dark and dank, smelling of rot. A short way off a foghorn moaned intermittently through the mist.

We lived in a bungalow-type hut and attended a school nearby. Dad worked from one of the army huts and there was a mess (club) for the men but nothing for the wives who lived at the post. Wives and families of the men in the forces were recorded as chattel. My dictionary gives the explanation of that word as: slave; bondsman; property of.

My mother sat by a black cast-iron stove in the evenings, darning socks or knitting, tears falling on the wool. My father loved the comradeship of the mess and the beer and would stay there while dinner got cold and Mother felt neglected. Sometimes he'd come home "tiddly" a common term for pretty well drunk.

By this time the family had increased with two boys — my brothers, Stanley and Gordon.

My mother had nobody to turn to. No escape route. In England, she was still considered "the enemy." And her father had told her that she was never to return to Germany if she ever married an enemy (English) soldier.

Even though I was just a child, I felt her unhappiness. As Peggy was older, Mother could talk a little to her and I knew they were close. I guessed that as I was "Daddy's favourite," they formed a bond without me. I sensed these things but I knew I shouldn't worry about it because I was loved by both mother and father and I went on in my Pollyanna way.

The teachers in that school were not dedicated to our learning and sometimes locked us out of the classroom, resulting in the fact that we had more play than school time. We told our parents about it. There was an investigation and new teachers arrived.

One teacher had a routine to gather us into a circle and ask if we had cleaned our teeth that morning. I didn't know how to lie and told her one day that I had not cleaned my teeth.

"All the children can enter the circle," she said, "except Doris. She's a lazy, dirty girl and will have to stay outside of the circle." She gave me a shoe box with some coal in it.

"Take this home to your mother and show her what your teeth will look like if you don't clean your teeth."

Oh! The pain of it.

I remember fishing off a pier with my father when the herring run came in. The water turned into a shivering silver sea and it was thrilling to catch a lot of fish.

Lots of wild donkeys roamed the fields. Some had been mistreated and had sores and bleeding cuts. They could be quite tame and one put his head in my open bedroom window one morning and "Hee-hawed," scaring the life out of me.

Even though small, I could tell the people in sod huts were poor. The squares of peat, taken from fields, were their source of heat, sending up thick grey smoke from the chimneys. But there were always the pubs and the men sounded jolly, singing ribald songs even though there wasn't any work for them and life was hard.

My uncle and aunt came for a visit from London and went up to kiss the Blarney Stone nearby. You bend over backwards up on the ramparts of a castle and kiss the stone that will give you good luck. Well, when they got back home, they won a lot of money in a lottery so all of us thought it really was true.

After two years, Dad was sent to London. He went ahead to find accommodation for us. He worked at Whitehall, near Buckingham Palace. He wrote to Mother regularly and she replied by mail but something happened to her letters to him; Dad never received them.

My father became frantic, thinking Mother was punishing him for his drinking. There was no telephoning in those days, at least we had no access to one. The up-shot was Dad finally found out what had gone wrong. It unnerved him enough to pay more attention to his family and from then on he always returned to the roost in time for dinner.

We were all happy to move to the large apartment over some stores on Regents Street in London. I loved the excitement and bustle of being in the middle of a big city. My father thought the same way and made the days count in the time we lived there. He took us to everything the big city had to show us while Mother usually stayed at home — she liked her quiet time. We went to museums, the science museum and Victoria and Albert Museum, pantomime, changing of the guard, parks, and the zoo. It was a continual merry-go-round of shared fun. We even went to a vaudeville show. Father had a zest for life and I loved the way he made these excursions a lot of fun. We went a few times to the zoo to see the chimpanzees have a tea party. They had dresses on and poured tea from a real teapot. Then they poured the tea over each other and went crazy, climbing over the tea table while we screamed with laughter, loving every minute.

I remember how the glass doors to the science museum opened even before we were close to them. We just couldn't believe there was such a thing as an electric eye that would see us and open doors for us.

Then there was the hologram. In a kiosk resembling a telephone booth, a figure of a man sat three dimensional as if he was real. I could hardly tear myself away from the miracle of it and wondered what the world was going to look like in the future if, using photography, they could reproduce people like that example. Would people be able to recreate their fathers or mothers who had died, to sit with them in their living rooms? It must have been when I was almost nine years of age when I saw these things.

Dad invited his mother and father to London. They had to travel by bus and he was to meet them at the last bus stop. They didn't arrive and it got later and later. My father ran up and down the streets looking for two seventy-year-olds in the middle of London! Eventually he found them sitting on the curb of a sidewalk. They had got off the bus too early and just waited like that figuring Dad would find them!

School was not memorable for me except for Christmas plays. I was always the main character, either a fairy doll who brought all the toys to life or the poor little match girl. That's when I felt the power of my audience's approval. Little boys gave me candy and followed me home.

Dad's next transfer was to Purfleet not far from the docks at Tilbury on the river Thames. It was a no-man's land. Mother must have wondered if she was ever going to lead a genteel life again. My brother John was born there and became our real live doll.

Peggy had a white angora rabbit. She combed its fur every day and could sell the fur when she had a bag full. One day the rabbit was gone and when we sat down to dinner we could see the pink flesh of the rabbit in Mother's casserole. We refused to eat and cried and cried. Father should have never killed a pet but what did we know at that time what our parents were going through? It was taboo to let children know of anything distressing. We knew of no adult problems.

Mother sewed all our clothes and my sister and I wore identical dresses until we left home.

I remember the apricot coloured organdy dresses she was making. They were to have two deep frills on the skirts. Mother sat at her hand-turned Singer sewing machine, mounds of stiff organdy around her. She would call us in to fit the length and waist and as I climbed out of the cloud of organdy I thought we would be the most glamourous girls in the world. I remember Mother with pins in her mouth and satisfaction on her face. In that backwater place she could create things of beauty. She not only made clothes for us but for our dolls and covers for our doll cribs. I kept a doll's wine-coloured velvet coat which had a white fur collar, until I was married.

Father also made our Christmas presents. He made wrought iron bassinets and furniture for our dolls and he would turn common things, like wooden matchboxes, into chests of drawers for our doll houses, gluing the boxes together to make furniture, putting on a bead for the drawer pulls. For the boys he made tiny trucks with wheels made from discarded thread reels.

He never once woke us up when we were sleeping Christmas eve. He had a second lot of army socks put away and he'd fill those ahead of time, hang them on the end of the beds in place of the empty ones without making a noise. The fillings were humble compared to today's Christmas stockings. To help fill them, the bottom always had nuts with their shells on, which Dad would crack later with his nutcracker and there would be an extravagant orange, some cheap candy and a plaything or two. Nothing elaborate. But later, when we got downstairs we would get to unwrap one larger gift. Those gifts would be like the doll cribs or castles or toy cars for the boys. We would never own more than one doll at a time. I believed in Santa Claus, until I was fourteen, yes it's true. I had to be told the truth even though my younger brothers had guessed long ago. We always had a Christmas tree, however poor we might have been. In those days we had tiny candle holders with a clip on them. We'd put small candles in them and when it was time, race to light them all. Dad would have a pail of sand and a pail of water nearby, just in case the whole tree caught fire. We sang carols quickly as the lights flickered and finally went out and then we opened our other presents.

We went to see our English grandparents, Margaret and Harry, in Yapton, Sussex. They had moved to a cobble-stone house which had an outside biffy. It also had a small landing on the stairs with a window which had a window seat that looked out to a bridge where, the rumour was, pirates had once hidden their treasures. The bridge was only two miles from the sea. I would often sneak away from what the rest of the family was doing and go to the landing to read Grandma's books; *A Pilgrim's Progress* and what's the name of the Lilliputians? Ah yes, *Gulliver's travels*.

My grandmother came from a genteel family. She was ostracized by them when she married a poor gardener. Harry was deaf and required Margaret to read the paper to him while he put this large horn, like a loud speaker, into his ear. He was always saying "Speak up Maggie. You're mumbling."

Harry was working down a well when he was younger and the walls fell on him. Consequently he had a rounded back. Every night he disappeared to go on his three wheel tricycle to the *Black Dog* pub, and there he'd recite all the old ditties he knew. I remember one my father learned from him

Oh! She was....
As beau - ti - ful as a butterfly
and proud as a queen
was that pretty Polly Perkins
from Paddington Green.

Harry and my two uncles were estate gardeners and gardening was in the blood of their descendants, through my father, to some of my siblings, and now down to my children. I was with my daughter Brenda recently when she moved from her country house to come to Mission: She had enough plants and seeds to start a nursery!

Margaret was a wonderful cook, although in those days we were not educated about calories and fat. We loved her suet puddings and her spicey sausages for breakfast. When we visited our grandparents, we would pile in the car and go to the beach at Bognor Regis. Some years we would even rent a seaside apartment in Littlehampton instead. Mother never really had a chance to rest there though, because she could never take a break from watching us children in case one of us would drown. Dad, on the other hand, would build the best sandcastles and take us to the Punch and Judy puppet shows. He taught me how to swim by throwing me into the deep water so I HAD to learn.

I can't emphasize enough how he made our learning fun. And I find it strange that Peggy and my brothers thought he was too strict and they fought against him. Maybe I can understand the boys feeling that way because Dad wanted them to know their next grade subjects before they'd conquered the present ones. But he taught them how to take a car apart and put it together again. And he never let them get away with not doing their homework. He made them steam engines with the meccano set and encouraged them to be innovative. Peggy was cross with him because he had pulled her from school (he was paying for us to go to the convent) and she loved being in school. And when I went for my job away from home, he sent Peggy, who had been enjoying her job, down to chaperone me because I was having too good a time with dating.

I think we were in Tidworth during the depression years and yet we were never aware of the poverty in the depression which many tell me about now. As Father was in the services, he was paid regularly. I remember a soldier delivering a roast of beef every week though, so maybe it was tough to look after five children. It's just that as children, we had no idea about it.

As Mother had been a chef, we always had nutritious meals. I didn't like them all because sometimes she had to use stringy, fat mutton and tripe. Eeew!. However Dad always, always kept a vegetable garden and we had never-ending fresh greens, carrots, onions and turnips so we were kept healthy.

Father taught us to ride bikes, never complaining when he had to fix broken spokes or punctured tires. He taught us to shoot and how to trap rabbits and he took us to raunchy army variety shows. He taught me a little tapdance routine. He wore a bowler hat and we somehow twisted our arms as we tapped away to go with the rhythm — I could illustrate some of it today if I was asked!

When we drove to my grandparents, we drove in a three-wheeled car. We would pass a tremendous-sized white chalk horse carved during ancient times into the hillside. In ages past, Stonehenge was to us just a lot of big stones. Nearby Salisbury Cathedral looked like a fairy castle.

While we were in Tidworth I was still in my fairy-tale world, imagining stories in books would come alive. I was always sure that one day I'd find a treasure. There was a comic strip in the newspaper and it was about a girl who had a fairy doll. This doll could wave her wand when no-one was looking and make wishes come true. I really believed it was possible to have a doll like that and every Christmas it was my wish to have a fairy doll so I would be able to make everyone's troubles disappear. (On my eightieth birthday my daughter gave me one!)

I believed in fairy stories and that strange things could happen. And when one day I looked up at our mantlepiece above the fireplace, I saw what I hadn't seen before: the clock had a little door in it like one from *Alice in Wonderland*. I climbed up on a chair to open it and inside the compartment as nice as you please, was a ten-shilling note. It had to be for me.

I knew I was supposed to keep this a secret. I went to the sweet shop, bought a good sized bag of candies and hid the rest of the money in a box where I kept some books.

The day came when Father went to retrieve what he had stashed in the clock and horrors! He knew he had a thief in the family, whereas I thought it had appeared by magic. We all sat around the kitchen table while he grilled us. We trembled because when he was angry it frightened everyone. He concentrated on Peggy: "Tell me; tell me" he ranted. Then even worse, he concentrated on Mother. Mother had trouble paying bills with her housekeeping money and he thought for sure it was her. And through all this no one thought it was me because I NEVER did anything wrong. Poor Peggy and poor Mother, but I was paralyzed with fright and couldn't for the life of me tell them how it came about that I got the ten shillings. So I kept quiet for years and years and quite often when talking about family stories the case of the missing ten shillings would rear its head and no one would see my cheeks flush and they didn't suspect in the slightest that I had been the culprit.

Many years later, when the family was gathered together, I confessed it had been me who took the money. It was like going to a catholic's confessional. The family was glad the secret was out and Mother especially understood my imaginative ways and forgave me.

In those days, children were not allowed in the living room except on special occasions. One of those was on Sundays when we could go in to sit on the carpet and listen to programs for children on the radio. The Ovaltinies were a group of young people and their commercial went like this:

We are the Ovaltinies
little boys and girls.
Make your request, we'll not refuse you
we are here
just to amuse you.
Would you like a song or story?
Would you share our joy?

We made our own entertainment, usually around the kitchen table. I always had paper, pens and cheap paint. I'd draw anything that came to mind. We played outside most of the time and biked everywhere.

Army schools were not considered of high quality. There was one student named Tom who was a long and gangly figure. He was always knocking things over where he walked and never got his homework done. The teacher often called him to the front of the class, told him to lean over the desk and whacked him with a long, thin cane. As he returned to his seat, he'd look at me and grin. I think he sensed my sympathy and knew the thwacks on his bottom hurt me as well.

I had skipped a grade because everyone except me thought I was smart. I was sent for an examination to get a scholarship. I was taken by bus to a large university-type building and told to sit at one of the thirty or so tables in a great hall. A man in black robes stood on a platform at the head of the room and snapped his cane loudly on his desk while looking at his large pocketwatch.

"Begin!" he yelled.

For me he might as well have yelled "Freeze!" because I did.

I looked at the papers on the desk and nothing made any sense. I did nothing. The hours passed while I looked around the room dreaming about the stone figures in the alcoves, wondering what their stories were.

Father was incredulous when I hadn't passed but I knew I wasn't meant to be an academic.

One day at home, Mother had a visitor. Now that was very unusual for our mother. A smartly dressed lady with a large brimmed hat was ushered into the living room and the door was closed. We strained our ears to make out what they were saying and came to realize that (a.) Mother was crying and (b.) they were speaking in German.

After the lady left, Mother was still sobbing. She told us this lady wanted to tell her about a man named Hitler who was making Germany almost a police state and families were turning against each other and informing authorities if they knew of someone not in tune with this Hitler's thinking. The country was hypnotized with his speeches and people were turning into fanatics.

Mother was sad for weeks after the visit. She couldn't believe that her home country had turned into such horror.

2:

A princess in Hong Kong

I was twelve years old when Father came home one day to say we were going to live in Hong Kong for three years.

For a young English girl to live in Hong Kong between 1936 and 1939 was the silver screen come alive.

My father was in the Royal Engineers and was sent to Hong Kong for something to do with defending it against invasion. So Mother got us all equipped and ready for the five-week journey and not one of us was sorry to leave Tidworth for places unknown and romantic.

The P & O Liner looked huge to us as we reached the docks but it wasn't long before we were familiar with it, John with Mother and father in one room, Gordon and Stanley in another and Peggy and me in another. Father sat us down and gave us all the rules, especially to the two girls. We mustn't speak to other passengers and must not stray too far from our cabins. We were allowed to participate in games of quoits and to have the tiny cup of beef broth the waiters brought on deck in the mornings but on no account were we allowed over the barrier into the first class area. And of course, that's where I wanted to go. Everything looked exotic there.

I couldn't wait to find out what we could do within those guidelines and took a walk around our part of the deck. About twenty or so marines were sitting together near a lifeboat and one of them called me over. "You're a pretty lass," he said while the others sort of snickered. "Where do you come from?" I thought it was rude if I didn't answer so I told him.

"I come from close to there," he said, "Would you like to see the photographs I have in my cabin?" I nodded. "I'll just go down ahead. Meet me at deck number three and my cabin number is fifteen."

"All right" I said, thinking how very handsome he was; almost like a film star.

I was walking along the corridor to reach number fifteen when a young girl who we had met at the dining table saw me. "Where do you think you're going?" She yelled at me. When I continued on my way she said "I'm going right now to let your father know where you are." Thank goodness she caught me because I later realized what might have happened to me. I ran back to our cabin.

The Bay of Biscay was the scourge of sailors. Terrifying waves reached as high as Big Ben in London then came crashing and twisting down, tossing the ship from one side to the other. Everyone went below-deck to bed, retching and moaning with sea-sickness. I wondered what all the fuss was until it hit me too and I staggered down as well.

Alexandria port thrilled me with the sense of the Orient. Zulus unloaded cargo. Their culture forbade them to comb or wash their hair and mud clumps hung on to the ends of it. All of them had a stick comb of sorts stuck in their hair to scratch their head. But how magnificent they were, their tall, almost black bodies lifting loads with the grace of dancers while chanting hypnotic songs, making the air vibrate with rhythm.

We weren't allowed ashore at some ports, but in Singapore and Penang we took a tour. As we walked on pathways to the sights, thousands of bold monkeys swung off trees in our faces.

Dolphins helped break the monotony of endless seas, they frolicked alongside our ship and we loved their playfulness. The sharks were not lovable. A crew member hung a huge cut of beef over the side of the boat when we anchored at a port. The bait caught a monster shark which the sailors hauled aboard. It had a huge, gaping mouth and rows of sharp teeth.

Hong Kong consisted of both the island and part of mainland China. Kowloon is on the mainland and was connected to the island by world-famous ferries. These ferries ran frequently until late at night with enviable efficiency.

We first lived in Kowloon in a large flat above some shops. It was spacious and cool, being made of stone. Windows had wooden shutters and iron slots at the sides for a large beam to be put across in the event of a typhoon. On Signal Hill, a tower structure would warn of oncoming typhoons. When one was approaching we would get ready to batten down the hatches and put the beams in the slots at the windows while sampans, junks and large vessels had to make for port. While we lived there, we survived two typhoons, one more terrible than the other, lifting ocean liners onto the shore and thousands were killed.

I remember sneaking away from the apartment to go down to the shop close by. It sold Chinese newspapers and American comics. I would sit on the floor in a corner reading *Dragon Lady* and *Terry and the Pirates* comics. I would feel as if I was in their fantasy world.

The climate being hot and humid created ideal breeding ground for infectious diseases. My brother came down with Hong Kong blisters. Mother was given a thick, mustard-yellow ointment. She was told to first scrape the blisters off with a wooden stick then rub in this stuff. Peggy and I hid in the bedroom covering our ears to block out John's screaming. Often the blisters re-appeared, sometimes covering his whole body. Cholera was easy to spread and of course tuberculosis was ever-present.

We had to be indoctrinated to the ways of that new country. My father went to see about getting a car. While filling out forms, the clerk told him "You are allowed two a year."

"Two what?" my father asked.

"You can run over two Chinamen a year."

"Good Lord! Why would I do such a thing?" my father said.

The clerk looked amused.

"They think the devil is always at their heels. They came up with the idea that they could run in front of cars, just missing being run over themselves and the wheels would catch the devil and kill him instead. So you see we can't very well blame the driver."

We were told not to go into certain areas under any circumstances. People there were desperately poor and would do anything for money. They'd cut the fingers off some Europeans to get their rings and some tourists had disappeared in those areas.

We were expected to act as superiors and to hire two or three servants. If we lived in a large house it was necessary to have a Chinese guard to protect the premises. Female servants were called amahs. Adiah was our younger servant and she and I used to communicate even though neither could speak each other's language. There was a closet-sized room at the rear of our apartment with two concrete slabs on which both servants slept. For pillows, they had a rectangular porcelain box with a hole in one end. They slept with a hand in this hole because their treasures were hidden in there. Adaih was Catholic and she had pictures of the Virgin Mary on the wall. But for good measure, they also had a statue of Bhudda where they burned incense.

Adiah was careful not to let Mother know we talked to each other, we were not to fraternize with the natives. But Adiah had a boyfriend who worked in a biscuit factory and he gave her bags of broken pieces that would have been thrown away.

"Dolesay! Dolesay! Come" she would call when she received one of these gifts. There was no way she could pronounce the word Doris. And I'd go into their little space and eat with her the broken biscuits with the pretty colours of the hard icing. It was a thrill of sharing the secret.

Some of these amahs dedicated their lives to European families, and it was heart-wrenching for them when the families returned to England. Very few went with the families, and those who did became strangers in a cold, new land.

It wasn't long before we left the mainland and moved to the island. We lived close to the only piece of flat land which was the race-course. An East Indian cemetery was behind our apartment and we could watch families burning their dead on funeral pyres. Neither servants nor renters of apartments could keep cockroaches away. We had to wear slippers if we got up at night and squish our way to the bathroom. The ice-box legs had to stand in small pots of poison otherwise the cockroaches would cover the whole thing.

Buffalo flies were round balls the size of a small potato and stone hard. They'd bump into everything like a drunk, even into one's face. They flew so fast, you were hit before you were aware they were around but believe me, when they hit, it hurt. I guess there were snakes but I never saw one, maybe the Chinese residents ate them.

The Chinese enjoyed theatre and we watched outdoor performances with actors fighting each other and when they pushed phoney daggers into their adversaries, fake blood would come gushing out like fountains and the audience loved it. They were always having a parade of some sort, wearing scarlet clothes with much gold trimming. Musicians played coconut violins and thumped on tambourines. One old fellow passed beneath our window every evening playing one of these violins and with the screeching sounds sing what sounded like "EPEE! Look chuck. Bow chuck!"

The boys would imitate this old fellow and we would howl with laughter.

During a funeral, women would be hidden behind a large black cloth and they would wail enough to make us shiver.

When we looked directly out of our living room window, we could see a hill across the road covered with squatting women, some with babies strapped to their backs, smashing large stones into small stones with a hammer, and putting them into a canvas sack. Every so often they vacated the area and the hill would explode with dynamite to release more large rocks, then back they came to take up their positions again. I was only fourteen but cringed when I saw them and the life they had to lead. I thought it was wrong for the British to come to a different country and subject people to such poverty that they would do anything to have food for their family. But the argument was that if the British weren't there, they would have starved to death.

TB was common in Hong Kong and men in particular had a habit of spitting with abandon. Double-decker trams had an uncovered upper deck and moved constantly past our apartment and around the race-course. People on that deck would even spit from there, letting loose a salvo to the sidewalk. You had to be careful where you stepped because it was easy to step into it, carrying the disease further. Notices were posted everywhere, warning against the spread of TB by spitting but to no avail.

Victoria, the capital of Hong Kong, was colourful and vibrant. Streets were allocated for different products. There was a flower street, a tailors' street and a bird-cage street.

Mother had always sewed our dresses but the Chinese tailors were so cheap, she would buy material and a pattern and take us there to be fitted. It was a known fact that the tailor would skimp with the pattern so he could have some material left over for himself. They knew how to make use of every scrap.

Mother spent her leisure hours knitting and embroidering. She knitted a terrific bathing suit for Peggy from apple-green wool and she looked good in it. We were swimming at the local pool when Peggy dived into the water with a splash, thinking she made quite the figure with her new suit on.

To our horror, we — and everyone else at the pool — saw the woolen bathing suit stretch out and float behind her! She soon realized she was naked to her knees and she struggled to get out of the pool trying to gather up the sodden, heavy mass that used to be that fine garment.

We just couldn't stop laughing, but it must have been one of Peggy's worst moments. And poor Mother was so sorry about it.

We had a beach just for Europeans where we had a cottage made entirely from bamboo. Even the "nails" were bamboo shoots.

Father went to a boat builder to order a rowing boat. He had drawn a rough sketch of it and the craftsman was so obliging he reproduced the bumps and curves which were in the drawing. As a consequence the boat was always tipping over in the water but we loved playing in and on it. My sister and I were like mermaids, swimming as if we were fish instead of human beings.

We belonged to the cricket club where only "whites" were allowed to belong. Peggy and I became terrific tennis players. I loved the "ping" sound of the ball hitting the racquet at the sweet spot. We went on boat parties to small island beaches and when I was fourteen my parents took Peggy and me to a ball in the world-famous Peninsular Hotel. I wore my first long gown and felt like a princess.

The British army used Sikhs as policemen. They were over six feet high and disciplined. When they carried their truncheons to hit whoever was causing trouble, the Chinese were terrified and ran as fast as they could away from the scene. The Sikhs were very loyal soldiers to England.

School for army children was mixed, boys and girls, and as it didn't have much of a reputation, my father enrolled Peggy and me into the all-girls school at St. Paul's Catholic convent. The teachers were nuns from Paris. We went only to the day-school, not to board there.

Many Philippine and Chinese girls were boarders, their families recognizing the importance of an English education. They got top marks in their subjects when they could memorize everything but if they had to reason, they didn't do as well.

The sisters at St. Paul's were cultured and placed a strong emphasis on the arts.

I was always drawing in my exercise books and I liked designing dresses. I thought my future might be as a dress designer. My schoolmates would ask me to design a dress for them and they'd take the drawing to tailor street and have it made from the sketch.

We were often asked what we were going to be when we left school and when Sister Henri, a tall, thin and severe nun, asked me that question I replied that I really wanted to be a model.

Everything came to a standstill as she drew herself even higher, slapped her cane on a desk and said, "Enough! We will not talk about such a thing!"

It reminded me of the joke where another reverend mother asked this question of a graduating class and the first girl said "I want to be a prostitute." The reverend mother fainted.

When she came to, she asked again what the girl had said. "I want to be a prostitute" she replied. "Oh! Thank the Lord," the reverend mother said "I thought you said you wanted to be a Protestant!"

We were Protestants and it wasn't easy to accept being told we were destined for Hell. It was essential for our exams that we knew the Catholic Catechism. We just parroted replies to those questions even though we felt like rebelling. There were subtle and not so subtle hints to "see the light" and convert.

I was asked to read my essays aloud and given high marks for them but I almost failed in art because I didn't want "to stay inside the lines." I always wanted to stretch the boundaries of what we were told to do.

The convent staged the only theatrical plays available in Hong Kong at that time. The scenery was professionally done and performances had ticket sales. I had always had the lead in school plays so when they found I could not only act but also annunciate well — and I had blond hair too — I became their trophy.

I became the Virgin Mary, a queen from biblical times, or Cinderella, or Alice in Wonderland. I danced in dances of the glade forest and I memorized ten or so pages of poetry to read on stage. One night I was reciting Sister Henri's favourite poem and I fainted. After that, the sisters eased up a bit with all I had to learn. My school work was suffering but they told me: "Don't worry about your exams Doris. You've been rehearsing too much and we understand you don't have the time to study for exams and do stage work as well."

At the final curtain of these plays I was presented with gifts from members of the audience — especially the opposite sex — and flowers galore. Once I received a natural pearl ring which looked important. Love notes were common.

I was only fourteen but was treated as a movie star. I loved it all, savouring the heady power of a favoured one.

During this time my father tried to keep me safe from trouble and trouble meant boys. They buzzed around me like flies to a honey cake. We'd be sitting down to dinner while the sounds of mating whistles calling me would float through our window. Father's face would become scarlet with rage because of his inability to stop it.

I was no longer looking like the ugly baby born to my parents, I was now pretty with naturally wavy blond hair and fair skin. As one admirer wrote in a poem to me:

Carved out of marble and petals of rose.

In Hong Kong, being fair and blond was in stark contrast to the majority of people living in that corner of the world.

Europeans were also a pampered minority.

There was an orphanage attached to the convent. At night, the sisters went out to collect the little baby girls which had been left in street gutters, discarded by mothers too poor to raise them. These children were brought up in the orphanage, baptized as catholics and trained in household or other work as they got older.

One of these girls had been trained as a seamstress. She was without arms. She was in charge of seeing to the costumes for the many plays we had and it was she who made my ball-gown when I was Cinderella. Sitting on a low stool, picking up pins with her toes, she fitted me into the white satin crinoline dress. It was a small miracle to watch her make tucks and put frills in place with her feet. She never spoke to me but over the next few weeks she sewed extra pearls into the bodice. She could never realize her own dreams so I figured she had transferred them to me and the Cinderella dress.

When I stepped out on the stage in the scene for the ball, the audience gasped "Ahhh!" in admiration.

Later, Reverend Mother called me into the sacred sanctuary of her office.

"Doris," she said, "No one will look lovelier than you in that Cinderella dress and we would like to make you a gift of it. However" she added, "we will only give it to you if you'll agree to become a catholic."

I was stunned. I wanted the dress badly but I knew it was wrong of Reverend Mother. I burst into tears and ran out of the office to my home. My mother held me and tried to make me understand the zeal the nuns felt for their mission in life but she was sad as well.

We would meet young English men at the beach and arrange to meet them when my parents were otherwise occupied. I remember being in a speedboat with one, singing love songs of the day — *Harbour Lights* was one. But my father turned down invitations for Peggy and me to attend dances on the visiting navy ships in the harbour. Wow! There would have been many more stories if he had allowed us to go.

A short while later my ever-watchful father happened to look out the window to see a car trailing me as I walked to school. He rushed to find a rickshaw. Rickshaw owners were fleet of foot and it wasn't long before he caught up with the car that was still inching along following me. I was just approaching an isolated area. My father jumped down from the rickshaw and went up to the car demanding to know who the man in the back seat was and what he was doing and threatened to get the police. The young Chinese man was nervous; I guess he had visions of the Sikhs and said in pidgin English, a convoluted version of English which colonials understood.

"Velly solly mister," he said, and drove away.

From then on, my poor father lived in terror of me being kidnapped. He had reason because I invited trouble. I had met a thirty-five-year old Englishman and secretly went to the movies with him. He ruined everything by sending to our house a gigantic basket of tall gladiolias. Father got down the leather razor strop which hung inside the bathroom door and strapped me hard. I don't care what they say in today's world that parents shouldn't spank. It was about the only thing that could contain me. He tracked down the fellow, threatening him with everything, but the man said he thought I was at least eighteen.

From that time on, my parents curtailed my activities and I had to go everywhere with them or stay at home. I was miserable. But I guess I'm able to write this story because of my father's vigilance.

It was about this time that Mother told me she was going to stay a while in Macao and that she was pregnant again. She was eight years older than my father and dreaded going through the up-bringing of another child especially as there would be no servants when we returned to England. I questioned my father about this later, and asked if there had been an abortion. But he said "Never." I think my memory is correct because how could I forget her crying with me when she told me she was going to have another child? However good he was as a father, I don't think he had enough understanding of her condition. He berated her for always having unpaid bills at the grocery store. He never went into those stores himself so how would he know the cost of having good food on the table? And how prices for everything increased with time, There were always rows over paying bills. She didn't smoke or drink or buy elaborate clothes; and how could she ever heal from the wound of never seeing her home again?

3:

Back to England and war

It was July 1939 and I was on the cusp of being fifteen when we got word we were to return to England. Little did we know our Hong Kong would never be the same and little did we imagine what horrors the people would suffer when the Japanese invaded.

For me it had been Shangri-la. I had been a piece of thistle-down lifted by a breeze of adoration and tossed about from one delicious event to another.

The serious side of life lay ahead.

We boarded the s.s. Rawalpindi and I was in full bloom.

The ensigns looked good in their white uniforms. Again, it felt like an adventure with the luxury of being on board and on the blue seas. This time it wouldn't take five and a half weeks to make it to England — just four.

We had the familiar beef consomme every morning on silver trays and played quoits on deck and lounged in deck chairs in the sun. Two of the ensigns tried to claim me and I played one against the other, being careful because they were not supposed to be friendly with passengers and my father lurked around every corner. He had one weakness though! He had a nap every afternoon.

We called into Calcutta and Bombay. Father bought a bronze bell in Bombay — nothing elaborate — but it stood as a reminder of our trip. I was nauseated with the sight of hopeless poverty and the destitution of people lying on pavements, covered with sores and old rags.

We were scorched going through the Suez Canal. The air conditioning had to be turned off because a sandstorm hit us and we could hardly breathe in the cabins as the sand came through the ducts hitting us like small needles. On the deck it was worse, everything got clogged with sand and we heard two crew members had died of heat exhaustion. What an experience! It was as if we would die too because the heat was unbearable and sand even found its way into our mouths.

We were in the Mediterranean when we saw a ship not far from us engulfed in flames. It was listing and sending word for help. Our brave ensigns and crew went out on lifeboats and managed to rescue the people on board. As we watched them return to our ship, the other boat sank. I was so proud of our rescuers and it felt terrible to see the boat go down under the sea.

On board we played a lot of table tennis and Peggy and I were top players.

We called into the port of Marseilles. "Now Doris," Father said as we went ashore, "let's see you order our meals in French. After all you went to a French convent and I paid for private lessons for you."

My parents didn't have a clue that I hadn't made good use of my tuition. Sister Michael, who gave me those private lessons, was a dear, plump nun who would never have sent a bad report home to parents. She sighed often during my lessons and was ever hopeful that I would speak French one day.

I thought I'd be found out but I should have realized that cafes had many travelers who stumbled around the language and waiters were expert in making sense of it. Using my limited knowledge I managed to fluke my way through and Father never did discover the truth of my deficiency.

I was stunned to see men's urinals on the sidewalks. The only parts concealed were the vital organs. Streams of urine were part of the landscape. I wondered if the sisters in Hong Kong had been used to seeing this.

The ensigns had been caught fraternizing with me; they were reprimanded and stayed in the background for the rest of the journey.

We docked in Portsmouth, close to where I was born.

Father was told he was posted to Chatham, in Kent. As our family had no accommodation prepared for us, we stayed in an army barracks where we bunked down for a couple of weeks. We slept on army cots with horsehair mattresses and what seemed like cement for pillows. After living in a warm climate, I was cold and missed my dream life in Hong Kong already.

Father bought a dear house in the village of Hempstead, near Gillingham. In England, many houses had no numbers. Instead, they went by the names the owners put on them. And mail was delivered to the name of the house. Ours was called *Homeleigh*. It could have been called "little heaven" or "comfort station." It was a stone bungalow with bay windows, a huge back garden and an orchard on one side with all kinds of fruit. As you opened the gate to go into the front garden, flowers and honeysuckle welcomed you with their perfume.

We had to find furniture and Dad let me help choose the type and colour for the living room. He thought with my connection to art, I would know better what would fit in our living room. It was a good feeling to put my colour sense to work but I think it wasn't good to upstage Mother. After the furniture came, I think she felt resentful but she grew to like the arrangement and put the episode to one side.

There were three bedrooms and a bathroom and of course, a kitchen. It wasn't long before my brothers made a cottage out of the shed in the orchard so they could have privacy and Stanley really needed it because he was forever studying. That enabled Mother to have one bedroom as a dining room. Dad made her a lovely rock garden and it was her joy.

Almost right away Peggy was offered a job as a nanny in London and that's when Father sat me down to see which school I would go to. Sitting opposite him, I said "No. I don't want to go to school anymore. I've had it. I want to do the things I want to do."

He hit the roof. "You will go!"

"I will not."

"I say you will."

"You can't make me."

After all, my stage performances were much more interesting and I wanted to have my own money to be able to take charge of my own life.

And I did not go back to school.

"What will you work as? You're only fifteen and have no training."

I found a job as a clerk in an electrical shop in Gillingham which was part of a co-op. There were large wooden boxes in the corner and I was told they were television sets. When they told me what television sets were supposed to do, I thought it was impossible.

I made very little money. Some went for bus fare and some for my board at home. The shop closed on Wednesday afternoons but we worked late Fridays and all day Saturday. The staff kidded me because I was so young and guileless, coming to work early in the morning and wishing a "good day" with a smile while the rest of the staff were overworked or overtired and not up to being cheery.

I saw my manager commit dishonest acts to make money for himself. Flashlights — or torches as we called them — were necessary in the "blackout." The blackout was in effect during the whole war years, requiring hooded lights on cars and heavy blackout curtains on all windows. Flashlights were the only means of seeing where you were going at night. Batteries were always in demand but they were in short supply.

People came in with old batteries left in their flashlights and the acid had eaten at the insides. The manager would say "It's hopeless — see where it's eaten away?" and they'd nod their heads, sigh and fork out for a new flashlight while he threw the old one in a big garbage can near the counter, insert new batteries in a new torch and collect money from the customer. After they left he would laugh, retrieve the discarded one, use a bit of sandpaper to get rid of the blight, put in some batteries, and sell it from home on the black market which was beginning to rear its head.

In all my fifteen years I had never seen anyone deliberately do a wrong thing. But I guess it was because we were always looked after and had enough to live on without resorting to doing wrong.

The country was in a state of nervous anxiety; would we be going to war with Germany or did Neville Chamberlain, the British prime minister, straighten things out? The Home Guard was called into order. Older men who were not going to be called to fight in a war were trained in control measures in the event England was invaded. They practised with pitch forks and shovels instead of rifles. There wasn't a stock of armaments on hand. It was sad to see these older men go through their drills but at least we knew that we had some sense of order if German parachutists came down from the sky — as we all expected.

On the 3rd September, 1939, Chamberlain's voice crackled out of the radio solemnly declaring "England is at war with Germany." Sirens wailed and church bells clanged. We didn't know what to expect and we were frightened. We were always looking up in case the parachutists were coming. We huddled around the radio waiting for any scrap of news.

But nothing happened. No parachutes, sheep grazed, people shopped and the children went to school. Cars were driven and food was plentiful. How could we be at war? One thing we were told was the church bells would only chime again if we were invaded or when the war would be declared over.

However, government plans were put into action to keep the populace healthy and happy and ration books were distributed without further ado.

It hadn't taken me long to have a boyfriend and before he was "called up" for the army, we would cycle to the beach or along Kent's country roads. We whizzed by orchards, hop fields or rolling hills, old stone houses and castle ruins feeling we were bursting with love and life.

The government was great with quickly organizing ways we could survive well in war conditions. First we were to build a bomb shelter in our gardens. If bombs exploded near buildings, people could be injured or killed with flying debris or collapsing walls. It was safer to be underground and away from the house. Everytime my boyfriend Bert came to call, Father would collar him to help dig our bomb shelter. "May as well make use of him" he said, while I took them lemonade and waited impatiently to be alone with Bert.

We had Air-raid wardens who would check to see you didn't have even a chink of light coming through your windows. The names of train stations were taken down. We heard there was something called the "fifth column." This was the name for the Germans having placed spies long ago in strategic places and in the event of war they would have knowledge of generators, railway stations, waterworks, political buildings, war offices and so on and they could sabotage those places.

I was enjoying my job and got paid every week. There were many posters in the streets and in the shops, saying such things as "The walls have ears," and "Careless talk costs lives." We were being made aware that who we talked to may be a spy looking for knowledge of the area.

Once again I was socialising and attracting the opposite sex so it was a nasty surprise when my father was promoted to major and told to move to the massive army camp in Yorkshire called Catterick camp. I was ready to work outside the home, but I couldn't afford to house and feed myself as well. My father would not have allowed it anyway so I had to give my notice at work and leave with the family. Our house was rented and off we went.

Catterick camp (1940)

Catterick camp wasn't a pleasant place to look at and even worse, Father told me I was not to go to work, even if I could have found it in this wall-to-wall nest of soldiers. I was told it was time for me to help my mother and should stay in the house to do housework.

Me ! A star from Hong Kong, a lover of social interaction, one who could not stand the brain-numbing work of a housewife. So it was a time for tears, frustration and misery. I was sixteen, beautiful and trapped in the depressing castle of home. I didn't know anyone. The only male I came into contact with was the milkman. He was young, freckled, had red hair and stammered and blushed whenever I could talk to him. Peggy was still in London and my brothers went to the school on the base.

Father brought home an old, clumsy Oliver typewriter.

"Learn to type Doris and we'll get you a job" he said absolutely fed up with my unhappiness.

Every day I tapped away with two fingers and despised every minute. But if it meant I could be free of being cooped up in the house, I kept at it.

When Father saw I could type a letter reasonably quickly and he could stand my tears no more, he set out to get me a job in the NAAFI (the only shop on the base, run by the Navy, Army and Air Force Institutes – an organisation created by the government to run recreational establishments and sell goods to servicemen and their families). He told them I was a typist and made sure they would pay me accordingly. I wasn't interviewed, only told to report the next morning.

It only took one morning at work for the boss to throw up his hands, advertise for a new typist and move me to an unthreatening position. I checked all the sales bills, finding adding mistakes — no calculators then — so the boss could reclaim the money when necessary.

I was away from housework, had some money and found adoring salesboys at the back of the store. One of the young men, Fred, kissed me not long after I was employed. I was ready for a bit of romance and we walked together and had romantic ideas such as running away to Gretna Green, in Scotland, where young couples could get married without the blessings of their irate parents. He gave me a jewelry box but Dad made me return it. "Men who give you gifts like that, expect something in return!" he said.

Our romance went along until he wrote me a letter heading it with "Dear *Sweat*heart Doris." Oh! The shame of having a boy friend who didn't know how to spell. I told him goodbye, all thoughts of romance crushed with the word *sweat*.

The family moved into a colonel's residence and I liked living in lots of space with rooms for servants, a butler's pantry, French doors leading to the dining room from the kitchen, and lots of large windows. I would go into the servants' quarters and I'd dance and sing songs until Mother asked me to calm it down because they couldn't hear the news on the radio with me carrying on like that.

Stanley and Gordon at this time were evacuated to Wales because the government thought many children would be killed unless they were sent out of bombing range. It bothered me. Did some parents think they'd save money if their children could be looked after somewhere else? Was it cruel of me to think that way? My brothers survived but Stanley was affected by it; something to do with the young woman he boarded with.

Off we went again — ordered to go to Beverley, near Hull. No forces base there so we rented a lovely house with a bay window which had little diamond-shaped panes of glass. There was a small airport at the bottom of our hill.

Peggy, who had joined the family again, got a job right away and me? I WAS TO WORK FOR MY FATHER as a typist. At least he didn't care if letters took a long time to be typed! I was therefore connected to my father twenty four hours of the day unless he was traveling. This way he could monitor where I was and what I was doing and restrict any young men from getting close to me. It didn't take me long to get fed up with the protectiveness and I started crying again.

The only thing that stopped the tears was when a man in the street, a painter, asked if he could paint my portrait. I told him to ask my father, who agreed if the man came to our house while Dad was sitting close by. I was fascinated by the medium he used which were soft pastel sticks of lovely colours. He talked about painting as he worked and after he had completed the project, my father bought me a box of pastels, like those the man used, and the right paper to work on.

My whole world changed.

I stayed up late at night copying photographs from magazines in pastel and nothing else mattered but that I could duplicate these pictures. The results were unbelievable. My family was stunned with these shockingly good paintings. So they let me alone and didn't prevent me from staying up till the early hours of the morning.

One night a German bomber got through defense lines and bombed the airport at the bottom of the hill. My father ordered us to cower under the staircase. I was so frightened that I started to laugh. My father slapped my face hard to bring me to order. The house was shaking as if we were in an earthquake and Father told us we'd better make for the air raid shelter across the road.

"All together: Run!"

We ran half dressed with my brother John screaming. We got to the shelter shaking and holding onto each other as tight as we could while John peed in his pants.

It became quiet and we heard the voice of an air-raid warden, those unsung heroes of the war. He came to the open door and shouted, "What the devil are you doing here? This shelter is falling down and will fall on top of you." The man picked at the wall with his pen-knife and mortar crumbled to the ground. We learned later that there had been corruption with the building of these shelters. The contractors had used weaker concrete than was contracted for.

The all-clear siren went off; the single bomber had left. There had been no warning sirens because it was what they called a sneak attack. The Germans were learning that if they flew low enough they could avoid radar detection. Our bombing experience was not like in London when the bombers came in droves with no relief.

I got a call from the young ensign who had been on the s.s.Rawalpindi. He wanted to meet me in Hull. I asked for permission and Dad said I could go as long as the next door neighbour fellow would drive me in his MG and act as chaperone.

The ensign WANTED ME TO MARRY HIM! He thought my flirting meant that I was serious about him! The fellow who had driven me stepped right up and said it was time to go.

Somehow I linked up with a group who had access to a home with a large room for dancing. We rolled up the massive carpet, put on the gramophone and danced to the wonderful Scottish folk dances. It was about the only time in the year of working for my father that I felt free.

Dad kept other young men from his office at bay. Little did he know the one he should have worried about was the humped-back dwarf who brought in cups of tea and ran his fingers up and down my legs if he could. I was always on guard when he came.

Once again I was miserable, caged in like Rapunsel with no young company. I thought I might join the services, but when my father heard what

I was thinking, he went through the roof. "They'll eat you alive!" he roared, "I won't allow it."

I had two cousins who were working for British Iron and Steel (BISC) in Leamington Spa. They had avoided joining the forces as their jobs with BISC were considered of national importance. With their help, it was arranged that I would join the firm and be a typist.

BISC controlled the shipping and distribution of iron and steel needed for munitions, aircraft and ship building. Most of these products came from Canada or America and they crossed the Atlantic in large convoys of ships, trying to avoid lurking German submarines.

Although I loved my parents, it was a glorious day when I left home for the next part of my life. I was almost seventeen years old.

The government was now in high gear, organising the country so it could continue functioning in spite of the bombing.

Cod liver oil and orange juice was given to pregnant women.

Children were given milk at school.

Ration books were distributed for food and clothing.

We were urged to start a "victory garden" even in our typically small front gardens. If possible we should have a few chickens which would help us have meat and eggs. That way the country could concentrate on producing the necessities for fighting.

Because most of the able-bodied men were at the front, the government created a land army to recruit strong young women to work on the farms. They were called The Land Army Girls and they were paid as if they were in the regular army.

We were encouraged to be vigilant with our health and, for example, put some soy flour in our baking for extra protein.

There were always lineups everywhere. Many food items were rationed. One exception was fish — which was "off rations" as we used to say — but only the earlybirds got any. Sugar was limited but the government gave extra rations at canning time when fruit was plentiful. It enabled women to have preserves for the winter.

BISC needed to get out of London and away from the bombing so it had requisitioned mansions and hotels to house their employees. The Clarendon Hotel in Leamington and the mansion belonging to Bryant and May (the firm who made matches) at Ashorne were some examples. They also took over Warwick Castle.

Warwick Castle & Leamington Spa *(1941)*

My cousins met me at the train station at Leamington Spa and took me to meet the manager who would be responsible for me — instead of my parents — because I was under twenty-one years of age. My cousins told me they would see me later that week and left us to have a cup of tea together.

While pouring me a cup of tea, the manager said it was necessary to quote the rules of the house. I was to have a temporary room for a couple of nights but then would move into my permanent room.

The rules:

√ I must be in the hotel by eleven at night.

√ No males were allowed in the rooms but may wait in the lounge on the main floor.

√ You would have a special table for your meals and on it would be a container for your ration of sugar.

√ The bus to work left at eight in the morning and would bring you home at four o'clock.

√ Meal times were posted on the wall outside of the dining room.

√ Telephone to be used only when necessary and limited to two minutes each call (This because the lines needed to be kept clear in the event of an attack by the Germans.)

√ Bath water must not be deeper than five inches.

√ Mail would be placed on a table by the dining room and arranged in alphabetical order.

After we finished the tea and scones, the manager took hold of my case, and showed me to the temporary room.

There were three women in the room and one was the most beautiful I'd ever seen. She looked like a Rossetti portrait. She had long, black, wavy hair and skin like a camellia. Her mouth was tiny, as a geisha.

I was very tired and glad to slip under the covers to sleep, but I felt frightened as well because I was without my parents or my sister for the first time in my life. The lights were switched off and I had just started to doze off when the lights were switched on again. Two of the women in the room were talking in an agitated way. I couldn't figure out what had happened but my heart was jumping. Then they told me.

The beautiful young woman had somehow got onto the roof of the hotel and had thrown herself to the ground. Apparently she'd been the mistress of one of the directors in the firm and his wife had appeared, threatening to ruin their jobs.

What a first night away from home! I hardly slept the rest of the night. I was to work in Warwick Castle!

The castle had lovely grounds and many species of rhododendron and azalea. Peacocks strutted and screeched their salutes. To enter the castle one had to go through the portcullis (massive iron gate) which was raised at sunrise and lowered at sundown. This was a handed-down tradition and an elderly Beefeater guarded a small door next to the gate to make sure no one came uninvited.

I shared a large room with Letty in the Clarendon Hotel. All our meals were looked after as well as the cleaning. A small remittance was taken from our wages to pay for this but the rest was ours. Rationing of clothes restricted how much we could buy. Even underwear was rationed and a dress could use up your whole quota. I made sandals from crocheted string with webbing (off rations) across the top. We did without wearing our silk stockings and we used scrap material to add flounces to older dresses when fashions changed and dresses became longer.

Weekends were our socializing time. Letty was a book-worm and a clever young woman. She didn't care to gallivant around like I did. But she was good to me and remained my friend till our mature years when she died in Chicago after being mugged on the street.

I was introduced to the boss and two co-workers. The boss was a middle-aged Scot with such a heavy accent I thought I'd never understand what he was saying. But I liked him.

This department was responsible for tracing shiploads of steel. We were to follow – on paper – the progress from the factory in Canada or America, across the sea in convoys and on to the delivery point. Sometimes the ship would be torpedoed and I'd write across the form "Lost at sea".

Once again I was paid as a typist who didn't type. The boss had motioned me to a new-fangled typewriter.

"This is your desk lass, perhaps ye'll start by typing this letter" he said.

As I knew I would, I made a mess of it and waited for him to fire me. But he only smiled and said, "Och aye lass! Dinna worry, you can take it to the typing pool and you can do the filing. Now gi'yr self a break and go to the cafeteria for lunch and dinna worry now."

I delivered the letter to the huge typing pool, feeling very much the new girl and went down a corridor on the way to the cafeteria. A young man was walking towards me and a shiver went down my back he was so good looking.

"I know you're the new girl," he said "Your name is Doris and mine is Derek. Will you go to the movies with me tomorrow night?"

"Yes… yes… all right… do you know where I live?"

"Yes I do, and I'll call for you at seven."

I found the cafeteria but my feet didn't touch the floor. I wanted to sing.

A girl in the lineup to get lunch tapped me on the shoulder. "I'm Gloria" she said "We've got a drama club here and there's an audition at four o'clock. Would you like to come?"

"Sounds lovely, the stage is my second home," I told her.

I auditioned and was floored to be given a lead part. But to my dismay, Gloria — who had always had the lead before — was designated to be my plain-looking sister.

But I had other things on my mind — seeing Derek the next day.

The hours finally passed so I could go down to the lobby of the Clarendon the next evening to meet Derek.

Sitting in the movie house, I turned towards him and found he hadn't been looking at the screen but was staring at me.

"Do you know you're perfect Doris? Your skin, your hair and your body. I adored you from the moment I saw you."

I had only been away from home for three days and already I had a lead in a play and had met a young man as good as any I'd dreamed about.

After the movie, Derek had to run for the last bus. He told me he had to register for enlistment in the navy the next day but there was a ball at Ashorne Hill on Thursday.

"Will you meet me there at eight o'clock darling?" he said.

Of course I said yes. BISC buses would take us to events such as this.

At work the next day, tracing orders of steel coming, I envisioned submarines trailing the convoy, sights trained on the ships and firing their torpedoes at helpless sailors. And if Derek goes into the navy, they will be trained at him too.

For the ball I wore a simple long dress but it didn't matter because I was in love and no one would notice my clothes.

He took me in his arms and we fitted together perfectly. The orchestra played in that oak-paneled hall, the gowns twirled round and round and I thought I was in fairyland. He guided me out to the garden, the roses were full of perfume on that warm summer night. He kissed me and the world was in tune with the moment.

We went back into the hall where a director's wife was playing the harp, looking like a Grecian wall painting in her ivory gown. Everything came together to make one of those timeless cameo moments.

I excused myself to go to the ladies' room.

I was refurbishing my lipstick when Gloria came in.

"Doris, I've got something to tell you" she said.

"Yes?"

"Derek already has a girlfriend."

I couldn't get my head around that announcement and thought she was just jealous of me because I got the lead in the play.

"Where is she then" I asked.

"Her name is Holly. She's six years older than Derek. She's had a nervous breakdown and attempted suicide twice. She's been called to her father's funeral in London. She won't be able to stand the shock of Derek leaving her as well."

I couldn't seem to think as I stumbled back to where Derek was standing. I pulled him outside again. The scent of the roses now made me feel sick.

"Is it true Derek? About Holly?"

He pleaded with me to understand and be patient.

"As soon as she's able to take it, I'll tell her my darling."

I felt cold and hard.

"One or the other Derek, you must decide."

And later, Holly came back to cling onto Derek's arm. Her huge eyes were dark and frightened and she didn't look well. He looked longingly towards me as they passed by but I did not relent. I soon had a new beau by the name of John.

Three months later, I saw a notice in the company's newsletter. The ship Derek was on was torpedoed and sunk. There were no survivors.

The windows of our room looked out on The Parade, which was the main street in Leamington Spa. I had a single bed with drawers underneath and a closet which consisted of a flowered curtain around an iron framework. We didn't need much space for clothes because the ration coupons only allowed a few purchases. I worked in what had been Queen Anne's bedroom in Warwick Castle – it had been made into an office.

Everyone was scheduled to be on fire watching duty at some time.

Germans were dropping fire bombs which created many simultaneous small fires. Watching out for fires and then putting them out quickly was something the populace could do during the night and we all took turns to be on watch.

While I was on duty at the castle one night, six of us started telling ghost stories. The weir (a small waterfall) in the moat made a rushing, whooshing noise. One of the girls told about her friend who had seen the castle's ghost. She had a nervous breakdown after the experience. We went down into the dungeon where we came across a gnome of a man with the skin of a white slug. He showed us the Doomsday Book and told us REAL horror stories. He was the night-watchman and he took us with a torch to where they had strung up prisoners. We saw crosses scratched in the stone walls, marking off the days. We heard rats scuttling and drips of water coming down from the walls. The musty smell clung in my nostrils and I was glad when that watch was over.

My father sent a letter:

"Dear Doris, I don't like you calling your boss by his Christian name. I don't like you being involved with so many young men we can't keep track of their names. You seem to be forever going to parties and I think you're headed for trouble.

"So we are going to bring Peggy down to keep an eye on you. She has been accepted in the accounting department of the BISC and we should be arriving soon. The manager says she will be in the same room as yourself. Pull your horns in and concentrate on your work, Doris. love Dad."

Whew! That letter made my hackles rise. How could he have done that? My sister loved her job and living at home. When she arrived, she berated me for letting Father know I was having such a good time.

"You could have pretended you were doing needlepoint or something," she said.

She was cross with me for disrupting her life and of course could no more hold me down than rein in a bluebird. She told Letty: "It's always been the same with Doris, she was given private tutoring while I was told to leave school. I never got the kinds of gifts she had. I know everyone felt sorry for her because of the pain she had with her periods but I was made to leave my friends and a job I loved because she can't simmer down."

In those days, we obeyed our parents regardless of our feelings, and truth to tell, Peggy worried that having escaped the protection of home, I would probably run into trouble. Even though she was irritated by my devil-may-care ways, she always loved me.

However hard she tried, she finally wrote to Father to say it was hopeless to keep track of me and if he wanted to do something about it he'd better come down and berate me himself. Well he did, but it didn't make any difference: I was in plays, going to dances, and making my own decisions.

The pain I had every month with my periods was more like labour pains. Anyone who saw me go through it told everyone I just had to have it seen to. My doctor said to get permission from my father for me to have an operation to cut the hymen. My father refused permission because he said my future husband would think I wasn't a virgin !

The doctor told my father not to be so backwards and I needed to have the operation done. The doctor finally got my father to agree. I went to the hospital and they put me under the knife. I woke up in a ward with about forty men and women in it. I asked to use the bed pan not knowing I was stuffed with cotton wool. A nurse came soon and started to haul out miles of this bloodied cotton wool. I just couldn't believe I could contain that much!

The operation didn't do any good. The pain returned and never left until after my first baby.

Letty, Peggy and I lived in our room at the Clarry for four and a half years while the rest of the world teetered on the edge of chaos. Being so far from the coast, we didn't fear the bombers as much. We had our bikes and thought nothing of riding many miles in the country. However, my parents were living in London and a bomb tore down one of the walls of their house.

We were close to Stratford on Avon and went to the plays that were held there. Air force bases were close to us and anytime we had a dance in the Clarendon, we could put in a call and order a lorryload of airmen!

A London stage director came to work as a director for BISC. In his spare time, he'd direct our local plays that were held in the nearby village of Ashorne. I was always chosen for a lead part and the local people recognized me if I was in town. My boss never expected much from me in the office, he just boasted about my accomplishments on the stage.

Art schools were closed because of the war but there was a hankering inside of me that wouldn't let me be. So I painted on sugar ration bowls in the hotel, putting gay flowers and the owner's name on each. I painted fire-screens and I portrayed swans and crinolined ladies and flower gardens. On the tiles over the sink in our room I painted a small boy bent double, looking at us through his legs. It was reportedly still there in 1990.

At the bottom of The Parade (the town's high street) was Jephson Gardens, a delight to the senses with its flower beds and fountains. The municipal hall, close to the gardens, was extravagant enough to be a palace. Friday night dances were held in the ballroom and there was always a good orchestra. No alcohol was allowed but we all loved those Friday nights.

It was my seventeenth birthday and there was to be a beauty contest that night at one of those dances. I brushed my hair till it shone, just in case. Just in case. My hair was my glory with its colour between platinum and gold. Only cheap women or film stars could have a hair dye in those days so it was rare to have the colour of mine.

The hall was packed with soldiers and airmen on leave. We were to parade in front of them and gradually the other girls were eliminated and I remained. I felt humiliated being examined like that. Then a greasy-looking man kissed me and declared me the beauty queen of Leamington Spa for a year. I was given a silver chalice but I had nowhere to put the thing — I gave it away.

The next morning an older woman who lived with us at the Clarendon Hotel came up to me.

"You have disgraced our corporation putting yourself on display like that — you are nothing but a tramp," she said.

Her friend told me I'd better resign from being the beauty queen because BISC did not approve of such tacky carrying on.

"What will your father say about that?" she wanted to know.

I hadn't thought about that and dreaded getting word from my parents.

Instead of being annoyed, I got a telegram from Father saying "We know you're the best!"

Telegrams were the fastest way to send messages to people. But usually it meant that a loved one was either "missing in action" or had been killed.

I didn't participate in any queenly duties and the matter died down.

And being so young, I didn't realize that those older women were JEALOUS. They were older spinsters and were always finding fault where none existed; judgmental in petty things, especially towards the young people.

My boyfriend John wore horn-rimmed spectacles, was dark-haired, shy and very loyal. Often he had to wait in the auditorium while I rehearsed my roles in plays. We cycled everywhere together, loving being outside after a week of working indoors. He wasn't my hero though. In the war, most eligible men were in the services overseas and as the song went,

They're either too young or too old
They're either too stale or too grassy-green

He was recruited into the army when he turned eighteen. We wrote to each other often but the days of him being away stretched into months. Often, his letters were held up while they were being censored – some arriving with words or even whole sentences blacked out. Then I'd receive a bundle all at once. But the day came when I was notified by the Red Cross that he was wounded and would I go to visit him in a hospital in Medhurst about thirty miles away. They included an address where I could stay overnight.

These billeting services were undertaken by volunteers who lived close to the hospitals where wounded servicemen were recovering. It boosted morale and at the same time made the volunteers feel they were really doing something to help the war effort by providing a place to stay for the families of the wounded while they visited their loved ones.

The BISC director sent for me.

"We want you to take this gift to John on behalf of our Corporation" he said. "Be careful to hold the box upright at all times."

The pale grey box was about eight inches square and not heavy. It was securely taped shut and I guessed it might be a glass ornament.

On the bus to Medhurst I struggled with guilt feelings. I'd been resenting the fact that being loyal to John meant I couldn't have fun the way my friends were doing.

Especially going to the American camps which were always sending vans to our hotels to take us to the dances they put on. The girls would return with nylon stockings and boxes of chocolates and say the food was out of this world.

I was glad to get to our destination in the bus because I was balancing my overnight case, my purse and the grey box. I asked where the hospital was. The letter had not elaborated on John's condition and I had no idea what I'd be faced with. I should make it plain that I led a protected life whereas Peggy could stomach anything gory. She was a volunteer in the hospital for returning veterans. I tried to take the training but every time the teacher told us how the blood circulated, illustrating on a chart, I fainted. So they told me I wouldn't be any use: If a chart could put me out, what would actual blood do?

The hospital where John was had been built of rose-coloured bricks and the grounds had very nice flower beds. Patients in royal blue dressing gowns, on crutches or with eyes bandaged were walking around with nurses. I went to find the receptionist.

"Can I leave my suitcase with you?" I asked, "and can you tell me where my boyfriend John is?"

I started to shake and was close to tears. The receptionist must have gone through this many times and she smiled encouragingly as she directed me to his room.

I've always tried to take the easy way out but there was no escaping this. I thought if he looked too awful I was going to faint.

The door to his room was open and I saw this cocooned figure with a slit for a nose and mouth and a pair of brown eyes at the top of them. They were John's eyes all right and they filled with tears when he saw it was me.

I leaned over to kiss the bandaged head but he let out a yell. He couldn't bear to be touched. I told him about the grey box and opened it for him. It was a bunch of green grapes from Ashorne's conservatory. John was grateful but I fumed with anger.

The Directors had made a fuss about sending something for John who had risked his life for them while they sat in their safe armchairs! They hadn't troubled to find a meaningful gift they had just reached up and taken the same grapes they routinely had for their dessert.

But John wanted badly to talk and patted the edge of the bed for me to sit there. John told me it had all been a nightmare with the D-day landing.

"A bomb exploded close to me and I was buried alive for an hour and a half. They were desperate to dig me out before I died, and while they were digging, they chopped off flesh from my side with the shovels. Just about every one of my bones is broken but I'm alive and you are here for me. Thank you! It's heaven to see you!"

It exhausted me to listen to him. He needed to talk but didn't have the energy left to even ask about my life. It wasn't long before he asked me to leave because he had to have more pain killers. And I wasn't sorry to get out of there.

The billet was a short walk from the hospital. The street had about thirty brick houses all joined together like many a mining town. When seen from a train window they look identical and boring with their chimneys and back gardens repeated exactly. But when you push open the gate to a front garden the individuality is there and usually the small gardens are charming.

The back gardens are enclosed with high brick walls, the tops often have shards of broken glass to stop anyone from climbing over.

I knocked on the door of number seventeen and a tightly-knit lady in a grey print dress opened it.

"The Red Cross says you have a room for me," I said.

She had a whispery voice. "Come in. My name is Mrs.Fairchild."

We went through a musty smelling hall. A spindly grandfather clock stood in the corner with the pendulum still.

In the kitchen sat a portly man on a wooden chair who was looking into the embers of a shiny black iron stove. There was a green velvet runner with a gold fringe on the mantlepiece, a clock and, out of character, three exquisite crystal vases.

It turned out that Mr.Fairchild had been a designer for cut-glass crystal. He showed me the book of his design drawings.

After that we all sat in the kitchen with nothing else to say to each other. Mrs.Fairchild sat stiff-backed with hands folded in her lap and the only sounds were the tick tock of the clock and the scraping of a piece of coal losing its balance before dropping into the embers.

Next morning I said goodbye to the Fairchilds and as I passed the parlour the next morning I saw the stuffed horsehair sofa and chairs. A lot of English people had these parlours which stayed the same for years waiting for company that seldom arrived.

It had been strange to stay in that place. I'm sure these people didn't have many visitors but the war brought out the goodness in people from all walks of life.

I went to see John before I caught the bus home. We both longed for the fighting to be over. It would take ages before he would be able to return to the front. He wanted only to get the job done with the Germans. I told him rehearsals were non-stop and I couldn't come back until they were over.

He wrote to say his bones were mending and when I next came to visit I should find him on crutches.

Once more I got on the bus but decided to get the late bus back and not stay again with the Fairchilds.

He wasn't in agony any more and as he struggled to walk with the crutches we went into the garden. Our conversation got around to our firm and how the men who had gone to fight would be reinstated after the war.

"You'll be one of the directors soon when you get back John" I said.

"I don't want to be a director Doris."

"You'll have to explain that one John. Where's your ambition?"

And I just couldn't believe it when he told me he didn't want the pressure of promotions.

"I'll be content to spend my life doing the same work I did before I went into the army" he said.

I didn't know what to think of this development. Maybe he was still suffering from the trauma of being buried alive. We had never discussed the future. We'd been so caught up with being young. Well, I couldn't let him know how disappointed I was because he was to be moved soon to therapy treatment and sent back to the front as soon as he was mobile.

I spent the bus ride home evaluating whether I should be tied to that relationship and concluded it wouldn't do any harm to go on a date or two as long as I still wrote to John. He didn't need to know about it and I'd make a clean breast of it when he was better.

One of these dates was with an airman named Rusty, named so because of his red hair.

Unbeknown to me he had asked a mutual friend, Mabel, to take me to a dance in a building close to the Clarendon. The place was BISC's camouflage department and the staff often put on the gramaphone so they could dance during their lunch break. Since I was supposed to be "untouchable," he bet Mabel that not only would he date me but he'd "bed" me too.

He was slightly built and not that great to look at. Oh! — but he was graceful and had such penetrating steel-grey eyes.

He held out his arms for me to dance. I was in a dream world, whirling and gliding around that hall as if I was born for it. I was on a cushion of air. Pure delight. And I didn't want it to ever end. But the record stopped and he turned to Mabel to dance with her, leaving me standing there. I wanted to tear him away and demand he come back to me. But he just smiled, tipped his fingers to his forehead and left. I was furious.

Next day he phoned "Will you go to dinner with me on Friday?"

Visions of his dancing flooded my brain and I put thoughts of John behind me and told him "Yes."

Would I be ready to face accusers? The ones who in the old days would tar and feather a girl who wasn't faithful to her man while he was at the front? There were rules of behaviour for women whose boyfriends were fighting and especially those who had been wounded. We owed them our very lives. And I had taken the first step off the straight and narrow path.

We had dinner at an old Tudor building which had been converted to a restaurant. The low ceilings and small rooms made for an intimate atmosphere. We talked in an agitated, excited way as if to catch up with the years we hadn't known each other.

Something happened to me as I talked with him. I seemed to be more clever with my train of thought. I was responding to an inquisitive, very intelligent person. It was as if he spurred me on to greater heights. He talked about books. My library choices were safe and not mind-challenging.

"I'll loan you one I'm just finishing," he said, "it's about Eli Cuthbertson, the fellow who came up with the bridge game system."

We walked home to the Clarry and warmth glowed between us. Rusty reached under my sweater and his hands eased up to my breasts, continuing to talk as though he wasn't burning up every fibre of my body. I pushed his hands away.

"Oh! Is that what you're about?" I snarled at him.

"Sorry Doris," he said, "I'm only human you know. What kind of sheltered never-never land have you been living in?"

There was an arrogant cynicism in his voice and a bitter hardness. I sensed trouble. We were quiet for a while and when he spoke, he was softer.

"I'll obey the rules but you don't know how I've watched you for months and longed to be with you. Maybe you now know that Mabel bringing you to the hall was no accident."

In the war you meet a man in uniform but he really isn't a soldier, sailor or airman: He's a farmer, mechanic, accountant or whatever. He's been thrown into the mill of war and wears a uniform to say he's a fighter. But his real identity is the one he left when he joined up.

"Can I see you on Monday? he asked.

"Would you like to go to an opera?"

Oh Glory! An opera. It was a dream of mine. My mother and I would listen to operas on the radio but I'd never been to an actual performance. I told him "Okay" and also that it had been a good evening.

We were at the door of the Clarendon hotel. Holding his hands behind his back, he slowly leaned forward and kissed me. I told myself I was ready to enjoy this as a thrill worked itself down from my heart to my groin.

As I pulled away, I saw a shadowy figure standing across the street. Was someone watching us? It would be awful if John got word of this. I hadn't let him know how I had changed my feelings about him.

Always when we met, conversation between Rusty and me resembled little fireworks working back and forth. It was exhilarating. We went to see *La Boheme* in Coventry. As the story went on, Rusty would explain what was happening. In the end, my handkerchief was soaking wet with tears. I died along with Mimi (even though she looked a mite too broad in the beam to be ill with tuberculosis). I loved every minute. We had to use the bus to get there and home because gas for cars was almost non-existent.

We went to Stratford on Avon some time later and found the last train had left before the play had ended. Everywhere we asked for a place to sleep, the answer was "full up." During the war, hotels were either requisitioned like the Clarendon or really full of travelers. Finally we found this wretched place. The manager only had one bedroom left with one double bed that he said we could share. But I said "no way." Rusty slept on the sofa downstairs and I was shown this dreary room with no lock on the door. The manager thought I was daft not to share the bed like any ordinary person.

I shivered in the bed with the threadbare blanket pulled up around my ears. The wind hissed through a broken pane of glass in the tall window. A string hung from the ceiling which held a naked lightbulb and every puff of wind set it swinging eerily. I tugged at the string to create some light and reassurance. I had visions of the manager trying to get in.

I was too scared to sleep and spent the time going over and over in my mind about what I should do about Rusty and John. I had to decide one way or the other.

It had been such a learning experience to be with Rusty and it had nothing to do with his divine dancing. He pushed my mind to go further. It felt like a massive oak door had opened for me, to reveal a land of delights. He poured out knowledge of so many subjects in a steady stream. Knowledge I was thirsty for.

But often, warnings pricked at me. He made hurting, sarcastic remarks about my friends or myself. Or when under stress his ulcers would start hurting. At such times he didn't want anyone near him and was miserable.

I found it was hard to write to John because I no longer found him interesting. My letters were sent less and less. I was gadding about and he was back again at the front facing those ungodly terrors. I couldn't imagine how he had to live with the memory of being buried alive. I felt awful about the whole thing and the naked lightbulb added to my feelings of desolation. Finally I switched off the light and drifted into sleep.

I dreamed that Macbeth came towards me in the form of that dreadful manager and his blood dripped on my blanket.

I woke to a knock on the door. It was morning and Rusty came in carrying a tray with a pot of tea and two cups. There was a rose in a bud vase. His eyes twinkled and traveled down from my disheveled hair to the shape of my body. Slowly and meaningfully he made sure I understood what he was not saying. "Did you manage to sleep?" he asked.

I chattered non-stop about how frightened I'd been. He looked down at me with such unguarded tenderness. He was dear to me at that moment and I could have dragged him down on top of me, but the teapot was in the way. Life went in a different path because of that teapot.

We caught the train back home, he going to his base while I faced the accusing mob at the hotel.

Peggy said "You didn't let our manager know. We were frantically worried about where you were".

I tried to explain about the pesky trains and how we had to take ages to find a place to sleep but I could tell they didn't believe any of it.

Mabel saw me at work. "I see he's won his bet" she smirked.

"Won what? What are you talking about?"

"Rusty bet everyone he would get you into bed with him. With you being so unattainable we were sure he couldn't do it but he obviously did."

"I did NOT sleep with him" I shouted and my face was hot with rage. What a fool I had been.

I unloaded my fury to Peggy and Letty when I got home from work but bless them, they believed me and it was some consolation "We just didn't know if you were all right," they said. "Anyway there's mail for you downstairs."

A letter from John. I took it into the lounge to read.

> *Doris,*
>
> *Today I received what so many soldiers dread to receive: a Dear John letter.*
>
> *This person told me you've been romancing an airman. He's been watching your "goodnight" activities and has been explicit. The only thing keeping me from killing myself is the chance it may not be so. I will wait to hear from you, praying it isn't true. Meanwhile I've asked for special leave*

and hope to see you soon.
    John.

I was to meet Rusty at Ashorne Hall for a dance. I would have to tell him goodbye.

We stepped onto the dance floor and once again I was completely in tune with him and loving the indescribable beauty of dancing with him. I panicked thinking about having to give him up.

He knew something was wrong and we went outside into the garden. I told Rusty about the letter and told him I knew about the bet he made and that I felt humiliated.

"Forgive me Doris," he said, "the bet was an act of bravado. It isn't the way it looks."

"Regardless, Rusty, John is in a bad way and I have to deal with that business before I do anything else"

"What would you say if I asked you to marry me?"

"I can't think of anything until I see John. I can't stop thinking of him, the way he was in hospital, and it must be terrible for such a sensitive man."

The war sometimes made everything surreal. Here we were with dance music playing inside and the scent of lovely roses surrounding us, yet bombs were being dropped on our beloved London and young men were being forced to kill.

When the bus came to take me back to the hotel, Rusty and I clung to each other until only the tips of his fingers connected to mine and soon he was gone from sight.

John came and I thought I'd never recover from his visit.

He kept saying "I don't want to live anymore. I never thought you would deceive me and I'm going to throw myself in front of a train."

But I knew suicide threats could be used to hold another person hostage. I held firm, told him we could write sometimes, but I felt the need to be free.

I wavered with remorse. Should I have said this? Should I have said that? How would I deal with the situation if he did carry out his threat? Maybe I'd have to go into a nunnery.

John left his bike at my storage place; he would get it again when he got another leave. When I watched him go, I felt years older.

Rusty phoned. "I have to know how things went with John."

I started to cry.

"Let me come and talk to you. Please."

So I said yes, I wasn't bound to anyone now. He came, and I told him I was wary about him after I learned about the bet but I guessed we could go out a few times. He was bitter. We parried words as I tried to avoid his clever, hurting stabs. I knew he was only being defensive but it scared me.

The Americans & Canadians

And that's how I joined the throng I had been envying. The jolly crowd of young women who climbed into lorries to go to the American base. The Americans held their dances in a hangar-like building and big bands boomed away. It was easy to see a different country's personality. They were so relaxed and ever ready to have fun.

Well, my feet were hardly inside the door when I was whisked onto the floor by a small cheerful sergeant. Not even having a chance to catch my breath or a "do you mind?" I was jitter-bugging.

Now I am NOT the jitter-bugging type. I prefer refined. No matter. I was thrown in the air, slid under his legs and whizzed around in complete disregard for what I wanted. How I ever did these things is a mystery to me. But it created a sinful excitement, letting loose to their music.

There were about twenty men to one girl so there were lineups of men wanting to dance. Faces blurred and there was no time to talk, wouldn't have been able to hear if there was, the music was so loud.

One of the men dragged me outside and produced a bottle of liquor.

"Quick, drink up" he said.

Another man had seen us go out of the door and tried to pull me back inside, "Don't listen to him," he said, and they got ready to fight. They were full of pent up energy and needed action to relieve the tension of waiting day by day by day to go to the front.

I was grabbed and hauled around again but the non-stop whirl was now irritating. The band seemed louder and more agitated. The energy that had excited me at first was now grating my nerves. Nothing like when Rusty and I danced, absolutely no comparison.

So I went over to the buffet tables which were swamped with food such as I hadn't see for ages: ham and turkey, salads and fruits of all kinds. I don't know how they got it all and it seemed unfair when you knew the whole of

England was on strict rations.

I sat with six young Americans and realized with a pang they were no older than me. Many were younger. They had left their homes and parents and everything familiar to them. They might never see their families or their country again. I smiled a lot and listened to their stories. I looked at their photographs. Those photos seemed to be their lifelines. They forgot their brashness and said they were lonely and they were dreading the future. It was a small thing to do, to be civil to these overseas men who came to help England win the war.

I tried going on dates with other men. One was a Canadian air force officer who was as good looking as Cinderella's prince. We danced at the town hall but his real interest was to get me to a little flat in town. He showed me photos of a large mansion where he was brought up and told me his father owned an aircraft factory. But we girls knew that in the war people came and went, no checking could be done and many lies were told. I said goodbye to him and others. I was careful and wasn't going to risk ruining my life for a few nights on the town.

Rusty became more agitated. If I didn't commit myself to him, he said he'd use his ulcer condition to get out of the forces and return home. He said he wanted me to belong only to him. He had been training to be a lawyer before the war and his parents owned a hotel.

I had a letter from John: Thank the lord, he was accepting the fact that I was no longer attached to him and, obviously, he had not committed suicide.

Now, for the first time in my remembered life, I was without a steady boyfriend and felt lost. I wasn't satisfied with a faithful, loving partner or a sarcastic, exciting one. No one would match Rusty and every day I would cry and cry some more.

Peggy and Letty were getting fed up with my dejected state. The dining room of the Clarendon doubled as a dance room when the tables were stacked at the back. We usually had a small orchestra and, as I mentioned before, there was always a lot of men available. I didn't have a partner and I didn't want to go to the dance one evening in May, 1945, but the girls said they couldn't stand my crying any more and I had to go with them.

I put on my Alice Blue dress and high-heeled black suede sandals and went downstairs. There was a somewhat wilted corsage laying on the table so I pinned it to my dress but felt tacky because one's fellow was supposed to supply this.

Everyone was having a good time, whereas I was in another mood. Some American airmen persuaded me to go to where they were serving drinks.

"Where have you been all my life?" one of them drawled. I was so sick of these lines. None of them had invented any kind of new introduction. "How about a scotch darlin," he said.

I only drank sherry or ginger-beer shandy (half ginger ale and half lager) and that rarely. I was so tired of boozy men and they all lacked Rusty's qualities. I thought I'd leave it all and go upstairs to our room. But then I heard a Canadian voice. I could tell it was Canadian because it wasn't the slower drawl of the Americans.

"Why do you wear such a tired corsage?"

Was there really a man on this earth who could say something different, even if it was rude? I turned to see a clean-cut air force officer with deep sapphire blue eyes.

"Will you dance with me Doris?" he said, finessing me out of the American circle.

"How do you know my name?"

"Your sister introduced us five minutes ago."

"I'm so sorry. So many people here. Faces get to be a blur."

"Her boyfriend is my pilot," he said.

The reason I didn't remember meeting him was because I was still wishing Rusty was with me and the tunes the band was playing brought back all the wonderful dances we had together. I didn't dare tell the man I'd even forgotten his name.

Dancing with him was different from dancing with Rusty. He spun me around so much I had to hold on tight and I became drunk with laughing. Was it really me laughing? It had been so long since I could feel anything but pain with John's situation and with losing Rusty.

When the music stopped, he talked non-stop and I couldn't understand most of what he said because of his accent. He spoke of jazz and big bands and Canada. He showed me photographs of his family and there were many pictures of his good-looking sister. I forgot my doldrums and had a jolly good evening and hoped he wouldn't ruin everything by pawing me when we said goodnight.

The orchestra played the last waltz and I went to the door of the hotel with him where there was a glassed-in porch and we sat there.

He leaned over and carefully kissed me on the cheek. When I tried to figure out what it was that I liked about him I decided his smile was nice and he seemed clean, elegant and idealistic. He asked to see me the next day.

When I returned to my room, the girls were putting their hair in curlers — something I had never needed to do. They were also packing away their dancing shoes and taking off their make-up.

"I don't remember you introducing me to your fellow's navigator" I told Peggy, "what the heck is his name?"

"Paddy," she replied "and they say he's just too honest to be true and that he's forever helping the underdog. They told me he kneels next to his bed at night to pray in front of all those men in the barracks."

Apparently not one of them teased him.

Yes I thought, this man sounded right up my alley. I could still feel us dancing, whirling around, with me in my Alice Blue dress. I thought the world might not be so dull after all.

The next day he met me in the Clarendon lounge and presented me with a box of Neilson's chocolates. It was rare to see a box of chocolates.

"What would you like to do?" he asked.

"We could walk to Jephson Gardens," I said, since the thing to do in England was to go for a walk.

We went out to the street and he put his fingers to his lips and whistled for a taxi.

"What are you DOING?" I said.

"We'll go by taxi" he said.

I told him primly, when we go for a walk, we don't go by taxi, we walk.

He waved the taxi away.

The gardens were lovely and the fountains spit water into the air with gay abandon. Whether in peace or in war, England kept its gardens with a dedicated legion of gardeners.

We were light-hearted but careful. Not knowing if the afternoon was to be a fleeting capsule of time or if we'd venture further with each other. He told me he had received a Christmas parcel from his mother which had taken six months to reach him.

"We can cycle to the country tomorrow and have a picnic" he said.

He was to borrow a bike and of course, I always had one. When he saw it he was surprised it was a racer bike with drop handlebars,

We were lucky to have a really warm day and took off along the country roads. Michelmas daisies were in the hedgerows and the summer sun was hot on our faces and arms. We passed through several villages with small houses and low-slung roofs. Oak trees by a small river offered us shade and Paddy took his mother's parcel off the bicycle rack.

The home-baked Christmas cake was dark and richly mellowed over the delayed journey to her son. There were cookies in angel and Santa Claus shapes, Christmas candies and home-made fudge.

Wrapped separately were pens, stationery and a bottle of aftershave lotion. He squirted some on his arm. I thought it smelled clean, like I expected Canada to smell — clean and full of possibilities: A place where dreams could come true.

"Mother writes every other day," he said, "and often sends parcels. It helps a lot."

I could see he was her darling boy, her shining light.

He had been a lab assistant at Courtaulds, the rayon manufacturer. His job would be kept open for him when he returned to Canada.

"I want to be loyal to the company but I want another career, maybe my own business," he said.

I had brought some sandwiches and bottled drinks so we started with those and then attacked that wonderful parcel.

"Doris," he said, "my pilot told me there's to be a dance at Ashorne Hill but you haven't invited me. Can I ask why?"

Truth was I was scared Rusty would be there and I knew if I danced with him, my resolve would weaken and I'd be in a mess again.

"You are invited now," I said.

Soon it was time to leave that pastoral spot and I had enjoyed being with him. Had I found a kindred spirit?

We cycled back to the Clarry and Peggy said "You've got a sunburn Doris." And it was true. My arms were flaming red but I knew my heart was beginning to flame as well and life had cheered up a lot.

When we met in the evening, Paddy told me he had some Nivea cream which would help the sunburn. He went back to his lodgings and returned to tenderly put the cream on my arms.

The balls in Ashorne Hall were elegant affairs. We wore evening gowns and there was entertainment during the interval. The atmosphere was of romantic times with gallant knights and gracious ladies engaged in love affairs. I met Paddy in the lobby and once again was struck by his freshly scrubbed look. I was moving towards him when Rusty appeared between us.

"Is this another notch in your rifle," he asked with a twisted smile and jerking his head at Paddy.

It was one of those moments that seemed to go on forever with danger signals zig-zagging between us. Paddy realised what was going on and deftly took my arm, maneuvering me onto the dance floor.

Rusty danced on purpose close to us, with a pale-faced girl. I knew there would be trouble unless I got out of his sight. So I told Paddy we should go outside for a breath of fresh air. It was a gorgeous night and we walked around the grounds with the moon making everything a silver wonderland. He brought me close to him and as I nuzzled against his shoulder, I could smell again his aftershave. It was called Bachelor shaving lotion.

We kissed again and again while my flighty mind was visioning Rusty with that girl.

The night ended and I had escaped the danger and never saw Rusty again. But even though I'm an older woman, I still remember the fascination he had for me.

Paddy had two aunts and an uncle in Edinburgh, Scotland, and had arranged to visit them. Aunt Jessie was driving an ambulance for the forces and Aunt Vi kept the apartment going. It was the same apartment they had been brought up in.

He wrote to say he loved me and couldn't wait to tell me what he'd been thinking about.

He was to be sent on flying duty for two weeks and to be stationed in the north of England. One never asked where, what, or why, because everything like that was secret. Half the time they didn't know where themselves until the last minute. He wrote lovely long letters saying he didn't know when he could see me next.

"Let's talk about it when we meet again" he wrote.

It was quite a long time before Paddy phoned to say he was coming but the time had passed quickly because I was rehearsing the role of Jane in *Pride and Prejudice*.

When I was on stage, my real life fell to the background. The footlights transformed me into my role. The Doris who lived in the Clarry, the Doris who had a boyfriend named Paddy, and the Doris who worked in Warwick Castle was no more. Acting surged in my veins.

"I'll see you tomorrow at the Portcullis" he said over the phone.

My heart flipped when I saw him waiting with a carnation and another box of Nelson's chocolates. His arms felt so good around me and our kisses were different now, hungry and reaching. We ignored the staff streaming past and I knew this was serious.

It was so good to see him again. He talked about his work as a navigator and how it was based on the stars and he named them as we walked the two miles to Kenilworth Castle. They were only the ruins of the castle but they were historic. We crossed the small undulating hills of the grounds and over the stepping stones of a brook close to Kenilworth Café. He had to stoop to go through the beamed Tudor doorway. He was five feet ten inches and people were much smaller in ancient times. We ordered tea and griddle cakes and held hands across the table.

"I can't wait to tell everyone back home about you" he said.

I said "You'll tell your grandchildren: 'One day during the war I met this blonde English girl and we walked by castles and talked about stars and danced in beautiful ballrooms'."

He smiled and said "I think my grandchildren will be your grandchildren." And he bought a photo postcard of the place and wrote a date on it for remembrance. He talked continuously. I was getting used to his accent.

"I missed the worst part of the war," he said. "I finished training in Lachine, Quebec, but then had a ruptured appendix and nearly died. My crew had to go ahead without me. My mother came to visit and couldn't even recognize me because I'd lost so much weight."

He said flying gave him severe headaches. He said he was homesick for his country and worried about his family. His father, brother and sister were all in a sanatorium for TB.

As he talked, I tried to imagine that large country of his and the people in it.

"I've got a confession to make as well," he said, "the photos I showed you and told you they were of my sister? Well it was of a girlfriend I had. I've just written to her to say I've fallen in love with you."

"Dear Me!" I thought "why do men have to play these games?" But I didn't want to spoil the short leave he had, so kept quiet.

I also kept quiet when he laughed at the small English trains and when he criticized English people for being "stuffy." I felt huffy about such remarks.

"English rivers are only streams compared to Canadian waterways," he said, "and your so-called historic buildings — where people actually LIVE

— should be torn down, especially the old places around the castle."

He had always thought he would marry at twenty-nine years of age, the age his father was when he married Loretta, his mother. He showed me a large photograph of his mother. Paddy was only twenty-two at the time. His home was in a town called Cornwall, on the border with America. When he told me this, I recalled a fortune teller had said I would marry someone who lived on the border of two countries; she'd also said that this man would have a lock of hair which was always falling on his forehead. Heavens! How could she have known Paddy would be like that.

He told me he was always the top of his class at school and as soon as he had graduated, Courtaulds had come to him with an offer to work with them. His chances of advancement were good. He had always loved sport but didn't have much time for it because he had to work after school. He had helped his mother with money since he was small, doing paper routes and selling Christmas cards door to door.

"She's had a lot to deal with, with visiting the 'san' and keeping the home going," he said. "She's always petrified that people will be sorry for us, so she made sure we were always dressed well and she made pretty well everything we wore."

We finished eating the griddle cakes and drinking our tea and walked to the Clarendon, crossing the brook again on stepping stones and walking over small hills.

We were tired when we came to the hotel and sat together in the lounge.

"What religion are you?" he asked.

"Church of England."

He told me he was a Catholic.

I had only met a few catholics in England and I remembered the convent in Hong Kong and how I had been doomed to hell because I was a Protestant. I took another look at him. He not only came from a far away country but he had a faith I didn't want to think about. I shook my head to get my thoughts to change direction.

"Such lovely hair!" he said, "we have a lot to ponder over, the squadron is due to go to Burma to fight the Japanese. It's guerrilla warfare and jungle tactics and there's a very hot, humid climate"

He had borrowed a motorbike to come to Leamington and it was a long ride back to Yorkshire. After he left, I couldn't stop thinking about him being in Burma. And the troops who did make it back from there were either severely wounded or missing limbs. The fighting there was not straightforward. Tunnels were built in the jungle and our men were ambushed from those.

John wrote to say he was coming for his bicycle. I dreaded seeing him; I didn't want to deal with his suicide threats and with him dredging up all my feelings of remorse. But he was an older, wiser version of the man I used to know. His physical wounds had healed. We spent a few hours in a sad and limbo way and finally he swung his leg over the bar on the bike and without looking back he was gone.

Paddy phoned from the Canadian leave house.

"See you in an hour," he said.

Life was like that in the war. Snatched hours or perhaps a few days, but then weeks or months of your man disappearing again. It felt as if there was a cyclone in my stomach when he came close to me and I smelled the freshness of him.

"What happened to John, Doris?" a girl passing us in the lounge said.

Paddy's face went red "Who is John?"

I told him the story and as he listened he slumped in his chair.

"Let's go to the movies" he said.

All quiet on the Western Front was on.

I found he was just as soft as I was when watching a film like this. We both cried. Tears ran down his cheeks and I sobbed as we were reminded of the tragedies of war. VE day (Victory in Europe) had been on 9th May 1945 and the European fighting was over, but how could we solve the problem of the Japanese? They were everywhere in the east, on outlying islands and in jungles. Their suicide squads felt it was an honor to sacrifice themselves to blow up small pockets of the enemy. Our men were brought up to value life. They were also worn down with the fighting of the European war.

We both had heavy hearts when we left the movie house because it wouldn't be long before Paddy would leave for Burma.

Back at the Clarry, he held me tight.

"Marry me Doris," he said.

We'd known each other for one month. A month of short hurried visits. We lived for each meeting and when together, spent the time dreading when he had to leave. Always in our minds the fact that anything could happen and knowing we were not masters of our fate. I didn't want to make decisions.

"It's too sudden," I said, sounding like a lady in Victorian days. But it *was* sudden and one thing that rattled around my brain was that he had been getting letters from his mother after he told her he wanted to marry me. The letters were little short of telling him it would be a betrayal to her if he went ahead with the idea. Now what — I ask you — would my life be like having a mother-in-law set against me before she even knew me?

"There isn't much time," he said, "I love you so much and I know you love me and we're made for each other."

"What about your mother? What about our different religions? Can I leave my family and my country? What about you making England your country? Maybe you're just lonely and you'll think otherwise once you get back to Canada."

"Darling, you know you're my ideal. I wasn't going to marry until I was twenty-nine but I didn't know you existed. Say you'll marry me."

I was scared. If I didn't make up my mind, things might change and I'd regret not being brave enough to chance being wrong.

"I'll see you tomorrow," I said, "and we'll talk about it then."

Of course I told Peggy and Letty about it.

"Dad will have a fit," Peggy said, but then she hugged me.

She said England was going to be a mess for a long time: Rationing would go on for ages and we'd have to re-build all the bombed-out buildings and Canada seemed like the land of opportunity. "As for knowing if Paddy is meant to be your husband or not whoever in the world knows these things?"

Letty went downstairs to get me a cup of warm milk. I could see she was wondering how a spoiled young woman like me would cope with the different country far from family and England and to be without the protection of my sister and close friends.

Peggy was always thinking about family and I knew she would miss me — even though I annoyed her by snitching her stockings — as I would miss her.

Morning arrived and Paddy bounded up the steps of the Clarry with the ever-present box of Neilson's chocolates. I had so many that I'd share them with our friends and they were impressed.

We went into the lounge, he crushed me to him and his kisses were so hard they hurt my teeth. It felt possessive and good at the same time.

"Well?" he said but he seemed to know the answer and was grinning widely. "Do you want me to go on my knees?" And he did.

He promised to love and to be good to me all my life.

"Yes," I said feeling as if I was falling off a cliff, "I love you and will marry you."

He got up and spun around in circles. He lifted me up in the air not caring if people were gawking at us — after all British people were not as careless with showing their feelings in public.

"Now we must get organized. And the first thing for you to do is to stop calling me Paddy."

He told me that his crew had decided that was his name but I was to call him Ted.

"Actually it's Edwin Fraser Paterson."

"I always thought I'd marry an Anthony," I said.

He sounded impatient. "My name IS Anthony."

"I thought you said it was Ted."

"A Catholic has to have as his first name the name of a saint and mine is Anthony. Edwin is formal for Ted. Fraser is my maternal grandmother's name. I only use Anthony for official records."

Well! Who would have thought it?

4:

Becoming a war bride

He had written to tell his mother that we were going to be married as soon as possible and had the letter in his pocket — he was going to mail it as soon as he had my answer.

"But I knew your answer would be yes because we both know, don't we? And I'm sending my mother money so she can buy you a diamond ring in Canada. Saves money. I know she'll like you when she meets you and now we'll go to have our photographs taken."

"Just a minute," I hushed him as he was making my head spin, "we'll have to tell my parents and you'll have to get permission from my father. It's not going to be easy when we've known each other barely a month."

"What do you mean, permission?"

"You'll have to ask for my hand in marriage. He has a right to know what's in store for his daughter."

I used the phone in the hallway — the only one for use by the Clarendon's residents. It took a long time but eventually I got through to my father.

"Hello Daddy, you know that Canadian I've been dating?"

"Yes."

"We'd both like to come down to see you because he wants to ask permission to marry me. When can we come?"

Silence.

"Daddy?"

"He will never have my permission," my father said in a voice encased in anger.

How could he ruin my happiness like that? My eyes pricked with tears. "What do you mean? You don't even know him."

"You can come tomorrow and he can talk all he wants but he'll never have my permission."

"Goodbye" I said, "We'll see you tomorrow."

"Goodbye."

I turned from the phone and stumbled back to Ted "He won't give his permission," I bawled.

Ted frowned, then as if a light went on he said, "Then I won't ask for his permission, I'll ask for his blessing and no father can refuse that."

He lifted my downcast face so I could see he was confident and wiped my tears away with his finger. I had to smile as I thought I had a pretty smart cookie there.

He arrived early the next morning to go to the railway station and was bursting with the news.

"The United States has dropped atom bombs on Japan!"

He told me all previous weapons were nothing compared to the magnitude of this. With just one bomb they had wiped out the city of Hiroshima and another one, Nagasaki — two large Japanese cities.

"We may not have to go to Burma after all: Japan has no choice but to surrender," he told me.

The train was absolutely crowded with troops with no room in the carriages, so we arranged our cases to serve as seats in the corridor like many others.

I love trains. The rhythmic sound of the wheels is like the pendulum of our grandfather clock. The placards with the names of the towns had not been replaced yet, but I knew the look of the towns we passed so I could tell when Gillingham was near. We caught a bus to Hempstead and Mother was at the gate of our house. I knew Ted would think she was sweet — I hadn't told him she was German born (I found out much later that his grandfather was German too).

Father wasn't sweet. He wasted no time to take Ted into the dining room, closing the door firmly behind them while Mother and I strained our ears to hear what was going on. Ted's voice held its own so we gathered he was doing all right.

My thirteen-year-old brother John, thought it was jolly good to have a colonial air force officer visiting. We had roast chicken (Father always kept chickens), peas and carrots from the garden, and Mother's Brown Betty pudding made with apples from our orchard. Questions were shot at Ted from every direction.

Father was good during the meal and afterwards walked with Ted to the orchard while Mother and I did the dishes.

"He's a nice boy," Mother said, "and I hope you'll have a good life together. But I must tell you it isn't easy marrying a man from another country, even if you won't have a language barrier."

Father had softened by the time he came back to the kitchen.

"I would have never given my consent to this match but I can't refuse my blessing," he said. "Ted's mother needs assistance and TB is very contagious you know. But I do wish you all the best Doris." He hugged me and gulped down his emotions. I knew he would soon have indigestion.

Ted slept on the "put-you-up" (bed-chesterfield) in the living room and when I took him in a morning cup of tea — a British custom — I asked if he had slept well.

"That stupid clock kept me awake all night. How can you stand it bonging away every quarter of the hour?"

Primly, I said, "We don't hear the bonging. It's part of our home life."

We played a game of cards and when Ted knew he was losing, he shocked me by losing his temper. Afterwards Mother took me aside and said it was a danger signal and to expect it to rear its head in our married life.

We said goodbye to my parents, feeling lighter because we were on good terms — unlike my mother's experience of being forbidden to return home if she married my father. We walked to catch the bus and when it arrived we got on together and Ted lifted me up in his arms.

"She's going to marry me!" he shouted to the driver and passengers, "Isn't it wonderful?"

And they all clapped and laughed. It was embarrassing but I loved his impulsive ways — such a contrast to the British.

At the train station we split and ran for our respective trains, each running backwards and blowing kisses until he disappeared amongst the steam of the engines.

July 9th was to be my twenty-first birthday and Ted said he'd do all he could to be with me for the celebration. I had invited about a hundred people which included the necessary truckload of airmen from the near-by base.

He came the day before and we had been out cycling but we rushed to make the hotel before curfew time. I was still under twenty-one and had to be in by eleven. He stopped and pulled over to a lighted telephone kiosk. "I must hurry," I told him, feeling a bit like Cinderella.

All of a sudden I was frightened. There were so many stories of men from overseas who had raped girls. Did I really know this man? He held out a pair of air force wings encased in an acrylic heart - it had a cord to put around my neck. "I made this for you," he said and I fainted dead away.

There was an awful screeching in my ears as I came to and a British Bobby was standing over me writing in a small navy-blue book.

"What I've got so far 'ere sir," he was saying to Ted, "is that you was a-walking your bikes when all of a sudden the young lady 'ere pitches fo'ard and went out like a bloomin' light."

Ted had phoned for an ambulance and in spite of my objections I was put on a stretcher and taken to hospital. He had phoned the Clarry.

It was midnight when they wheeled me into the women's ward. Two nurses were whispering and looked at me in a disparaging way. Patient's overhead lights were turned on and I could see I was in a dormitory-type room. I saw with horror that they were looking at me because they thought I had been raped.

The Sister came and said I must have some tests.

"No," I said "I have a big party organized for tomorrow and must leave in the morning."

Ted was supposed to come and get me at ten a.m. if I was okay. I dressed and sat in a straight-backed chair, waiting. The minutes ticked by and the buzz of whispering on the ward started again. I knew they were thinking "Poor girl; he does what he wants and then scrams."

But Ted arrived and all of them saw how concerned he was and I was just thankful they couldn't smell his breath which reeked of beer.

Now when I say "reeked," I'm one of those people who think two pints of beer will reek, reek and reek. I wondered if this was another danger signal.

He apologized.

The party was a great success and my parents gave me a gold locket and watch: We never wore costume jewelry; it had to be real gold and real precious stones or nothing at all.

Ted's mother had still not sent the ring for me.

Worse, she was bombarding him with letters telling him not to marry me. She tried every device. His sister had joined in the condemnation and

Ted was absolutely crushed by it.

British Iron and Steel Corporation was able to return to London because, of course, the war was over. And Ted could be sent home anytime, so he wanted to set a date for the wedding. Everything seemed to be on quicksand.

Ted's father wrote to me to say he was happy Ted was to marry me and oh! the letter meant so much to me I thought maybe I had a friend over there after all.

But we had much to sort out. As a non-Catholic, I was told I could only marry a Catholic if I took instructions in the Catholic faith. We had to go through a sort of indoctrination so we made arrangements to go to a nearby convent and meet with the mother superior.

There was no question of Ted changing his religion. He'd been an altar boy and was deeply attached to the Catholic religion. I would have to swear to bring up any children in the Catholic faith and abide by the rules of the religion. Fish on Friday. No birth-control. No divorce and so on.

As I had been educated in a convent, I already knew the catechism — a book of questions and answers about the Catholic teachings. The mother superior welcomed me with a hug crushing me against her stiffly starched bib. Her protruding white bonnet scratched my face. We would repeat the catechism like robots although I didn't believe any of it. One day Ted joined me and was taken aback by the way she was teaching me. He refused to let me go anymore.

Coming down with the flu

I still didn't have my engagement ring from Canada.

I was walking up the hill on the main street of Leamington Spa when my head started to spin and the pavement rushed up to hit me in the face. I had to stagger the last few steps to reach the Clarry and collapsed inside the door. Blurry faces over me carried me to a van. I didn't care where they were taking me and absolutely nothing mattered anymore. It felt I was carried along in the under-current of the earth.

When I somewhat recovered two days later, my hurting eyes could make out slim tall windows with curtains of olive-green brocade. A nursing sister came through the door and, crossing herself, said "Glory be to the Father, the son and the Holy Ghost! She's back in the land of the living!"

My lips were parched and flaked with dead skin.

The sister murmured "You've had the worst case of 'flu. You almost died."

I then could see that I was in Ashorne Hill's infirmary, overlooking the familiar rose garden. I drifted back to sleep.

Two days later, the sister nudged my arm. "Doris, a Canadian air force officer wants to see you. Are you up to it?"

My legs felt like jelly but I put my housecoat on and leaning on sister's arm, I went out to see Ted.

I don't think he knew how ill I'd been because he was talking a mile a minute and I had to concentrate to figure out what he was saying.

"Mother's letters are getting more harsh. I think she's worried she won't receive any more money from my paycheque when we marry." he said.

I wasn't well enough to care a fig about anything.

After a few days they allowed me to return to the Clarry to recover properly. Ted had to return to base but I didn't want him to go. I seized on the idea that I could go with him as I still had sick-leave. He was ecstatic. I hurriedly left a message with the manager of the Clarry and asked her to tell Peggy. I threw my clothes into a suitcase and like honeymooners, we were off to Yorkshire where Ted was based.

A place was found for me for the two days. During the war people opened up their extra rooms to billet visiting spouses and girlfriends of members of the forces. Ted carried my suitcase up to the bedroom and it was hard for him to leave but I was nervous and didn't want to abuse the host's kindness.

We danced that night to a large orchestra similar to Tommy Dorsey's band. There were at least twenty-five musicians and they played all our favourite war-time songs. We were in a large marquee and they had a makeshift dance floor. It was wonderful and sad at the same time because most of the dancing men were to be sent back home pretty soon. But for the moment, we danced and danced and the pulsing swing music surrounded us with its hypnotic spell. Our sexual desires were reaching a dangerous level and there was a hunger to throw caution to the wind and find a way to sleep in each other's arms.

Next morning he borrowed a bike and came to say he got a telegram from my father demanding to know where I was and I was to phone Peggy at the Clarendon and Dad at Hempstead. I wondered how on earth my father had tracked Ted down like that.

I phoned Peggy first, maybe I could put off dealing with my father.

"Hi Peggy! what's up?" I asked after I got through to her.

"What's up? What's up?" she shouted. "We've all been going crazy here. No one knew where you were. What the heck are you doing in Yorkshire? Have you eloped with Ted? How could you worry us so much?"

"I left a message with the manager at the Clarry, Peggy."

"Well we never got the message. The manager was called to London because her mother died suddenly. We had no idea what happened to you. Father is going round the bend, it was no small job to track Ted down. Now you phone Dad right away."

I told her it was all above board but, as I stood there, I realized once again no one would believe me, believe I was as pure as a white dove!

I got through to my father and had to hold the phone away from my ear because of his angry, booming voice. He ended with "I wish you'd learn responsibility and consider others' feelings. First you're deathly ill, Ted visits you when you're hardly out of bed, and then you disappear. What's he thinking of? It's disgraceful."

I tried to explain and guessed no one could have such a great time without something going haywire. Ted was to fly on a mission so I high-tailed back to the Clarry with the reputation of a stained woman. At least we had snatched a little extra time together.

Soon after I got back to the Clarry, Ted phoned from Yorkshire. "Dody, we can't go on like this, tell me when we can get married. How about the end of August?"

"We can't do that because Peggy's wedding is going to be on the 23rd September. I couldn't upstage her and besides, my poor parents have to foot the bill for both receptions."

I was starting to realize that I'd be leaving everything I'd known.

So we aimed for the 10th November as that would enable Ted to start procedures and then, when he next came down to Hempstead we could get the marriage licence.

He had to go on a mission. The crew was piloting VIPs here, there and everywhere but he managed to come to Peggy's wedding.

The church was made of stone, centuries old and quaint. Denys was in the army so members of the guard of honor held their swords over the path leading to the church. She would now be Mrs.Grasby. The reception was in an old Tudor lodge with ceilings so low Ted had to duck under them to dance. It was good to see Mother and Dad. We thought we should tell them the date of our wedding now and thankfully Dad took it well enough.

To be a bridesmaid for Peggy's wedding, I had to find a dress but I didn't have the coupons for one. Judy, who worked in the office next to me was teaching me to sew. She was a seamstress and offered to loan me a bridesmaid dress she had. She brought out a pale-grey box from her closet and slipped the string from it. She removed the lid and pulled away the tissue paper. Slowly, carefully, she lifted the dress from its sleeping place.

It was azure blue and the material was chiffon. The movement caused by being lifted from the box made it flutter and billow as if it had a life of its own. There were two small blue doves to be worn in the hair. "Let's see you in it," she said.

It floated over my head and hugged and released my body in a caressing way. I stepped up to the full-length mirror and felt the breath being snatched from me. It was beautiful! The dress was meant for me! The blue accented the colour of my eyes and the doves nestled in my long, wavy blond hair. The chiffon trembled, waiting to be asked to dance. I knew Ted would love me even more when he saw this vision of loveliness, and I knew I would never look so good again.

I turned towards Judy. "Thank you Judy, it's wonderful."

Her face was sternly set. "Doris, you can't have the dress. It's your sister who is the bride. It's her day. No one would look at anyone else if you wore that gown."

I knew she was right so I took it off and we folded it carefully back into the grey box. When Judy tied the string around it again I wanted to cry because Ted would never know how I could look.

I borrowed a dress from someone else and no one else knew about the azure blue beauty which had made me a princess for those few minutes.

And Peggy looked lovely.

After the wedding reception and Peggy and Denys had left for their honeymoon, I changed so that Ted and I could go for a walk. He seemed distracted and depressed and I asked him why.

"Mother says it would make more sense to hold off getting married until I return to Canada, get settled and then send for you."

I froze. I couldn't talk. Visions of this woman told me she wouldn't let her boy go without a fight.

"There seems to be so many hurdles," he went on, "there's the question of religion and where will I find accommodation in Canada? The money I always give my mother. Can I afford that and afford to set up house with you as well."

I felt an awful cold run through my veins. Was this the man who had begged and begged me to be his? I could not believe what I was hearing.

I was well and truly in shock.

I went to sit on a nearby stone wall turning my face away from him.

The grass looked greener this year. The first bronze leaves of autumn sailed down lazily from the oak trees. There was a tinge of cold in the air and I didn't want to hear what Ted was saying.

At last I said in a hard voice, "Perhaps it's best if we call the whole thing off. I have doubts too."

His face panicked and he reached to hold me as if he would never let me go. "We'll rise above the obstacles, Dody. Don't let's give into other influences. We won't let anything stand in our way."

BISC was to return to London. All personnel were given a choice. Go with them or leave with a bonus. As I'd be going to Canada and probably never see my family again, I opted to take the bonus and said goodbye to the Clarry, which had seen me from a seventeen-year-old girl to a twenty-one-year-old woman. I went home to Hempstead where we would be married. Peggy was to go to London with the firm.

Getting married *(10th November 1945)*

Father came with me to find a Catholic church to be married in. We found one and the priest was outside chasing a chicken on the grass. The walls of the church were propped up with beams. When we went inside we could see it was dirty and in a state of disrepair, one had the impression it could have been a chicken coop. Father was horrified and without giving me the chance to say anything, made excuses to leave.

"No daughter of mine will be married in that flea trap," he said, burping with an upset stomach.

So that's how we found the church in Rochester (close to where Charles

Dickens had lived).

Two small children were kneeling in prayer and I thought the Catholic religion can't be all that bad if small children can feel at home going to pray without their parents being there and no service going on.

Father Thomas agreed to have the ceremony and said he'd read the banns — the announcement of upcoming weddings six weeks before the ceremony. This tradition was from the old days and gave a chance for anyone who disagreed with the wedding to speak up. "Of course," he said to me, "you're not entitled to a mass because you're not a Catholic"

Father arranged for the reception to be in the Swan Hotel and my parents paid for it all. Ted went to get a marriage licence in Rochester. It was horrible. The Dickens character of Uriah Heep was behind the counter and snarled at Ted. During the war a lot of Englishmen resented the Americans or Canadians taking the best looking girls away from England.

"So!" he said "A colonial thinks he'll be a somebody if he carries a genuine English product back to Canada does he?"

I was proud of Ted not to retaliate but it was nasty.

Well, what do you know? Ted's mother finally sent the engagement ring. It was almost time for our wedding by the time I'd had it enlarged and it was put on my finger. How could I like it when someone who hated me had chosen it? We bought the wedding rings together. They were plain narrow bands and stamped with the "utility" symbol. During the war all manufacturing was only of a useful nature. No frills. Chinaware, clothes and jewelry were good, basic stuff and reasonably priced. It was possible to get more elaborate things but they would cost one dearly and they were in short supply.

As I wasn't able to splurge on a wedding dress, I felt I could put my coupons and my bonus money to good use by buying a going away suit, the outfit one wears after the wedding reception.

We were going to visit Peggy in London when I espied a beautiful suit in an exclusive shop window. Definitely not utility. It was a tan colour with a subtle checked design; the pockets had pleats and were edged with brown velvet. The collar was velvet and the shoulders were padded, the very latest thing. I stopped in my tracks and pulled Ted into the shop. The price was equivalent to a month's wages. Undaunted, I tried it on, asked for the skirt to be shortened and put a deposit on it. Once outside of the shop Ted lost his temper with a vengeance. I tried to explain a girl needed to feel special on her wedding day. I had to borrow my wedding dress from my cousin's wife and besides, the bonus I had from BISC would cover the cost.

He turned me towards him in the street and said, "You'll have to realize that from now on, money belongs to both of us and we'll need every penny to start our lives in Canada. You make me scared when you spend money like that on the spur of the moment. What am I to think of our future?"

So I bawled my head off all down the street. There was nothing I could do about the suit now and by jingo, there's nothing I would do about it because I felt justified in buying it. We didn't really know each other after all. When we reached Peggy's apartment she knew right away that we'd had a row. She ushered us into the living room and closed the door, so we could work through the problem. The temper and tightness with money worried me and my spending petrified him!

Letty had asked me why I didn't move to London with them until I was called to Canada. There were hidden reasons. There had been a couple of older men in the firm who had persisted in bothering me. One was a department head who had chased me up the stone tower in Warwick castle while feeling up my legs (I heard later that he'd cornered lots of young women). His wife was our friend and we refrained from reporting him because she would have been devastated.

And another thing, we would be living in the center of London's theatre district and I'd be tempted to go on the stage again. I loved the smell of it, the excitement and the fantasy-land of the stage. So if I was faced with the temptation to be a star again, would I be able to resist it?

My mother had been right. Ted had a temper which could erupt suddenly and if I had doubts about our marriage, I figured, as a Protestant I could divorce him if things didn't work out. But Ted seemed to read my mind.

"Don't think you can be divorced from me and if there's any possibility of it in your mind we'd better call everything off right now."

Whoops!

Meanwhile, I had received a parcel from Ted's mother, Loretta. It was a lovely white nightie and dressing gown. I thought she may be softening.

And so we reached the 9th November. Ted went into a hotel close to the church for the night. He phoned and said he would be giving me a diary on our wedding day: A diary of all the days we'd spent together; every movie we'd seen; every dance we had gone to; the walks we took, and highlights of our times together.

Many years later, as I became frustrated with his drinking, I wanted to hurt him some way and when he came home one night in that state, he found the torn apart pages of that diary strewn across the living room.

His best man had been sent on a mission so he'd asked Wes, who had lived close to him in Cornwall, Ontario, to fill in. This man had also married an English girl and I would meet her when I arrived in Cornwall.

I woke up on the 10th to hear Mother starting a fire in the kitchen stove. She was always the first up and had the place warm and a cup of tea for Father in bed before everyone got underway. She had a heart condition but everyone ignored it. She was expected to carry on doing all that she had done before the diagnosis. I used to get angry to see her carrying a boiler full of chicken feed. She'd take it to the end of the garden huffing and puffing with the strain of it. I wondered why the doctor didn't set the family down and insist we understand the danger signs.

She'd had the first signs of heart problems while I was home after my hymen operation. Dad had told her to lie down because she was having pain in her chest.

"It's only indigestion," he had told the doctor when he came.

I had gone up to her bedroom and she was gasping for breath. Her left arm and leg was numb and she was frightened. I massaged them until they returned to normal. I was not only relieved but proud that I had done something right. The doctor told my father not to be so insensitive and it was a heart attack, not indigestion.

But now it was the morning of my wedding.

I looked through the lace curtains to see it was a bright autumn day and birds were singing. My heart was fluttering. I saw my dress and veil hanging in the open closet together with borrowed satin shoes. My going-away suit was there too arousing a feeling of pride and rebellion.

Mother knocked on the door, she had a tray with some tea for me. Her face was sad and she looked on the verge of tears. She had such a sweet face with large brown eyes and a poignant look about her always.

"Good morning Doris, there's two letters here from Canada," she said.

Mother sat on the side of the bed as I opened the first.

> *Doris,*
>
> *I want you to know that we in Canada are disgusted with the way you tramps of English girls run after and snare our boys. Ted is a long way*

from home and lonely for us and he has fallen
prey to you.

I'm sure if he came to Canada before
marrying you he would change his mind.

I can't stop your wedding but I will always
know you trapped him.

Loretta

I handed the letter to Mother.

I opened the second letter from Ted's sister. It told me that I was responsible for making the whole family miserable and must have coerced him into marrying me. That his religion was everything to him and it was despicable that he would even think of marrying a non-Catholic and they will absolutely not welcome me into the family.

Doubts. Fears. Hurt. Sorrow. Uncertainty. All these emotions crowded down on me. I thought of more hurdles to be overcome. This spite was waiting for me. What a mess. Mother couldn't speak after reading the letters.

The phone rang, thankfully it was Ted. I told him what was in the letters and he was hurt too.

"It's hard for Mother not to be involved in such an important time," he said, "let's just think of us today Dody. My darling, tonight you will be Mrs. Ted Paterson and nothing anyone can say or do will alter that."

He had arranged for us to go to Torquay for our honeymoon and have five days off and had booked a room in the Regents Palace Hotel in London.

"They've got a new movie out called the *Wizard of Oz* and do you know what? Halfway through they go into colour instead of black and white. It's okay Dody, with us together we can lick the world!"

Father read Loretta's letter and his face turned beet red. He looked like a raging bull.

"I'll keep that letter as proof of the reception you will get," he said, "It's not too late to change your mind or at least hold off a while."

But as usual, I blithely plowed on, hoping things would improve.

Peggy and Letty, and Margaret — my best friend who was always by my side — would meet us at the church. They were at the Swan Hotel. I put on my virginal white gown and crowned my head with a plaited halo and veil.

Father gulped air as he helped me into the car. He had sworn never to "give the bride away." But everyone told him not to be an old poop and at last he agreed. "Such a silly thing to say, 'to give your daughter away,' as if a father wants to do that," he said.

So down the aisle I walked, carrying red roses, and Ted was waiting at the altar in his air-force-blue uniform. Slim, slightly elegant, watching me come toward him with loving, approving eyes.

It was as though I was on a stage playing a part unfamiliar to me. As I said "I do" it all seemed unreal and the morning's letters came to mind like a curse in a fairy tale.

"I pronounce you man and wife."

I came to my senses and we kissed — my first kiss as Mrs. Paterson pledging our lives to each other. We signed the register and were driven to the reception at the Swan Hotel.

Everyone was in a jolly mood. I met Wes. Poor Ted. Only one person to represent his side of the proceedings. What a lovely wedding cake it was. Mother had so much trouble getting the cake made, the family had to give up some ration coupons to make it and to have it iced with marzipan and royal icing. Mummy and Dads gave us the traditional present of a silver tea-service. We had said we wouldn't drink on that day (Seems to me it must have been my idea).

A waiter came to me and said, "In all the time I've worked here, I've never seen such a beautiful bride. May I drink a toast to your happiness?"

"Of course," I said thinking how sweet of him to do that.

"And of course," he continued after downing the sherry in a split second, I'd like to drink to the lucky man."

Another glassful disappeared.

"And...," he started again but I twigged to his game. Darn it: I thought he was genuine. But the man who was now my husband was not like that, he was always honest.

I changed into my travel suit and knew I looked great. It was worth the fight. We hopped on a train to London and our future.

I expected we'd be by ourselves on the train to London a-hugging and a-kissing but instead Wes joined us and the men talked sports and air force as if we were on a shopping expedition or something. After we reached the London station we were finally alone, free of outside interference, and I had him back for myself.

I was suddenly terribly shy as we registered at the Regent Palace desk. My cheeks were flaming as Ted unlocked the door to our room. Once we were inside he took me in his arms and I knew with horror, he had felt my girdle. I wore it to give me a smooth shape but if he went to undress me I wondered how he would deal with a live girdle?

The bathrooms were not adjoining our room but down the hallway and thank goodness he left to have a shower. I frantically tore the ruddy thing off and pushed it in my suitcase.

He did undress me.

"I wish I was an artist so I could paint you just as you are now," he said.

I had to turn my head away from his hungry scrutiny and oh! how I wished I had had a sherry at the reception because I knew he was to penetrate me and it would probably hurt.

Sure enough the sheet was stained red in the morning and I'd forgotten Mother's warning to use the foaming stuff she'd tucked amongst my nighties.

I had to ask Ted to get some Kotex for me. Nobody warned me about that. And I mustn't use Mother's stuff because one of the vows I made for the Catholic church was that I couldn't use birth-control.

The following morning was Armistice Day and we walked to the central cenotaph. It was misty cold with a hint of frost. Marching bands and dignitaries came to put wreaths on the cenotaph remembering those who died in the war. Sorrow was still raw and bleeding with so many people gone. A lone bugler played Taps and guns boomed their twenty-one-gun salute. The blood red poppies glowed through the grey mist and all of us shed tears.

We were standing in the eye of history, battered London surrounding us. There had been so many heroes, not only at the front but also in the city and the country. And what a spirit we had! Rich or poor, aristocrat or commoner, England had fought against all odds. I was proud. It was wonderful to belong to each other and both of us felt it heightened our happiness and awareness of life, everything seemed sharper, clearer and magical.

We saw Judy Garland in the *Wizard of Oz*. Before the movie there was a cartoon with Donald Duck and Ted actually rolled in the aisle with laughing. American comedy for me left much to be desired.

We stayed in a rooming house in Torquay on the south Devon coast. It was cold but we visited the caves of stalagmites and stalactites which I found pretty scary as they were deep down in caves. We went to a football game and the place was so crowded you couldn't move an inch.

"How do you get to the toilet if you need to?" I asked.

"Why do you think the men have rolled up newspapers" Ted replied by way of explaining.

We walked along some trails by the sea but heavy fog obscured everything. Before we knew it, it was time to return to London, from where Ted was posted to Yorkshire and I would return home. He was to find furnished rooms for us in York so I could join him. He was to be there for a short time.

In spite of her awful letter to me, Loretta sent a card. I guess she just had to accept we were married.

Ted phoned for me to join him and off I went to be a married woman and housewife. I didn't know how a housewife filled her time. I knew she cleaned and cooked and fussed with everything, but half the time Ted wouldn't be there and when he was, he was so clean and neat that nothing was disturbed. I found it hard to think I'd be in a house with only that prospect in mind. I loathed cleaning but liked cooking.

The house we rented was a side by side (duplex) and nicely furnished, it even had a hand-operated washing machine. Of the two bedrooms, one was jammed with the owner's stuff and locked. Ted told me they still had the key to the house and from time to time they might let themselves in to get things from that room. We had to accept that condition otherwise there was no accommodation to be had.

I hated to be alone when Ted was flying. All my life I had someone with me. Making matters worse, I didn't have any money of my own. During that time I found that all my jewelry had disappeared and I suspected the landlord's son but how was I to prove it?

Later I would get a cheque each month from the Canadian government as a wife's allowance but when we were in York I had nothing. I tried to work the washing machine but nearly wrenched my arms from their sockets turning that stupid wooden churner. I wasn't made to do those sort of things, I was the pretty girl on the stage, I had no use for physical work. I hadn't brought my paints with me and there was nothing to sew. Only thing left was to cook.

Ted came with me to get un-rationed items like powdered milk, powdered eggs and some flour. I learned to make the best omelets and different sauces to enhance the little meat we were allowed. I learned as long as you knew how to make a white sauce you could adapt it for all kinds of different sauces.

When Ted took off on his flying junkets I paced the floor and wondered what other wives did and whether they were as lonely and as bored as I was.

Ted showed me one could actually toast marshmallows, which seemed impossible to me. Lovely taste.

The owner's son came in one day and found out I had committed the worst crime. I had broken the coronation teapot.

To English people, coronation teapots and such are considered holy icons. These had the faces of the king and queen and the date inscribed and were usually kept in glass-fronted mahogany cabinets, preferably lit from behind and handed down from father to son. The landlord hadn't thought to leave an ordinary teapot for us and I had used the coronation one and broken off the spout when I emptied the leaves in the toilet. The owner's wife came, and said she would have never rented the place to me if she had known I was so careless. I just felt helpless in my new role. I didn't know that things like that were precious, our home had only one thing that resembled that teapot and that was an ashtray from Bognor Regis which we considered a carnival amusement trinket.

Days dragged by, relieved only when Ted would come through the door and I would jabber my head off and couldn't stop for all the crown jewels.

But it wasn't long before he was sent to another base and there wasn't any accommodation for wives so I went back home. There were odd times I would visit him by train. I remember one time when he had said he loved butterscotch pie. I found a recipe and was making it when I thought it wasn't like toffee at all, so I kept putting in all the brown sugar I could find until it was sticky and sweet like butterscotch. I carried it on my lap all the way on the train to his base. I thought he'd be thrilled but he made a face when he tasted it and said: "It's nothing like OUR butterscotch pie!"

Sometimes it would feel strange because he would leave me in bed at night and by the time I woke in the morning he would have been to Italy or some other country and back again.

He had some time off for Christmas and came to Hempstead on Christmas Eve. He took part in lighting the tiny candles on the tree and tasted Mother's wonderful cooking. We went for a walk in crisp snow and mainly talked about what it would be like to live together in Canada. For New Years', we visited Yapton and the old cobble-stone house which used to be my grandparents home. Ada, who had looked after the old couple when they were ill, lived in the house now.

It was smaller than I remembered. I showed Ted the stairway window where I used to sit to read books. We walked to the bridge where we played as children. I learned that the pirates actually did use this bridge as a hiding place for their ill-gotten gains.

Ada had never met anyone like Ted. She'd never married and was shy. As they say "she was backward in coming forward." We were sitting down to dinner but she was still fussing in the background. Ted picked her up bodily, she was just a slip of a thing, and plonked her in a chair. Her fluster was a delight to see, she pulled her black apron over her face to muffle her giggles. After that she wasn't as shy.

We went to Brighton and walked on the pier against bitter wind. The waves sent giant sprays of tangy salt into our faces. I told him of the many summers we spent at the beach when we were young.

"Have you ever ice-skated Dody?" he asked when we came to an arena. And I hadn't.

We went in and he rented skates for both of us, he tied my laces so tight it cut off circulation. "You've got to have them tight to support your ankles" he explained.

With that, he jumped onto the ice and as I watched in amazement, he twirled and zoomed backwards in confident, graceful motions. The audience looked at him in awe and some young women were trying to get close to him. He broke his speed with a cutting sound, sending up showers of ice particles. He was happy and exhilarated.

"Come on Dody - I'll show you how," he said as he held my hand.

I stumbled, slipped and slid helplessly every which way, my wrists hurt with grabbing hold of him. We tried a few times but I'm a timid creature and I was cold and couldn't feel anything below my ankles. He had to be on his own in this so I sat down on the bench and watched him take centre stage.

He went back to duty. I didn't know what or why he was flying. Something about taking people to be juried in Europe. Life with him was all bits and pieces of days. He seemed to be always taking off. I wondered if he would find it hard to settle down when he got back to Canada.

For me the days dragged in Hempstead although one thing I was thankful for was the opportunity to get to know my mother better. We developed a stronger bond because of it.

I resented my father and my heart ached for my mother when she ran to get the mail before Father saw it. If there was a bill she hadn't paid he'd have a fit and the house would echo with his bellowing. I couldn't see she ever spent money on herself while a lot of the grocery items were bought just for him. He could buy beer or a new car without any question and the house was paid for, so why didn't he relax? I decided I never wanted to live in a situation like that. She was nine years older than Father and didn't want sex anymore. She couldn't run home to her family and she didn't have friends because she was STILL considered an alien in England. She attended the small church next door to us but sometimes she was the only one there and the minister told her it wasn't worth his while to preach to a single person. Sometimes when she had a nap in the afternoon, she took a sleeping pill. She hadn't told me and when I went to wake her one day, she just would not come to. It worried me that she needed to take the pills.

Word came that Ted was to fly back to Canada in early May, 1946, from the base in Prestwick, Scotland. He asked me to travel there to be with him until take-off time. A crew-member's wife joined me and we took the train up to Prestwick.

We stayed in an old Scottish mansion and it was wonderful. The bath tub was as big as a swimming pool. The porridge was cooked all night and served with rich cream in the morning.

We only had the two days and all our talk was about finding a place to live, to write often, to be good. And pray it wouldn't be long before we'd be together. The other wife and I stood at the end of the runway fence and we waved and waved goodbye.

There were four hours to wait for our train to return home so we decided to rent a rowboat. We clean forgot it was the open sea and a wicked current caught us, carrying us far from shore. We looked back to see the beach was far, far behind and we were drifting further every second. We had lost our moorings in more ways than one. It took every bit of our reserve to strive to row against the pull of the water. We were both crying with frustration and thought at one time we had lost the battle. We redoubled our effort and, trembling and exhausted, we managed to make it to shore. We cried with relief as we put our feet on the beach. It was one way to forget about our men leaving us.

5:

On my way to Canada

It was 1946 and I was a war bride now, waiting for a space on a ship to join Ted. Time dragged and I thought I was in limbo.

For Ted, it was exciting and yet traumatic. His mother could put some of her responsibilities on Ted's shoulders. He learned that as well as TB, his father had heart trouble. Ted had rehabilitation leave, time to reconnect with relations and work.

At first, he wrote every other day but gradually letters were spaced further apart. He went back to his job at Courtaulds and looked for a place for us to rent. He went to dances which had big bands. I tried to come to terms with that. Didn't he know he was married? Maybe I should go to dances too. That would create problems for sure. I'd never been to a dance that men didn't crowd around me. I argued with myself not to be childish. I knew he was getting pressured from Loretta and if it came that I had to wait a long time before I joined him, she might find a way to win.

He wrote that he was lonesome for me and missed the comradeship of his flying crew.

He told me he'd given up looking for a place to rent and the Canadian government had given permission for us to stay at his parent's house until he found something. Ouch! That wasn't good news for me. He told me that there had been no building during the war and the country was trying to absorb the influx of so many veterans returning with their wives.

I packed my belongings in a large green canvas covered trunk with a rounded lid. My parents could hardly bear to see it sitting there, reminding them I would be going far away.

I got a letter from Canada House in London telling of some wives of Canadian servicemen who had been killed in air raids or had died in other circumstances and the children of these men needed to be escorted to Canada. They asked for any of the war brides to undertake this service. If so, we would have priority on our passage. I volunteered.

It wasn't long before I had a reply asking me to escort a young boy and my passage was confirmed for the 13th August, 1946, in the s.s.Aquitainia.

I was on my way to mail a letter to Ted when I heard this, so I wrote on the back of the envelope "Sailing on 13th August with child," not realizing the effect the word "child" would have on Loretta.

I savoured my last weeks at Hempstead. After I left England, I never saw my parents again.

The green trunk was sent ahead. My instructions for the journey along with traveling clothes, presents for the in-laws and toiletries were packed in a suitcase to travel with me.

Finally it hit me! It's something like the night before you get married. What have I done? How will I be without the love and protection which surrounded me since my birth? How will I bear to part with my dear, dear parents. How will I endure living with Ted's mother who hates the very mention of my name? I know I will have one friend and that's Ted's father. Although come to think of it, that might make matters worse with Loretta.

Would I ever see my country again?

It was time to leave and my brother Gordon was waiting to take me to the train. At *Homeleigh*'s gate, my mother and father waved and cried goodbye. Tears wouldn't come to my eyes and I couldn't speak. I entered a trance-like state. This happened when I had to go through something unbearable. Walking, getting on the train and the taxi in London was all done automatically, my brain and feelings numb. I told myself it'll soon be over and I won't be able to turn back.

I arrived at the designated place. It was a large, red-brick house.

A group of about thirty women and children were gathered together to be escorted to the boat the next day. I was shown to a large sparse room. There were bunk beds in four tiers against three walls. I asked if I could sleep on the bottom bed.

A lady called my name, loudly:

"Your sister is here to see you," she said.

"Oh Peggy," I cried out when I saw her. The numbness which had held me was melting, "It's so good to see you!"

"Letty has come too," she said, trying to be cheerful. "Let's go for a cup of tea."

"I must be back by eleven," I said, "we leave early tomorrow."

We went out talking and crying while looking for a restaurant. We settled down a bit over cups of tea and crumpets and held a horrible ache in our breasts. Soon it was time to return to the house.

"Good-bye Peggy," I moaned. "Know that a little of me stays here with my family and England."

Even Letty had tears in her eyes.

It was strange to sleep with so many people. Not like my dear home in the country with only the sound of birds. A child was fretful. Heavens! It would be hard to explain to a little one. Apparently I was to meet my ward on the boat. I hoped we'd get along well. I had nightmares. The lady in the bunk above me was crying. At last six o'clock came. The children picked up a sense of adventure and played happily and chattered as we boarded a bus for the train station. The train would take us to Southampton.

The carriage wheels went clickety-clack, clickety-clack, a comforting sound. No matter what else changed, that sound was always the same — clickety-clack, clickety clack. I talked to the other brides in the carriage and we showed photos of our spouses and the people we were leaving behind. By the time we reached Southampton we had made new friends.

As we approached the docks, we saw the ship. I smelled the familiar aroma of salt water, the tar and sisal ropes. I remembered going to Hong Kong and the sense of adventure that accompanies going up a gang plank. And I remembered that feeling of being suspended in time when on board – no outside news, no responsibilities, everything catered. Time to dream.

But when I got on board this ship, it was obvious we were NOT on a cruise ship. Partitions were put up and bunks squeezed in everywhere to accommodate as many people as possible. I was allotted a bunk. We were to go to lunch and I had the first sitting at meals. The dining room was as I remembered in the cruise ships. Everything elegant. And could you believe your eyes! WHITE BREAD. We hadn't seen white bread since the onset of the war. It tasted like cake. We were reminded that we were to go to a land of plenty compared to England, poor dear country.

On deck I met up with two ladies I knew from my district who belonged to the British War Bride Club. We welcomed each other as if we were long lost friends. We talked non-stop. The Captain was on the intercom and asked for Doris Paterson. My heart lurched. One of the girls had told me the Captain had just informed one of the brides that she was to return to her family because the husband did not want her to come to Canada.

I went to the Captain's office. He was with a soldier.

"This is Mr. Clark," the captain said.

Mr. Clark shook my hand and said, "I want to thank you for offering to look after my little boy but I was allowed to take him to Canada myself. My wife was killed in the bombing."

I felt sorrow for him and relief for me. Now I could lie back and enjoy myself without the worry of a little one.

After the end of the first day I found it wasn't so bad to be on the sea. If only the girls would stop telling all those horror stories about what to expect when we got to our destinations: A mother-in-law in a wigwam, smoking a pipe; A husband regretted marrying and now had a Canadian girl friend; The picture he showed of the lovely mansion he lived in was just a photo he took of a wealthy person's home; The real truth could be awful.

But I knew my Ted. He would never lie to me. He was as straight as a plumb line. One of the reasons I fell in love with him was because I heard that on one of his flights he had made an error as navigator and when the pilot told him to change the figures as no one would be the wiser, he refused to do so.

The second night was terrible. There was something wrong with the milk on board. The babies were all upset, vomiting and crying.

The sun was wonderful. Without being aware of it, the sea air, the sun and wind combined, tanned my skin. I was starting to get excited to see my new homeland and to be with Ted again. It had been three and a half months since I'd seen him. And I wondered again what reception I would get from his family. His father was now home from the TB sanatorium, thank goodness. I wondered if they would like the gifts I had brought for them. An antique brooch for his mother and I had knitted sweaters for father-in-law and Ted's brother Frank.

The third day, we were now more than half way there. The babies were losing weight and the mothers were fretting. The ship's doctor was concerned and prescribed a milk substitute. My new found friends and I felt as though we had always known each other. One came from Holland. She was beautiful and I adored her accent. So charming. She told me she hated it. Her husband had thought it was cute to begin with but by the time he left he was yelling at her, "Get it straight, for Pete's sake!" he complained that the accent got on his nerves. War time brought horror and dread, but it also brought adventure and romance. It's only when you've had the romance for some time that you face reality.

Day number four. Finally the babies were a little better, if thinner. We were getting used to being on board and the sounds that go with it. Tomorrow we would dock in Halifax. Tomorrow — tomorrow — the stomach churned. Nervous and excited. What could I expect of this Canada? Open spaces, grandeur. (The posters of Banff Hotel lingered in my mind). Fresh-faced people. Men who don't expect so much of their wives. Lots of hopefulness for the future without the depression of having to rebuild all the ruins of war. Lots of ration-free food. Ah well! We would learn if this was true.

My first day in a new world

We left the Aquitania. The Citadel of Halifax was visible. Our papers were checked on the dock-side by warrant officers who stamped our landing cards* "Landed Immigrant." Our money was changed. Some soldiers came to help carry our cases. I waved goodbye to my friends, they were to catch a different train. Some of us were taken to the train station. My stars! what an immense monster that engine was. My heart lurched, I wanted my dear little British trains. The soldier held out his hand for a tip. I looked through the new money. He poked at a five-dollar bill. I gave it to him. I climbed up into the Monster and was pleased with the comfortable surroundings. I will only have to stay on the train for two days and I would be in Montreal and "Ted will be waiting, Ted will be waiting," the wheels seemed to say.

The train moved fast and swayed back and forth making me nauseous. When the porter came to call us for lunch I told him I was sick. Geraldine, another war bride in the compartment with me said she felt the same. The porter told us to go to the dining room and he would bring us something to make us feel better.

* This card is the same one I tore up for use in the collage on the cover of this book.

The dining room was pleasant. The waiter brought us soup bowls with red liquid in them.

"What is it?" we asked.

"Good old tomato soup," he said smiling broadly.

We had never heard of tomato soup but we sipped cautiously and sure enough it settled our stomachs. I wondered what other strange foods we were going to find.

I marveled at the efficiency when the beds were made up for the night and had to admit those monster trains were comfortable. For no reason we could make out, the monster stopped near a village. There was French writing on a sign above a chemist's shop. Geraldine asked the porter how long we would be stopping there and he said, "About an hour."

She tugged at my arm. "Let's go and see what shops in Canada are like. Let's see what we've been missing during the war."

We climbed down the steps of the train and as my feet touched the earth I was conscious that this was Canada. It was a delight to see the selection of make-up in the shop and Geraldine squealed with joy. I bought some face-cream just to say I'd made my first purchase in Canada. Geraldine just couldn't make up her mind what to buy and I got nervous as time ticked by. At last she was done and we went out of the door TO SEE OUR TRAIN LEAVING! It was going without us.

We were in the middle of nowhere, all our stuff was on the train and our men were waiting in Montreal. Even if we ran, we wouldn't have been able to catch it, the train was too far away. We stood horrified until we saw someone's head hanging out of a window of the train and their arms waving frantically. Someone had pulled the emergency cord. There was a massive screeching of the brakes and we ran and ran to climb aboard.

We sat hunched in our seats and waited to be fined or at least scolded but no one came.

The journey seemed endless. Great stretches of land between any sign of life. I didn't expect such vastness, it was frightening really.

As we came close to Montreal, lineups for the washroom formed because we all wanted to replenish our make-up and look our best for our men. Everyone chattered and no one listened. We gathered our suitcases to be ready when the train stopped. As it slowed, the city emerged with warehouses and the backs of houses which had iron steps going up three stories.

Excitement turned into a panic as I wondered if I'd recognize him. I'd only seen Ted in civilian clothes a few times. The Ted I knew was connected to the air force blue uniform. The train ground to a halt and we all went to the windows to search for our loved ones. I saw him and gulped; he had on a ginger-coloured suit and a tie that was at least six inches wide with gaudy colours. But his eyes found me and my heart melted. Those eyes were the bluest in the world: clear, honest and reliable and all was okay again: He was still my Ted.

It was indescribable to feel his arms around me and he kept repeating the words, "You're here. You're here."

He took me to a hotel and as we climbed the stairs to our room everything faded into the background except the fact that we were together. Love for each other rose in intensity and it seemed as if the room would not be able to contain it.

He had brought presents for me, three pairs of nylon stockings (a new development to replace silk stockings) and six oranges. "Remember how we used to tease each other on the different way we pronounced oranges?" he laughed remembering my clipped "o" contrasting his prolonged sound.

He had bought me a music box. He'd shown and played the tune to so many people he had worn out the workings and he had to get another piece of music to put in it. It played *Claire de Lune,* my favourite tune. We didn't sleep much, we had too much to say and had too much love to share.

I was tired and my head spun. The first part of my journey was over and I now had Ted beside me. We were to spend one day in Montreal and then go to Cornwall, Ontario. His hand closed over mine. Such wonderful hands, I knew everything would be all right.

After that passionate night we went out on the streets of Montreal. I had forgotten how much fun it was to be with him. He had a jaunty way and a smile creased the corners of his eyes. He talked so easily and on so many subjects. He was clever and made me laugh often.

I saw elegant shops, but didn't dare ask if I could see what they were like on the inside. I don't think we had ever been in a clothes shop together, other than when I bought my going-away suit. Montreal seemed cosmopolitan, the sophisticated clothes on the women made them look as if they'd stepped out of a movie set. Oh! Oh! I was going to have competition here. I only used a dash of lipstick, mostly cut my own hair, and never used curlers. My clothes were simple and sensible. My suits were expected to be worn for at least ten years. I started to feel frumpy and made a mental note to smarten up.

"Where would you like to go, Dody? What would you like to do? Shall we have lunch first? You can choose something that you haven't been able to get in England since the war," Ted said. My stomach had been grumbling because, other that an orange, I hadn't eaten since getting off the train. I guess Ted didn't realize I'm not used to going without supper and breakfast, even if love seemed to take up all our senses for a while!

We found a restaurant. I ordered bacon and eggs with white toast. Of course we had bacon during the war but my father enjoyed it so much, so we used to let him have our rations. The smell was wonderful. The atmosphere in the restaurant was friendly and different — Canadian.

I see a gorgeous concoction of pink in a tall glass topped with ice cream and a cherry. "I'll have one of those," I said. "It's a strawberry soda," Ted told me, and sat back grinning, enjoying my delight in it. "Now, say the word," he said, "where to now?"

"I'd like to go down in one of those funny little basement bars I see," I told him "and have a rum and cola." His eyes widened. His jaw dropped. I saw a look of concern cross his face. "Is this my girl?" I sensed he was thinking; "Do I really know what she's like?"

The popular song of the moment was *Drinking Rum and Coca Cola,* and I wondered what it tasted like, because they wrote a song about it. I'd never had a drink called Coca-Cola but I'd heard all sorts of stories about it. Like it would rust through tin if it was left in a can. It could rot your teeth. And that people got addicted to it. That it was the most famous recipe which was a closely guarded secret.

"You don't want to go there," he said, "anyway, it's almost time to go to the baseball game. It's such a grand day for it too. We'll ride on top of the street car and on the way you'll see a lot of Montreal."

We started on our way and passed the horse-drawn buggies which took you sight seeing. I tested Ted out: "It looks like such a romantic way to see the city" I said.

"Romantic it may be" Ted replied, "but they charge far too much."

We caught the street car and it was grand to see the buildings and the flower clock and the people in the streets.

We reached the Stadium. Ted was getting antsy with excitement.

"Do you realize, Dody, we're going to see history in the making. This is the first time the big leagues have allowed a black man to play. His name is Jackie Robinson."

All the time we'd known each other there wasn't much mention of sport. My sport consisted of tennis, table tennis and swimming. Period. I do remember one occasion when we were with others in a park in England and the Canadians suggested we play baseball. I went up to bat, hit the ball straight to the pitcher who caught it, and I waited for a better pitch to come. Everybody screamed "Out! Out!" I was outraged. In rounders, our English equivalent game, we were allowed to take a choice of three throws. I spent the rest of the game way out in the field. So I didn't have much love of baseball. Nor did I have any idea that my lover of the previous night could turn into this excitable, screaming creature who is all but ignoring me and concentrating on this asinine arrangement of chasing a ball around.

"Have some pop corn," Ted said, not even looking away from the game, handing me the bag he'd just bought. He threw a handful of these fluffy things into his mouth. I took one piece and put it in mine. It took forever to get rid of those little hard things. I studied them. They were as hard as egg shells. One could choke on them. How did Ted manage to throw so many in his mouth and not bother spitting out this chaff? It certainly had a wonderful nutty smell, but I'd rather not spend all my time worrying if some would stick in my throat.

"Hot dogs! Get your hot-dogs here," young boys were shouting, as they wove in and out of the seats.

"What's a hot-dog?" I asked Ted. He actually looked away from the game and turned to me. "Imagine you not knowing a hot-dog!" he said, and ordered me one. A greasy looking reddish sausage on a long bun. I was surprised because it tasted good. The smell of the hot-dogs, the pop-corn, the rising and falling of the crowd's voices, the warm sunshine, not having slept much the night before, all combined to make me feel very sleepy.

Ted tried to explain what was happening in the game and just when I thought they were speeding up a bit, everyone rushed out to the center of the ballpark and argued with the man in stripes. "Oh! Please ! Get on with the game!" I said to myself. "I'm so tired and it's going on so long."

Hallelujah ! Everyone got up ready to go. I reached for my sweater.

Ted laughed. "No, no, Dody, it's the seventh inning stretch. Just gives people a rest from sitting."

The game went on. Jackie Robinson didn't look too hot, I didn't know if I could stay awake.

"We're going into overtime" Ted said, and we did!

87

It was over at last. I did make it after all!

"I know you won't mind," Ted said, "it's a double header. That means we get to see two games for the price of one."

My heart sank. I was starting to think of the future and wondered if it would entail sitting through many sessions like this one.

Five and a half hours later we left the stadium. Evening shadows were approaching. Tomorrow we were to meet his parents and reality would strike.

My bottom was sore from sitting so long but he took my hand and I had his attention again and I was ready for our future.

6:

Married life in Canada

In the afternoon we caught the train for Cornwall in Ontario — Ted's home and my new one. I wondered what kind of reception I'd get.

Ted's father was born in Scotland and I knew what Ted's mother looked like. She had dark hair and the same brilliant, keen eyes as her son. What I had garnered about her was that she was tiny, just five feet high and she dressed well. She was quite deaf but wouldn't admit it. She sometimes guessed at what people were saying, leading to embarrassing situations.

Mr. Paterson's name was Arthur. He had been a prisoner of war in the first world war, and was in the occupational forces in Northern Ireland. His brother, who had emigrated to Canada, had persuaded him it was the land of opportunity and that he should move here. He worked in a men's wear store and met Loretta in Ottawa. He joined the RCMP and had some sort of job to do by the canal which ran through Cornwall. He told us he thought he had contracted TB from lying in wait on the grassy banks of the canal for boats which used the canal illegally.

He had lost one eye in a car accident. However he had trained the muscles so well that no one was aware he had a glass eye. Arthur could not understand why Ted could spend so much time with sport, especially baseball. He tried to teach him carpentry but when Ted fumbled, Arthur lost patience. Although Ted admired his father, he felt dismissed by him.

We arrived in Cornwall and Ted flagged down a taxi. We whizzed by a nice shopping area then came to streets with single houses. Instead of English, walled-in gardens, there was one continuous green lawn. How did people

89

know where their property began and ended?

Ted's home was one side of a semi-detached house, it had a nice big balcony in the front and I wondered why England didn't have them because they looked so inviting.

The family was in front of the house, waiting for us. Frank, Ted's brother, had been allowed home from the "san" for a short while. Young Helen, Ted's youngest sister, was there too. She was twelve years old. Loretta kissed me on the cheek and Arthur hugged me. I knew he would help me if I needed it.

Loretta had a talent for making a real home: flowered wallpaper, ruffled white-dotted curtains. The dining room was set for dinner with a sparkling white tablecloth and yellow rose chinaware. There was a large boxed-in stove in the corner which sent out black pipes across the ceiling and into other rooms. The kitchen was large and full of good smells.

We were shown upstairs to our room. Mr. and Mrs. Paterson had given up their larger room for us.

Dinner was scrumptious. Loretta sure was a good cook. Everyone peppered us with questions but Ted wanted to tell them about Jackie Robinson. I offered to do the dishes but was made to understand the kitchen was Loretta's domain. There was going to be a lot of working out about what I was allowed to do.

After dinner Ted turned to me and declared, "I've got to go now."

"I don't understand, go where?"

"The days we had in Montreal were my days off. I work different shifts. Tonight I work night shift."

Shift work? Night shift? Tonight? my first night! I was to be left alone with people I don't know? How could he DO that? All these questions tumbled around my brain. He left and as I was still tired, I excused myself and went up to our room to cry and it wasn't long before I fell asleep.

I awoke with a feeling that something was wrong. It was dark and I didn't know where I was. Fear over took me because I smelled the awful smell of wartime gas. I froze as I thought the Germans were coming. We had dreaded the thought of it so long during the war and now there was no doubt — we were being gassed, the room was full of it. I tried to calm down, I thought I should wake everyone up but as no one was disturbed.

I lay awake and fully dressed until morning light. The smell of gas had gone and it was now the smell of Loretta cooking bacon. After he finished his breakfast, Ted came up to find me sitting up in bed.

"What's the matter Dody? You've been crying."

I told him about the gas smell and he laughed and laughed.

"I guess I forgot to tell you about a lot of things we take for granted," he said. "When the wind is in the right direction the smell of the paper mills covers Cornwall."

He rocked me in his arms but he was ready for sleep and his mother had my breakfast ready.

And so the days became routines and I could tell that Loretta was really trying to accept the situation. But as soon as she had rushed around doing the standard household chores, she would escape from me to her next door neighbour. Same thing after lunch.

However, Arthur liked to reminisce about the old country and his prisoner of war experiences. I think he felt that as I had come from almost the same country, I would have a better understanding. I didn't know. All I did know was that when we talked together, Loretta would slam things down, making a racket and making sure I understood she was not happy about it. He liked to go for walks, so at first, I went along with him — I wasn't used to sitting at home, and the walks gave me fresh air and I enjoyed his stories.

One day Mr.P. and I returned home from one of our walks to hear pots and pans crashing in the kitchen and Loretta's face scarlet with rage.

I understood. Not only had I had taken her son but now her husband liked me. I guess she figured I was a little snippet who had led a spoilt life while she had struggled all of hers. The family always got smacked with another set-back just when they were getting on top of things.

Money was tight for them and Loretta, such a proud woman, was forced to accept rent money from Ted and put up with having me around her. It was starting to be uncomfortable for me. I tried to know where I could be of help but house keeping was not my best skill — to put it mildly. I hung out the washing but she hauled it all back in. White sheets first, pillow cases, men's shirts and so on. All whites were dosed with Javex (Consequently all the whites quickly wore out). No neighbour could accuse her of grey sheets.

I tried dusting and I must admit while I did it I moved the chairs to different positions, thinking it was more elegant. I didn't really blame her for throwing the furniture back — hard enough to break them — to their original positions.

I didn't have money of my own, a situation I hated because I couldn't make any decisions. I asked Ted for some money to buy sheeting material so

I could make and embroider a banquet sized tablecloth. I ironed on transfers of roses around the edges and filled in my time cross stitching and writing letters home.

Ted's shift changed to days so I could meet him downtown and we'd walk home together. We would go into Woolworths to sit at the milk bar and have an ice cream soda. He loved giving me the small luxuries we didn't have in England. Walking home I felt overwhelmed with this bountiful land; smells of jelly making, bushel baskets of apples and peaches. Grapes, purple and green: They reminded me of taking grapes to John when he was wounded in the war.

I had my own war with Ted's mother. I wanted Ted to understand but he just smiled tenderly and told me it wouldn't be for long before we would find a place to live by ourselves. There were absolutely no places to rent in the newspaper. "Just hang in there Dody," he said.

If we walked in the evening there was usually a game of softball going on. If they were short a player, he would join them and I would pray for darkness to come so I would have his attention again.

We went to Ottawa to visit the wonderful Aunt May and Uncle Fred, as well as Ted's cousins. They told me when Loretta was small, she had been sent to live in a convent as her mother was ill. She became deaf after having the measles. The sisters would hit her knuckles with a cane if she didn't answer what they asked, never realizing she had become deaf. Since that time she had concentrated on lip-reading.

All the cousins were French-Canadian and they sat around an immense dining room table. Platters of food were brought in and everyone talked at once and I couldn't understand a word of it. It was all about sports, names of players, scores of different games, odds on future games, who was traded and who was not. It was noisy and I felt strange and alienated. I wanted to go to bed and have some peace. Even though they were lovely people, it was just too much for me.

Next day the women were cutting, scraping and cooking up masses of food, talking all the while. We were going to their summer cottage on the river. We piled into cars and came to a shell of a building standing on the edge of a river. I love swimming and could hardly wait to dive in.

"Watch out for the strong current," Aunt May called out.

The river was a mess of weeds that pulled and sucked at my legs. It didn't have the buoyancy of the sea and the current really WAS strong.

The food tasted good though. Everyone was a good cook over here, but of course they could have much more sugar and butter than the English were allowed. Rationing was still in effect over there.

The cousins became frantic to get back home in time for a baseball game in a park. It was a double header again! And worse, we had to sit on the grass. Ted was in his glory, not only could he watch the game but he could compare notes with the cousins. He kept jabbing my ribs saying, "Look at that! Look at that!" I could look, but I wasn't interested in the slightest. And I wasn't used to sitting on the grass so long. I was stiff, sore and miserable with the whole thing.

When we came back to Cornwall his mother refused to speak to us, banging things around and holding her hand to her heart. After he produced a large box of chocolates for her she became civilized with us again.

"Let me go out to work" I pleaded with Ted, "I can't stand this anymore."

"Definitely no," Ted said, his mouth set in a hard line, "I would never allow a wife of mine to work. Don't talk about it again. Anyway, what could you possibly do?"

"I could work in Woolworths or something," I said, at which point he got red in the face.

And church was another thing. Every Sunday morning Loretta gave me a book on the Mass, some white gloves and a rosary and off we'd go to the Catholic church. I had always belonged to the Church of England but I never saw any indication that there was such a church in Cornwall. How would I get to it even if there was? And so every Sunday morning, like a sheep, I followed Loretta and Ted to the Catholic church remembering the convent in Hong Kong.

The whole family was always dressed very well and one of the reasons was that Loretta made all the clothes for them. She was fond of telling how she stayed up till two and three in the morning to do so. Her sister Helen in the States was with a cleaning firm and a lot of clothes were never picked up so Helen boxed them up to send to Loretta. It was amazing to see how she undid the seams of suits and made pants and jackets for the boys and she took dresses and altered them for the girls.

The church was St.Columbans and Ted was a member of the young people's club. Ted really was fond of his religion and devout. He would go to confession and then to communion and there was an aura about him as if he was complete with his prayers. He was still going through rehabilitation from the forces and he wanted the best for us.

He was torn between his loved ones. His mother had pressed another rosary into my hand because I wasn't making use of the one she had given me. I thought about the situation and knew Ted was unhappy, so I picked up the rosary and tried to look religious.

Ted's father wasn't doing well. He worried about Anne and Frank in the sanitarium. People wouldn't come near you if TB was in the family for fear of catching it themselves.

The whole family went under cover when Loretta had one of her sessions about being cross with someone or other. She wouldn't talk to anyone for days after. She had high blood pressure. When the children were younger and she wanted to bring them in line, she would pretend to be dead. They told me she was so good at it she wouldn't even breathe and she could roll her eyes back in her head. She only "came to" when they ran to the neighbours for help. I know it was a thorn in her side to have me in her house and I just hoped for both of us it wouldn't be for much longer.

Arthur removed himself from Loretta and her temper by making a small space in the back garden shed where he constructed small tables and book shelves from orange crate wood.

A new event

Loretta had cooked steak for dinner one night. I took one look at it and for no reason felt sick.

"Don't you like steak Doris?" she asked

"I'm sorry Loretta, I just don't feel hungry."

Her face turned red and I felt there would be a storm coming.

"I work and slave to make you a nice dinner and what do you do? You go to Woolworths to have ice cream sodas and make me waste food."

There were lots of banging pots and pans that night.

I missed my period but thought it was because of the change of climate. I thought if you were pregnant you only felt sick in the mornings but it hit me every dinner time and honestly I just couldn't eat what Loretta had cooked even though I'd given up the soda drinking with Ted.

I waited till I was alone in the house to phone a doctor's office. The receptionist wanted to know the reason I was coming.

"I think I might be pregnant," I said.

"Please bring a sample of your urine with you and we'll see you in two days' time," she said.

I'd never had to take a sample before and didn't know what quantity a sample meant. I thought I'd better err on the side of more than less, so I filled a quart bottle. At the appointed time, I put the bottle in a paper bag and took off for the appointment. The receptionist smiled at me as I put the thing on her desk.

"What is that Mrs.Paterson?" she said.

I tried to whisper because the room was full of people.

"The sample."

To my utter horror, she took it out of the bag, exposing it to all those eyes and started to splutter and giggle. She didn't even lower her voice as she said, "We only require an ounce or two, not a whole quart!"

I finally went into the doctor's room, he seemed pleasant and efficient as I lay on the examining table.

"Now Doris, you think you might be pregnant do you?" he said. "Let's have a look here."

His fingers fussed to undo my cami-knicks, a combination of pantics and a slip which opened with little poppers between the legs.

"Dammit all!" he said, "How on earth do you undo these things?"

I was mortified even more.

After examining me, he estimated I must have conceived on the first night in Montreal and was now two months pregnant.

I could hardly wait till Ted came home. I felt different now I was going to be a mother. A child would cement our relationship. I would have plenty to keep me busy and I'd shower it with love. My parents and Loretta would be grandparents. I felt on top of the world and when Ted and I were in our room in each other's arms on the bed I burst out with the news.

"Teddy, I went to the doctors today and we're going to have a baby."

I thought about the movies and how the husband gets excited when he gets the news but instead there was dead silence.

"What's the matter? Aren't you glad for us?" I said.

"How can I be glad?" he said and pointed out we didn't have a home, that we should really stay with his mother because she needed the money and that he hadn't even thought about his future. "And now, I will have the responsibility of having children."

We'd never talked about having children and assumed we'd both want a family. I turned to face the wall and tried to hide the hurt.

After a couple of weeks we told the family that I was pregnant. Loretta took it as a personal affront because now everyone would know she was old enough to be a grandmother. She told me not to tell the neighbours. She told me Ted wasn't old enough to have the responsibility of having children and suggested I tell him not to come near me (meaning no more sex) until I myself was older.

I may have looked like an innocent girl but I wasn't stupid.

Uncle Ward came up from Gananoque to meet me and bring gifts from Loretta's sisters Maud, Kay and Daisy who lived close to each other. This was a real surprise and I delighted in the way each gift was wrapped with paper printed with brides and grooms or wedding bells. And they were tied with silver ribbons all curly-cued and bowed plus little gift tags with wedding wishes. I must remember to do something like this if I send presents; it's not something we did at home.

Uncle Ward was about six feet seven inches. He used to be the engineer on the small train from Gananoque to Kingston for many years but was now retired. He was the husband of Aunt Maud, the eldest of Loretta's family. He came by bus, seventy miles away, and will go back the same day. He doesn't think the journey is any big deal. He's a jolly, caring person and I feel good that he made the effort to welcome me.

One of the things that made me unhappy was I had no money of my own. I hadn't been in a position like that since I was fifteen years old and I hated it. I made none of the decisions and there was no way to fill in time other than embroidering red roses on the tablecloth.

And I thought about Ted when I met him and what a romantic figure he was to me. I thought of the time when we were to get on the bus in Hempstead and he scooped me up in his arms in front of all the passengers and told them he was so lucky to have me. And when he sent telegrams he'd sign them, "From your Teddy Bear who loves you."

Courtaulds gave Ted a job in the lab to measure the chemicals for rayon. Management told him to keep his nose to the grindstone and he would be promoted. But he hated the work and could see that workers became not much better than zombies after a few years. He joined the forces when he was nineteen and was twenty-two and a navigator when I met him.

He was forever getting acid spills on his clothes at work where they happily ate away little holes and there was no rescuing the pants, shirts or jackets. He also had strong hands and beakers would break easily when he handled them.

Ted had an aquiline nose and a gap between his front teeth. Yet one didn't think of his looks because of his strong personality. He was graceful and of course he had those blue eyes. Ted returned from work one day and wanted me to go with him for a walk.

"Since we're expecting a baby, we may get priority to rent a veteran's house." he said, "we'll just hope my darling."

When we got back to the house, Loretta was in a raging turmoil. "I had a twenty-dollar bill," she said with an angry voice and looked straight at me. "I've looked everywhere for it and its gone. The only one who could have taken it is you!"

"Don't say things like that, I wouldn't steal anything" I said.

"Hold on a minute Mother," Ted said, "Let's go through everything."

"It's no use. I've gone through every nook and cranny," she said, pulling out the washing machine to do the wash. Whenever she was upset she would either wash the clothes, the floor or even the walls.

Lifting off the lid of the washer she saw what we all saw: a twenty-dollar bill sitting on top of clothes to be washed.

"I guess I forgot," she said.

Ted spoke in a guarded voice: "We will be leaving soon Mother. It's likely we will have a house of our own."

It was a powerful blow to her and her breathing worried me. She clutched at her stomach and then her chest and I thought she was going to have a heart attack. It wasn't nice to see someone suffer like that and I knew she was wondering how she would manage without the money from Ted.

The bad taste left from me being accused, affected everyone but Loretta. She put it out of her mind, never said sorry and busied herself for a visit to the "san" to see her children. It was the day of the week when Loretta went to visit. She baked and fussed, filling up baskets of goodies not only for Anne and Frank but for other patients. Some of them never had a visitor. For years she'd done this with something to say to many patients and she never forgot a name or the circumstances they were in. They looked forward to seeing her because she made them laugh and was never lost for conversation. Back then, there was no cure for TB.

Anne and Frank started to receive an experimental new procedure that a Canadian doctor, Dr. Norman Bethune, who had TB, himself, had been self-administering. The doctor inserted a large needle into the infected lung to collapse it, giving it a chance to rest and recover.

Ted took me to visit his brother and sister. Anne was a lovely girl with long, blond hair. She had been disappointed that Ted had married an English girl but we became friends. She had been an all-round athlete until she was diagnosed with tuberculosis at fifteen years of age. She obviously adored Ted. "We think Ted is the greatest," she said, "he would come home from air force training before going overseas and we'd all gather round him on the bed while he told stories about his life.

Finally on our own (November 1946)

Ted got word we could move into a wartime house in mid November. It was in the north end of town and quite barren around the new development. A streetcar stopped a quarter of a mile away. These houses were built especially for veterans and the streets in the area were named after places the Canadians had fought in during the war. It was a beige coloured house with wooden siding and brown trim. There was a coal-burning iron stove in the kitchen which was for cooking as well as heating that area. The living room had a heating stove with the same pipes as at Loretta's place, going along the ceiling to other rooms. There was an enclosed back porch for coal and everything was nice and new.

When I lived at home, my mother and my sister were sure I could never keep a neat house but I knew I could do it.

The government had reserved some of the veteran's money for them to use on their return. Some went to university with it but we spent most of it on furniture for the house and a washing machine. I bought some material they called monks' cloth and crocheted the edges in dark green for curtains.

Some kind-hearted ladies in Cornwall wanted to bring all the war brides together and they arranged a place where we could meet once a month for a social evening. These ladies said we should hold fundraising teas and showed us how to put one on. Members baked cakes and pies to sell and brought their best chinaware. Visitors paid an entry fee to a hatted lady sitting at a table and another lady sold raffle tickets.

I didn't attend these sessions often and I never found out what they did with the money from the teas. I figured if I was going to be a Canadian, I'd better get on with it and not belong to a separate club.

Ted took me to a lacrosse game and I actually enjoyed it. Cornwall was playing a team of native indians called the Caughnawagans.

Lacrosse was initially an Indian game and it's actually Canada's national game, not, as most people think, hockey. The players whizzed a cement-type ball from a stick which had a curved loop at the end, laced with leather. The native Indians who lived near Cornwall were known to make the best sticks. To my surprise, I was on my feet yelling and screaming just like Ted. He was secretary-treasurer of the league and went to all the games.

After she heard we were to move, Loretta became softer towards me.

There was a formal dance planned for the church youth group. I hadn't danced with Ted for ages and I didn't have a formal gown. The only one I found downtown was too big for me but Loretta altered it to fit. "Did you get Doris a corsage?" Loretta asked Ted. "Am I supposed to?" he said. So on our way to the church hall he stopped at a neighbour's garden and picked a peony. It was at least six inches across.

When we danced, we turned and turned. His face remained in focus but the rest of the room became a blur of colours. We were in our own world. We walked home flushed with the memory of a special evening, that left peony petals scattered all over the dance floor.

When we moved, I had to get used to being alone. I'd been longing to get away from Loretta but at least she'd been a presence in the house. For all her difficult ways she was a strong and vibrant personality.

The drapes weren't in place yet and the floors looked up at me with their hard shine. I tried to light the kitchen stove but it went out every time. I was too scared to use the washing machine, I was nervous of all mechanical things. The house was too large and, without much furniture, it made me feel lonely.

We continued to give Ted's parents some financial help.

I was always writing letters home just pouring out my feelings that spilled over pages and pages. Mother planned to visit me but her health was worsening. Father who was wonderful in so many ways could not abide her being ill. I recalled one time when she had the flu and he stood at the bedroom door saying, "I think it's high time you got up!" He didn't understand she was a lot older than him and had a heart condition.

When Ted came home from work, the washing machine was still in the middle of the kitchen with the clothes in it but not washed. He told me not to be so scared of it. He attached an extension cord to reach the socket and when he plugged it in the sparks flew and the fuse went off. The extension cord had a broken wire and had shorted out.

"Never mind Dody, I'll do the washing if the machine worries you," Ted said. But I cried.

"It isn't only the washing machine," I said, "I can't get the stove to go and I haven't cooked dinner.

"Just watch me Dody and you will learn."

He moved the damper and jiggled the grate but the thing died again.

"Tell you what we'll do," he said, "we'll get some charcoal bricks and they will get it going. Meanwhile, we'll just have sandwiches."

"Can we get a small rug for the living room to make it more like home?" I asked him, "and maybe a hotplate so I can at least boil water for tea without lighting that big old monster?"

So I learned to cope with the stove and the washing machine. I was sorry I knew about the washing machine though, because Ted volunteered to bring home his whole lacrosse team's sweaters and pants for me to wash. I had never smelled such obnoxious odors!

He loved getting together with the "boys" playing softball and "winding down" at the pub afterwards. I wondered if I was to ever have him to myself.

He took me bowling and didn't understand why I wasn't spectacular at it. I'd never seen the game before and he made me worse with all his instructions how to bowl properly. "You were such a good table tennis player, I wonder why you can't bowl," he said.

Mr. Paterson came for a visit walking all the way and he didn't look well. He told me he was thankful I had married Ted. I was glad he could feel comfortable to come without worrying if it was a good time or not. And I hoped he knew how much it meant to me to have him as a friend.

I thought I was ready to have Loretta and family come for dinner. I bought a Puritan cookbook put out by the flour people and studied all the recipes. Ted didn't mind spending money on groceries as long as I didn't get things like whipping cream or similar frivolities. I worked towards having a good meal for them and practised how I would serve the meal without unnecessary fuss.

I made a chocolate cake the new way which involved throwing all the ingredients in a bowl and beating them six hundred times — by hand. I was pooped making it but it turned out light and lovely. You had to use cake flour and measure everything properly.

The night arrived and the family came. They examined the house and thought we were very lucky to start out living in a three-bedroom house — all spanking new. Mr. and Mrs. Paterson had rented the same house for twenty-five years and could not think of buying. My family bought the house in Hempstead and I grew up to think it should be that a family had a safe haven, a little piece of earth that was truly theirs.

My tablecloth with the crossed-stitch red roses covered the table. To my surprise, Loretta spoke to me in a friendly way. I had made stuffed pork tenderloin rolls with mushroom sauce, carrots and peas. And for dessert, I served fruit salad and the chocolate cake.

It was a success and I heard later that Loretta told others she had never had such a good cake. She even asked if I would make one like it for her friend's birthday. At last I had done something right.

Winter came. Boards in the house creaked and cracked with alarming noises. I woke Ted up often, telling him there was someone downstairs. He would say, "There's no one there," and go back to sleep.

"But I'm scared."

"Oh all right!" he said, "I'll go and see." But no one was ever there, so I lay shivering until I was worn out and at long last fell asleep. The cold seemed to seep into the very walls. Ted was hot-blooded and didn't need many blankets but I was the opposite, I didn't know if I'd ever get used to all of it.

I wasn't feeling settled, it wasn't really my home and I felt so alone. The house was a long way from downtown and I didn't know anyone. I found I was going from room to room like a moth batting itself against a lampshade. First this side bzzz! Then that side buzz! Feeling trapped and not knowing how to get out of it. There wasn't enough for me to do. I lived for Ted to return from work and sensed this was irritating to him. I listened to Ma Perkins on the radio in *Life can be beautiful*. When Ted came home I'd recite in detail what everyone had said. He laughed at how engrossed I could be. If I told him the story when we were in bed, it put him to sleep.

I thought it would help if we had a puppy and Ted got one for me. He was a black spaniel we called Paddy. He was good company and I could take him for walks but didn't have the heart to train him. Ted would hit him on the nose with a rolled up newspaper and I would cry. I wondered what kind of mother I'd be when I couldn't even discipline a dog. My sister had been wonderful with children but I'd always been a bit nervous around them.

Paddy was a great help. I took him for little runs and I could talk to him.

The government gave new mothers-to-be an information book, it was called *Canadian mother and child*. It was a help to me because I'd never been close to anyone having a baby. The book said that at four months you could feel the baby move, so I lay on the bed and held my breath. I wondered if there was a flutter of movement or was it gas? It felt like butterfly wings — surely, I thought, it couldn't be little feet or fists.

Ted was sweet when I put on my first maternity dress. He said it really seemed that I was going to be a mother now. His face was full of emotion and he was tender with me. But I felt it was all taking too long and I could hardly wait for the day when the baby would be born. I hadn't told a soul I was afraid because they would laugh, but I couldn't figure out how a large baby's head could come out of that small opening.

My parents looked forward to the event but Mother wasn't well. They had to amputate her leg because of a blood clot. It would have been lovely for Mother to have come for a visit to Canada as she had planned, but now that wasn't going to happen. Loneliness is exaggerated when one is away from support at a crucial time like birthing. It's a time when women band together since history began.

Loretta bought a length of flannelette from the lady who worked at the cotton mill. It was a mill tradition that the working women could buy enough flannelette to make diapers and crib sheets at wholesale prices. We bought a sewing machine and Ted had to show me how to hem diapers.

Anne was home from the "san." Pneumothorax (Dr. Bethune's collapsed lung treatment) was working and we lived in a time of miracles when this scourge of society could be wiped out. Anne was weak but started to knit a pink outfit for the baby.

I saw in a book I should be wearing a maternity corset and wondered where I'd get one. As I wanted to do everything right, I called into a pharmacy.

"Yes, lie down in the back there and we'll fit you," the lady in a white coat said.

She brought out a monstrosity of a garment. It was eighteen inches in width, had two openings on each side and long, long laces that were crossed such as you do up shoes. As one gets larger, these laces can be let out. Whale bones are inserted at intervals. I was supposed to put it on when lying down and secure hooks together.

The lady clucked approval and I stood up utterly and thoroughly miserable. How on earth could anyone enjoy being pregnant while encased in that contraption?

"Ah well!" I told myself, "If *Canadian Mother and Child* said it was necessary and it would secure the baby, it would be a small sacrifice."

My first Christmas away from home

I can't describe how unnerving it was to have the standard routines of Christmas in England to be changed into those of another country.

December 1946 was my first Christmas away from my family and I was five months pregnant. Ted bought a Christmas tree and told me their family opened all gifts on Christmas morning. My mother, who came from a German heritage, always had our special time on Christmas Eve. Our gifts were humble; socks, gloves, scarves or shaving cream for the men.

Following Canadian routines, we went to midnight mass and the church was packed. The priests wore robes for celebrating and the smell of incense was everywhere. Afterwards, we found that it had snowed and the air was crisp as we walked to Loretta's house for tortiere (minced pork pie), shortbread cookies and hot chocolate.

Next morning Ted and I unwrapped the presents from each other. I had had to ask him for money to get him a pair of skates. As I wanted it to be a complete surprise, I had hidden them in my closet and left a note in a small box under the tree to say his gift was in the closet. To this day I can't make out why he should lose his temper about having to go upstairs for his present, but he was angry. It didn't last, thank goodness, but it did damage my feelings.

My gift from him was a saucepan. I acted pleased but it seemed symbolic of what I had become, a housewife. I longed for the times when I had been treated as a star and when Christmas was a time for magic, not anger.

We spent the day at Loretta's with Arthur, Frank and Anne who had been allowed home for the occasion. Loretta's tree was two feet or so taller than the ceiling so they had to cut the top off. Her lights were in the shape of long icicles and bubbles went up and down in them. It was laden with every imaginable decoration. The house was a-jumping with smells of Christmas and Loretta was in her glory. She had sewed clothes, baked gingerbread men with funny faces. Made Christmas cakes and puddings. The child in her had turned her house into a wonderland for all who came through the door.

We all lived in fear of giving her a gift that was not to her liking. She had no qualms about pitching a gift across the room if a relative had given her something which didn't suit her!

Loretta excused herself and went up in the attic to bring down a cardboard box which she gave to me. "This Christmas decoration was bought for Ted's first Christmas and I've kept it safe so I could give it to the one he married," she said. It was a silver bauble the size of a grapefruit and I was happy that she had given it to me.

After we left the house I took the bauble out of the box to wonder at it again.... and DROPPED it! The sidewalk had been cleared of snow and it hit the concrete with a smack and shattered into a hundred pieces. I cried and I cried. But Ted consoled me and said we'd never let his mother know. But just the same, it had been a sort of building block for our togetherness and I was sorry about it.

My first child, Mary *(2nd January 1947)*

Early January brought a bitter cold that clamped onto my bones. The washing froze on the line and when I brought it in the sheets were like boards. I stood them up around the room until they collapsed like ghosts exhaling their misty breaths. I was tired and despondent and my back ached. I went to lie down but the pain didn't ease. Whichever way I turned it didn't help and then I felt a warm sticky rush between my legs. I called for Ted and he ran into the bedroom. "Oh! Teddy, pull back the covers." And instead of there being a white sheet — there was only a sea of blood. I panicked and Ted beat his fist on the wall. I heard him stumble down the stairs to phone for an ambulance. It came and rushed me to the emergency and as the trolley wheeled me down the hospital corridor, I lost consciousness.

We lost our baby.

Ted came to visit me and was as devastated as I was. Loretta came, all

Kate Hampe, Doris' mother, age twenty-nine, in Germany. Ernest fell in love with Kate when he was in Germany during the army of occupation following WWI.

Doris (left) and her sister Peggy in an English pram, Gosport, England, 1924. This was likely taken when Kate took them for walks while Ernest studied. They were living in one room at the time.

Near Cork, Ireland. Peggy, Doris, Stanley, Mother Kate and Gordon in 1931, when Doris was seven.

Hong Kong, 1938. St.Paul's Convent productions were lavish and professionally produced. Doris (front, right of centre in apron dress) played Alice in this rendition of Alice in Wonderland.

On a Hong Kong beach reserved for Europeans only, in front of their "mat shed" or cottage made entirely from bamboo — even the nails were made of bamboo shoots. Doris (standing, left rear), with her brother Stanley, guest naval officer, sister Peggy (front left), mother Kate, and friends.

Warwick Castle office staff of BISC (British Iron and Steel Corporation) during WWII when important companies were evacuated from London, away from the bombing. Doris is on the left in the middle row. Peacocks still roam freely on the castle grounds.

Ashorne Hill manor circa 1941 (above) and its lounge (left) were a centre of activities during Doris' war years.

The Clarendon Hotel faced the Parade in Leamington Spa, Warwickshire, England. The middle two windows on the top floor looked out from Doris' room.

Ted and Doris (at right) at one of the air force bases in England with one of Ted's crew members and his wife.

Kate Pearce, Doris's mother, wearing her favourite dress of navy chiffon with embroidered white daisies, 1945.

Ernest and Kate Pearce — Doris's parents — in 1946, in front of the family house Homeleigh, in Hempstead, near Gillingham, Kent, England. Ernest bought the house when they returned to England from Hong Kong.

Doris, aged twenty-one, and Ted, aged twenty-two, had these photos taken and hand tinted professionally in Leamington Spa in 1945.

Ernest Pearce escorts his daughter, Doris, to the church, November 10, 1945.

The wedding party outside Rochester Catholic Church. Ted and Doris (centre), with her best friend Margaret (left) and sister Peggy (right), and her parents at each end.

Doris with her first child, Barbara, in Cornwall, Ontario

Neighbours give Doris a baby shower shortly befor e Mark — her seventh child — is born.

The Paterson family in Winnipeg, Manitoba, 1967. Rear, from left, Scott, Brenda, Joy, Ted and Patrick. Front, from left, Mark, Pearce, Barbara, Doris, Paul, Laura and Ted Jr.

Omachi, Japan. Toshi Yoshida and Doris in woodcut printing room.

Doris and Willy, Mission, BC, 1990. Willy comes to Doris's rescue, helping deliver and collect her art work from exhibitions.

Doris with publisher Mary Dixon of Portage and Main Press, during the signing of the contract for The Life Series and Willy and Me books. February 1994.

Noboru Sawaii and Doris renewing an old frinedship during Noboru's visit to Mission in 1998.

friction gone for the moment. She too, hurt for us.

Two days later I was told I could go home and Ted and I sat on a bench in the hospital waiting room, waiting for the final billing and for a friend of Ted's to drive us home.

A sister came towards us carrying a shoe box and presented it to Ted.

"This is your baby," she said, "she lived for an hour and a half. We baptized her Mary so she is registered as a child and as a member of the Catholic religion. You will have to see that she's buried properly." She turned and walked away.

Ted held the shoe box in his lap.

No one had told us the baby had been alive. The friend arrived. Ted said, "Just take Doris home, I will follow later."

In my heart I thanked him for I could have never traveled with my baby in the car. I would have had to open the box to hold that little soul. And I know I could not have stood it. I cried and cried and prayed God would hurry up and heal that loss of ours.

Ted bought the tiniest white coffin for Mary and arranged with the cemetery, for fourteen dollars, to bury her in an infant grave, two feet by four feet near the fence.

But this is a cruel country in the winter time with the frozen ground. Mortals who die at this time of year have to wait to be buried until the ground thawed. And I knew I would grieve until the sun warmed the earth and our little girl could be put to rest forever.

Two weeks later there was an express letter from my father. Mother had a blood clot in her other leg. That leg had to be amputated as well and now the clot had gone to her brain. He didn't know how to cope and asked me to come home both to help him and to see my mother again.

My brother Gordon had been nursing her at home but now she had to stay in hospital as Gordon had to return to work.

Gordon was a loving son: He had learned German so he could converse with Mother in her native tongue.

He and I were close to each other in the family and later, he came to wrok in Canada. He marreid a girl — Fernande — from Chicoutimie, Quebec.

Ted found a ship was sailing from Montreal within three weeks and he booked a passage for me while I went through the motions of living. I didn't know how long I'd be away or when I could get a passage back home to Canada. I wondered if our relationship was secure enough to withstand the length of time I'd be away. I wondered if Ted would look for other companionship while I was in England.

Two days after booking my passage, someone came to the door and I heard Ted converse with a man. When Ted came towards me with a telegram, I just knew my mother had died. My father said that my sister would stay with him for a while and I was to cancel my passage as there was nothing I could do.

I wanted to go and shake Mother alive and tell her how much I loved her. I hadn't asked all the questions about her life. I saw how she had endured a great loneliness being the enemy to her husband's country. I could not stop crying. I just could not. Ted shrank from me, helpless to help while I hurt with crying.

We'd all taken her for granted. I wondered if everything I loved was dying. I gathered Paddy into my arms and begged him not to die as well. He made little whining noises so I stifled my sobs.

Ted was glad to go to work because he couldn't stand that I was giving myself over to grief and he didn't know how to help. He stayed out later at night "playing hockey with the guys." Of course drinking afterwards.

The sun got a little warmer and my heart accepted what it had to accept. I was determined to get pregnant again even though Loretta's friends warned me, saying it was dangerous to get pregnant so soon after the other case. I wanted a child so much and I didn't know what to do with my time. I wasn't allowed out to work and the house was always neat and clean.

So I thought I'd make a vow to God. If He would let me have a successful pregnancy, I would become a Catholic. Then I felt better.

Six weeks after my mother died, I received a letter from my father saying he had married Agnes.

I couldn't believe it. Agnes was a regular visitor to Mother when she was ill and Mother had suspected she was after my father. Mother made my brother promise that after she died, he would stop my father from marrying Agnes but of course there was nothing he could have done. It was ironical because my mother's mother had extracted from her the same promise about her father!

Father said he was selling *Homeleigh* and would move in with Agnes. At least I was spared the thought of Agnes living in Mother's house. I now had a stepmother called Agnes.

Ted was to go on retreat with the Catholic brothers.

"I need to ask for strength to be a better person," he said. He was referring to his drinking.

I felt sorry for him. Did I think I was the only one with trouble? He knelt in front of my chair, his head in my lap and I began from that time to recover some sense of balance again. I prayed that it would soon be spring and we could put that horrible winter behind us.

Another chance *(June 1947)*

The winter blues had gone. I presented a urine sample like a pro to the doctor's office. I was pregnant again.

"Hello Doris," he said. "I hope things work out well for you this time."

He told me not to do any hard work or lifting if I wanted this baby to live. I was to rest every afternoon, and remind myself my baby's life depended on it.

Ted said we would have a cleaning lady every two weeks to do the floors. I found the name of someone and she agreed to come. I saw her approach from down our street, she was wearing what looked like a cat-fur coat. It looked like Joseph's coat of many colours as it was made of pelts from all kinds of cats. There were four dogs trailing after her and sniffing at it as she batted them with her purse.

I felt awkward to be in the same house while she was cleaning my home. Ted told me he wanted her finished by the time he came home. He didn't like the idea of anyone else in his house while he was there.

I had a lot of time on my hands so I bought another cookbook about making cakes.

Ted was dissatisfied with his job. Actually he hated it. He told me he just had to go into business for himself. He felt that was where he belonged.

"What sort of business did you have in mind?" I asked.

"Anything, as long as it's a business," he said.

He spent weeks thinking about ideas but nothing jelled until he rushed in one day, very excited.

"There's a small store for rent down the road and I figured there's something everybody wants, hot pies."

"Just a minute," I said, "who's going to make the hot pies?"

114

"I figure like this. Mother makes great pastry. She's known for it everywhere. You make the meat or the fruit fillings and I'll deliver them hot from the oven on my bike. If we don't get orders, I'll cycle around, knocking on doors."

"What about when the baby is born?"

"I've thought of that. Peggy said that her husband Denys hasn't got work at the moment. There's lots of work for Denys here and Peggy could look after the baby while you make pies."

I rushed to the phone because I liked the fact that Peggy might come to Canada to live with us.

The phone line was full of static. I could hardly make myself heard. We couldn't understand what the other was talking about and Peggy was shouting "Hot pies Doris? What are you doing with hot pies?"

I was now screaming into the receiver.

"Madam," the operator broke in, "if you're trying to scream across the ocean, I can assure you it won't work. I'll see if I can get a better line."

Peggy got the drift of the idea but she told me that Denys had a job now, thanks all the same.

Ted was disappointed but still determined to leave his job.

"I've seen men who have had the life sucked out of them," he said, "they just work like robots and I don't want to become like them."

He knew about rayon and lab work and he knew his sports. He actually wrote a weekly sports column for the local paper but the pittance he was paid would not support a living. He was good at selling because he'd been doing that since he was a small boy. Finding the right idea without requiring money to start became an obsession.

I started hemorrhaging again. I put pillows under my feet in bed and lay perfectly still; it eased up and finally stopped and I was glad I didn't have to think about hot pies at that time.

The convent people had stressed it was a sin to be vain and look in a mirror and I had never seen myself nude, but getting out of bed one morning I saw my reflection. My waist had disappeared and my breasts had developed alarmingly. As I got closer to my due date in early February, 1948, I experienced back pain and cramps in my stomach. Ted phoned the doctor. The doctor said we were to wait until the pains came closer and then go to the hospital.

"I don't know what he means" I told Ted, "it's just one continuous pain."

Ted figured there was something wrong if I wasn't having pains the way I was supposed to have them, and he hovered in the doorway, ready to sprint at a moment's notice. I couldn't stand him being so petrified. Awhile before, I thought he should feel the baby kicking. We were in bed at the time and he put his hand on my stomach and the next thing I knew he'd leapt over the end of the bed and run downstairs. He just couldn't handle it.

The pain became very bad so Ted called a taxi and we registered at the hospital. I went to a room where they shaved my pubic hair and gave me an enema. I was upset because I was afraid of soiling the sheets. I asked what had happened to Ted and they told me he'd gone to work and to phone him if he was needed.

I cried, the pain was unbearable and the sister was impatient.

"Well," she said, "you had your fun and this is the way you'll pay for it."

Everyone seemed to know what birthing was about except me. I was taken to a private room and once every so often a sister came in and peered up my legs, dismissing me with "Heavens! You've hours to go yet."

Barbara's birthday *(5th February 1948)*

I was frightened and lonesome for my mother and my sister. I thought it would never end but finally they took me to the delivery room. They put straps on my wrists and strapped them to the sides of the table. There were stirrups at the end of the bed. "Put your feet in these!" someone said. I did but the pain was worse. They told me to push and I didn't know what to push. But nature let me know when it was time and they put a mask over my face. It smelled of rubber and the world spun out of control and I didn't care anymore and there were piercing blinking lights and I slowly came back down to earth and I heard a baby crying.

I looked over to the corner and there was this skinned rabbit of a baby. "It's a girl," the doctor declared. And love poured out of me to that little mite and I thanked God that all was well and I told Him I remembered my promise.

I was taken to a private room and Ted came and they brought the baby in. She was to be named Barbara. Ted held out one of his fingers and Barbara gripped it. His face broke into a grin. He noticed her ear lobe had the same small hole as he and his mother had. It was a wonder.

Loretta came clucking and fussing and adoring the baby in a way even she didn't understand. I told her I was to go home on the fourth day and she thought it was ridiculous because she had been kept in hospital fourteen days when she had her babies.

When Ted brought my clothes to go home, I thought it was going to be wonderful to wear ordinary dresses again but I couldn't even get a dress over my head. I had to wear the maternity dress again and went down the hall to weigh myself. The scale said one hundred and seventy pounds and I remembered all the cake-making. I gathered up our dear baby and decided, like Scarlet O'Hara, to think about it tomorrow!

Everything changed after Barbara was born. Loretta was kinder and Ted and I felt more bonded. I was kept busy with the baby and set myself the goal to learn how to sew all her clothes. I stopped resenting the Catholic church and started to prepare for my conversion.

But best of all, I felt I belonged now to Canada.

We had never discussed how large a family we should have but since I was to become a Catholic it would be in God's hands. According to the church, sexual intercourse is not for personal gratification but for procreation (making lots of little Catholics).

My Protestant baptism was considered okay by the Catholics but I would have to go to confession, receive holy communion at mass and receive a special blessing from a priest. Going to confession loomed as threatening as the guillotine. I had observed Catholics disappear into those closet-like arrangements and now I would be doing the same.

There were two kinds of sin: one was mild and called menial and the other was deadly serious and called mortal. Penance is usually a matter of reciting a few prayers as designated by a priest. The day came when I was to go into that closet. I knelt on a small step which activated a dim light to warn the priest that I was there. I could make out the silhouette of a figure behind the grated window.

"Bless me father for I have sinned," I said as I had been instructed.

"What do you have to say my child?"

All other sins paled by comparison to the fact that I had masturbated before my marriage. I felt tremendous guilt. The air in the confessional closed in on me and I wanted out. But I remembered my vow to God and this was part of the process.

And I told him that I had told white lies.

"Go on. Go on," he said.

And in a rush, I confessed.

Silence.

"Is that everything?"

"Yes father."

"Say your act of contrition and go through the rosary."

I parroted the act of contrition while still kneeling.

"You may go and the Lord be with you and sin no more."

Loretta had given me a pearl rosary but I didn't like reciting with it. I wanted to talk to God in my own words. I told myself nothing was perfect and later, at mass, I took communion alongside my husband and felt I was beginning a new phase of my life because my sins had been wiped clean.

Baby Barbara wasn't happy. It was three months since we brought her home. *Canadian Mother and Child* told us that you should only feed a baby every four hours. I put her to my breast but she only sucked a little and then fell asleep. She would wake up again in a short time to be fed. When I took her to the doctor for her shots, he told me to leave the house and go for a walk when she cried but I couldn't bring myself to do it. She didn't seem to be gaining weight either so I put *Canadian Mother and child* to rest and gave her formula in sterilized bottles. She soon gained weight and was content. Barbara was baptized with Arthur and Loretta as god parents. Afterwards Loretta turned to me and said, "Now if you die, I will have the baby."

Trouble with my brother John

My father wrote that he was having trouble with John, my youngest brother who was now seventeen. He wouldn't go to school and rebelled against my father. He was resentful and rude. My father was at his wit's end and didn't know what to do.

So I talked with Ted and asked him if we could suggest that John join us in Canada. Without hesitation Ted agreed. Not everyone would take in a rebellious teenager, especially if you were just starting your own family.

I wrote to my father and suggested he discuss this idea with John and if he agreed, to put him on a ship to New York and then by train to Cornwall.

I hadn't lost weight so I stopped baking and went for walks with Barbara in a pram. I saw there were classes once a week in the school to teach sewing. I was always a bit of a klutz about sewing. The teacher was strict and complained because no one did their stitching small enough. I went home and stitched the little dress I was making with stitches so fine you would have thought the fairies had done it. When the teacher saw what I had done she let out a squeal of excitement. "But be careful Doris," she said "if you value your eyes, you'd better stitch a little larger."

Barbara was now getting into a routine with feeding so I burned a larger hole in the nipples so she would get milk more easily.

Twice I'd met Loretta downtown and she turned her back to me. Once I was with Ted and she made a point to only recognize Ted. I asked him why he didn't make it easier for me but he just said that his mother was like that. I got tired of trying to understand why she did these things. It shouldn't have bothered me as much, but it did.

My brother arrived and he was still the brother I knew. Didn't take long for him to blurt out how our father showered his new wife with luxuries that Mother never had. The schools were bombed out and he missed a lot of schooling so he was afraid of trying again. My father sent fifty pounds but no word if he was going to send on-going financial help for John.

Ted took him to the high school but after testing him they said he had only a grade five education and would never fit in. Ted took him to the Catholic brothers' school and they put him in grade eight and constantly worked with him till he was able to join the high school.

I could now enjoy the baby, she smiled at us and brought sunshine into our lives. My sewing was improving and when I finished the dress I was proud. I could do it! I could sew.

Ted liked John being with us and taught him to play lacrosse and softball. I was starting to slim down and John adapted to being in Canada.

My father decided that he would go to Australia with Agnes. He had a brother and a sister out there and his pension would be worth more. They sold Agnes' house which enabled them to buy a farm. As they were selling nearly everything else, Father sent me some of Mother's jewelry and her dressing-table set of crystal and silver. I wondered what had happened to her lovely silk nightgowns which she kept "for best" in our cedar trunk.

It was good to have John for company and I now really thought I was a Canadian. It didn't happen overnight, it had to come of its own accord and I didn't feel the pull of my homeland as much anymore.

7:

Owning our first house on Vimy Street

Nine months went by and I was pregnant again.

John was doing well at school and had joined air force cadets and it was there that he gained confidence.

Nearly every day, I took Barbara in my arms and went around rooms pointing out different things and pronouncing words carefully so she would remember them. I made a few clothes for her.

Her hair was blonde and silky and she had a quiff that curled in the middle of her forehead, so I sang the song:

> *There was a little girl who had a little curl,*
> *right in the middle of her forehead,*
> *and when she was good, she was very, very good,*
> *but when she was bad she was horrid!*

We had been renting the house on Dieppe Street but received word that some of the war-time houses were up for sale to people like us. I told Ted it was a chance of a lifetime and we had to take advantage of it. The house on Vimy street wasn't as large as the one we had but it only cost one thousand dollars with a down payment of fifty dollars. Ted had to take out a loan for fifty dollars. The house was just around the corner from where we were living and the government was to put footings under it later without charge.

My father wrote from Albany, West Australia, saying the warm climate was heaven. There was no mention of him helping us with John's keep so I put it out of my mind.

Arthur had to return to the sanatorium. Frank got a job as a night clerk in a hotel. Everyone liked Frank. When he was a youngster, he would perform when asked. He sang ditties and did little dances. But one day Ted and I were at Loretta's when Frank appeared and Loretta said, "Frank, a crazy woman told me on the street today that you had married a girl from the san. I told her she must be thinking of Ted. I told her off, the silly old coot!"

Frank's face went red and he shuffled from one foot to the other. I motioned Frank to the kitchen and mouthed the words "Is it true?" and Lord Almighty, he nodded and said "How will I tell her?"

I thought it would be easier if he did it while Ted and I were there but to tell the truth I just wanted to run. Ted came in, saw the look on our faces and said, "What's up Dody" and I said that Frank had to tell them himself.

So Frank told Loretta: "Yes. I am married to Marcie."

Loretta still didn't believe what she was hearing. "But you sleep here every night," she said.

"I was afraid to tell you," he said "and I've got to go now."

Loretta took it very hard and it was understandable. Two sons had been married without her being there. The worst thing for Loretta was that now, the neighbours would know!

Marcie had known Frank in the san and they were great together. They drank quite a bit though, so it put a rift between myself and them.

But Marcie was now part of the family. She loved house keeping so she would be Loretta's friend.

We had to get ready to move to Vimy Street and it would signal another beginning to our lives.

Ted rented a sander to take the varnish off the floors in Vimy Street. It was wet weather so the new varnish wouldn't dry. He left the windows open to get rid of the smell but the rain came in, making the floors a sticky mess.

It was my first experience of moving household accumulations. In what I assumed was a Canadian ritual, someone had spread the word we were moving and a crowd of men appeared at the door on the designated day, each one complete with a case of beer or a bottle. Someone had produced a truck and it was a merry crew that took off down the road.

I looked around the empty house. It had been a good home. I took little Barbara's hand and locked the door for the last time.

Our new place was quite a bit smaller and it sure was cluttered until the men put up the beds and moved all to a tidier look. The men left singing bawdy songs.

The floor finish had finally dried. This house was closer to the last tram stop and when Ted came home from work on the tram, Barbara and I walked to meet him. At the last few yards I let go of her hand and she ran towards him, It never failed to delight him.

Yes, Barbara was walking. At first she had difficulty moving one leg so she would go round and round in one spot. Something twigged in my mind that it wasn't as it should be, even though she recited nursery rhymes and could count at an early age.

Polio epidemic hits Canada

It was a hot, humid July and terror was in the air.

Polio.

All mothers were scared to take the children swimming or to mix with other children. High fever, stiff neck and legs, sometimes paralysis and sometimes nothing else for it but to go in the so called "iron lung," a machine that could breathe for the person. They had to live with this thing up to their necks. There was no cure.

One day we attended a carnival and loud speakers had been connected to someone in a tent who was breathing in an iron lung. Every breath was long and drawn out and it added to our discomfort to know that person had no relief.

Barbara had a fever one day and I went to her because she was crying. When I checked her the next time, her eyes were rolled back and she was jerking in spasms. The noises coming from her made my blood run cold. I rolled her in a blanket, ran to the bathroom to wring out a washcloth in cold water and went to the phone while washing her forehead. Oh! I couldn't find the number to phone the doctor and all of a sudden it was there and I was dialing the number and washing her down at the same time and he was in his office and I could hardly get the words out.

"Doctor, this is Doris Paterson, my baby's in a convulsion. Tell me what to do." As I was talking, she was coming to, moaning and shaking.

He told me I had done everything right but to give her a baby aspirin as well. He told me if she didn't get better to bring her over to his office.

I was in charge of myself now and what do you know? I did all the right things. I held Barbara for hours and thought it was okay to cry now she was sleeping well.

Not long afterwards, I phoned Loretta to ask what you should do if a little one had a sore throat because Barbara was having trouble swallowing. And bless her, she came over on the tram to show me how to make a poultice of fried onions. She fried some onions and put them in gauze and secured it around Barbara's neck. She covered it with a woolen sock. She also had some liniment and told me if it went to her chest, to rub some of it on her. Loretta was in full charge.

"Some children fight off a fever by going into convulsions, it's natural," she said.

Someone, who I'll call W, asked Ted to go into business with him as a partner. He already had an exclusive dress store in Cornwall and wanted to start another. And so we went over the pros and cons. I wasn't partial to this man and I told Ted this. I also told him that I couldn't see him selling ladies dresses. But he really wanted to do it, so I relented and said that if that's what he wanted, he'd better do it.

They had to decide in which town to start this new endeavour and took off across Ontario to find a place which had the most money per capita. They settled on Sudbury, the nickel-mining town.

Then it was a matter for Ted to be trained in accounting and to find out about selling dresses.

It was mid-August and the baby was supposed to have been born by this time. It hadn't rained for a long time. Meanwhile men contracted by the government came to jack up the house to put a concrete foundation in as promised. Water and electricity was cut off and we were suspended in the air with no bathroom available.

I pleaded with the doctor to induce the birth and relieve me of this extra burden in the oppressive heat. But he said that nature must take its course. He said I could take castor oil and that might help, but as I had to use my neighbour's bathroom I wasn't about to do that.

It was the 22nd of August and I remembered the Suez Canal with the hundred-and-twenty-degree heat. It seemed worse than that day and the men were taking forever to re-connect the pipes and finish the basement foundation. Then all of a sudden I heard thunder clouds and I took off my shoes and went into the back garden, the earth cooled the soles of my feet and at long last the rain came down. Suddenly it poured and it poured and poured. I stood in the churned-up earth and tipped my face to the heavens and the rain cooled me down and I felt like laughing. Ted ran out: "For goodness sake what are you doing? Your dress is soaked and you'll catch a chill. For God's sake, don't make a spectacle of yourself," he said.

And he pulled me inside but I didn't care and my waters broke and I was ready for us to have our second child.

Brenda's birthday *(23rd August 1949)*

We took a taxi to Loretta's place. Barbara was to stay with her while I was in hospital. When I asked for a kiss goodbye, Barbara gave me a look which said, don't bother me. She was in the place where they treated her like a princess.

Going in for this birth was easier because I knew the process. They had cut me for Barbara's birth and a couple of stitches had come apart so I knew the opening was larger. And also it was agony to be pregnant in Cornwall's humid heat and I was glad to get it over with.

I was tied down on the table as before so I couldn't move my legs or my arms. I turned my head from left to right, back and forth until my head went numb. It gave me sadistic pleasure to know I was upsetting the sisters. I thought it was inhuman to tie women down.

"It's a girl Mrs. Paterson!"

And the baby let out a lusty cry. She looked like a six-month-old baby because she was chubby. She had red-gold hair which actually curled. Big blue eyes.

Ted came to my room. He had seen the baby and there was a softness in his face. I had wondered if he would be disappointed because it was another girl but he said, "No, Barbara will have a companion and if she brings us as much happiness as Barbara, we will be fortunate."

I was happy with his reaction as I'd heard of men blaming their wives for not having a boy.

Brenda nursed well but Barbara sensed the attention had gone from her to the baby and she pouted.

Arthur became extremely ill and they told us it was more his heart breaking down than the TB. I went with Loretta and Ted to visit him. When they left the room to visit others, I could see that Arthur was trying to tell me something but talking was hard for him.

"I'm worried about this upcoming business plan of Ted's. Why can't he stay at his job? You'd have a nice home by the plant."

I was truly sorry that Arthur was not realizing all the sacrifices Ted made to keep the family going and here he was looking after my brother as well! Ted was painfully aware that he was never going to change Arthur's mind however hard he tried.

When we got home from the san, Helen (Ted's youngest sister) seemed distracted. She said she was frightened because Brenda had been violently throwing up – a pile of soiled baby's clothes were heaped in a corner where she had left them after cleaning the baby a few times. I went to Brenda's crib and, as I lifted her up, she wretched and her vomit shot to the other side of the room.

But then she was hungry again and I didn't have any milk left. I made some formula for her as fast as I could and she gulped it down. As soon as I sat her up, the same thing happened again.

What was I to do?

Next day, the doctor told me some babies have that problem – it's called projectile vomiting.

so I would have to make a weak solution of cream of wheat, cut a larger hole in the nipple of the bottle, and feed that to her.

I was thankful that the solution worked but I had to give up the thought of nursing. I wondered why, if nursing was a natural thing, did I have trouble with it? Maybe it was because there was lots to worry about. Arthur would die soon. Ted was staying out late and now John, instead of following me around and feeling lost, was feeling his oats and had become the life of every party: the phone rang for him over and over.

One day he was mowing the lawn and I went out to talk to him. His face was turning red and a look of agony crossed his face. A thin trail of smoke curled up from his hand. The butt of the cigarette was burning his hand!

Two United church ministers came to our door about him. I had made sure that he went to the United church every Sunday. At least I thought I made sure. Apparently he'd only gone once.

"Mrs.Paterson, are you the guardian of John Pearce?"

"Yes I am. Please come in." (I'd been brought up to show respect to anyone wearing a turned-about collar).

126

"We are here," said the taller of the two, "to demand that you not coerce this young man into the Roman Catholic religion."

"What are you talking about?"

"You are Roman Catholic?"

"Yes."

"Then it's obvious you are the cause of your brother not attending church."

I told them that I sent him every Sunday and asked how they knew he wasn't there.

"We have people to check who's attending," the smaller man said, "and he has only been once."

It sounded like the Gestapo and the informers of Germany.

"I want you to leave and not return here," I said, while inching them to the door.

As soon as they left, I sat on the chesterfield and cried. I thought everything was going well with John because he had been promoted to sergeant in the cadets and topped his class at school. He was just about the most popular kid in town. He would have to choose his own way but I had to prepare to be disappointed.

Brenda seemed happier now on cream of wheat and dear Barbara helped by bringing diapers and together we sang to the baby. Being so busy, my weight had gone down and despite all of the worry, I felt good about myself.

Arthur was dying. Ted had been going to the sanatorium after work to stay with him. Ted looked worn out himself. He came home one day to say it was over and Arthur had died while he was with him. I looked for signs that Ted would give in to his grief but there was no crying, no reminiscences. Nothing. I wondered how he could be so callous, I excused it because he was caught up with the funeral arrangements. Loretta also was matter-of-fact. I guessed it was like when I went into robot mode.

Loretta's friend Mrs. Miller had a funeral business and Arthur was laid out in her building. I'd never seen a dead body before, let alone one I cared about. I had a nightmare thinking I was alone with Arthur while he was still lying in his casket.

With my blood running cold, I went into the chapel room and prayed my legs wouldn't give way. I went up to the casket and was glad to see him look peaceful. I tried not to think of all the things the undertaker did to make him look peaceful. I patted his coat-sleeve. Loretta's sister, who lived in the

United States, gave him the suit he was dressed in. It was the only one he had. Everyone thought Arthur was always well dressed — and he only had the one suit. He had such pride and kept it clean and well pressed.

The chapel room was booming with talking and laughing. I saw that Frank and Ted were laughing together as well. How could they DO that? With Arthur laying there. They all acted as if it was a party. All the Ottawa cousins were there getting caught up with all the news.

A voice close to me made me turn around. It was a nurse from the sanatorium who was with Arthur for a long time and she told me, "I can see you're troubled by the conduct here. I hope I'm not revealing a confidence but I want you to know something. When Mr.Paterson died, Ted ran out to the wooded area behind the san. I felt I should keep an eye on him. He threw himself to the ground and cried like a baby for at least an hour. So don't be fooled by his actions here."

Poor Ted; I wondered if I would ever REALLY understand him or know his true feelings.

We made our way to the church and mass was said. The casket went into the hearse. There were lots of cars around and everyone was saying "You take that one," or, "no. You take that one." Everyone got in and out of cars. Ted was with Loretta, Frank and Anne. The cousins were accommodated but I stood alone on the stone steps of the church. I felt an outsider. If Arthur had been alive he would not have let that happen to me. Finally a cousin backed up her car and told me to get in with her.

The day was bleak and grey as I watched the coffin lowered into the cavity of the earth. I tried not to think of maggots and worms and thought instead of how he was such a help to me and I was glad he would have some peace. He was fifty six years old — the same age as my mother was when she died — and ten years older than Loretta.

Her life would be different now.

Brother John goes to Australia

A letter from my father. He'd bought a farm in West Australia, near Albany and he wanted John to leave Canada and join him in Australia. I could hardly believe what I was reading! Doing that to John who had overcome all difficulties and was doing so well. I told John what Father had written: His face went white and his eyes were angry. "I don't want to go and that's that," he said.

"Are you sure John?"

"Absolutely. No way."

So I worked on a letter to reply to my father, telling him it would be cruel to ask John to change yet again.

I'd been taking advanced sewing lessons and had learned to smock. Smocking took a lot of time and used many yards of material for little dresses for the girls. I also made a blue coat-and-bonnet set for Barbara with white embroidery. I was proud I could do it.

I received a reply from my father.

"Am sending fare for John to catch a boat from New York. You'd better obey my instructions or else I'll get the lawyers on to you."

This was from the father who, all of my life, I had thought was fair and wonderful. I just couldn't believe it.

I talked to John again.

"John, you can see from this letter that Dad means business and I've got to think of Ted. You've been living here by Ted's goodness. He's thinking of going into business and we need every dollar. Maybe you could get a part-time job to help towards your keep?"

"I wouldn't know what to do"

"What about a paper route?"

"No. I don't want that."

So I told him he could think about it but I couldn't see how we could afford a lawyer to fight my father in the courts.

"Well then," he said "I guess I'll go to Australia."

It was with a heavy heart I accepted the loss of my brother. Frank went with him by train to New York to see him off on the boat, first to England to see Peggy, and then on to Australia.

Ted was gone for a week and John was gone too, so I had time to sew. I saw an ad in the paper asking for someone to smock a nightgown. I thought I could make some money and phoned the lady. She came to the house in a Cadillac. Gave the impression she hadn't two minutes to spare, handed me a length of pure silk, said she'd give me twenty dollars to make a nightie from it with smocking and took off with a flourish.

A man came to the door. He had heard the house was to be for sale and he wanted to buy it for two thousand dollars. We would make a profit of one thousand dollars. He gave me his phone number and Ted would see to it when he returned.

Ted came back and told me they'd put the first month's rent down for a store in Sudbury. He was glad he didn't have to advertize our house for sale. The man who had come to the door still wanted it. Ted cashed in his pension money at Courtaulds, gave in his notice, and he and his partner thought they would soon be rich.

Ted would leave and try to find a place for us to live, meanwhile I'd get organized for the move.

Loretta took all this badly. She thought it was all my doing, whereas I had been skeptical of everything. She laid the guilt trip on Ted, saying families were meant to be together.

It was a real blow to her.

Anne was home by this time so Loretta didn't have the continuity of visiting that dreaded building. Visits to the san were finished with. It had been a miracle to have Anne and Frank survive the curse of TB. Helen was at home as well but Loretta wanted Ted near her too. Anne had actually been going back to work again.

Moving to Sudbury *(February 1951)*

After Ted left for Sudbury I was lonely. I made myself set goals so I wouldn't miss him. He had much to do, setting up stock, advertizing and getting staff. They planned on having a big fashion show in the local cinema to celebrate the opening.

Ted phoned, told me he missed us terribly and said he'd be home for Christmas. He said he'd bought presents for each of us. He'd been sleeping in the back of the store. Renovations were done and everything ready to go and he found us a place to live, the upstairs of a large house in the city. He will paint it before we move in.

I finished the smocking for the lady and phoned to see if I could deliver it. I had to catch a bus then walk about a half a mile. Her house was the size of a library. I rang the bell and a maid answered. I told her my mission and she let me in.

There was a rotunda lobby with a spiral staircase. The tall ceilinged rooms were off-white. It looked as if I was watching a scene from a play as uniformed maids and man-servants dashed here there, and up and down the staircase carrying clothes and suitcases, shouting orders to this one and that one and going in and out of doors that led off the hall. In the midst of all that, the lady came down the stairs in a state of agitation to deal with me.

"Let me have it," she shouted above the din.

I unwrapped the tissue paper to show her and she said "There isn't as much smocking as I wanted."

"But madam, you would need more material if you wanted more."

She shrieked "And I'm supposed to give you twenty dollars for that?"

I stood there, conscious of my older clothes and my extra pounds. My face felt naked against her professionally made up one. And I felt shame that she didn't think it was a good job. She looked me over from head to foot as I shriveled in front of her. She shrugged.

"Haven't time to argue with you, I'm off to Greece."

She addressed an older woman in black, "Give her twenty dollars and get her to leave."

Salt tears stung my eyes as I left. I was humiliated and not treated with dignity. I made a vow that for the rest of my life, I'd do my best to undermine anyone who acted that way to me or anyone else. But through the tears I smiled: I made twenty dollars!

Ted made it home for Christmas. We met him at the railway station and waves of his love enveloped me when he reached us. Oh! How happy I was to have his arms around me again and we were both talking at once and he hugged the girls over and over saying how big they'd grown.

Next day we went to Loretta's for opening of presents and for the big meal because goodness knows what we would be doing in up-coming Christmases. Loretta and Christmas fit like a hand in a glove: The too-large tree with baubles, fruit cake enough to make one tipsy, decorated cookies, red bows adorning lamps and pictures.

It was just like a Christmas card from the good old days. It was also snowing and the local church bells were chiming.

Ted had bought a wind-up clown that played a drum for Barbara while for Brenda he had a pull-along grey elephant with floppy ears. For me, there was a make-up case: Burgundy leather with a zipper and it was filled with quality make-up.

After the meal we walked home pulling the children on a toboggan and we were filled with Christmas spirit.

Paddy, my dear little dog, had been trotting over to the neighbour's house a lot. At first I was annoyed because they were feeding him steak. But then I realized it was the answer for our upcoming move to an apartment where dogs weren't allowed. I talked to the neighbours and they said they would love to have Paddy.

I also had to sell the English-style pram and buy a fold-up one which I could carry up the stairs.

The sale of the house was complete and we were to move the first of February. I would start packing.

I had a gate across our front verandah so Barbara could play in safety. A couple of little girls saw me and asked why I kept my girl in a cage.

"I want her to be safe from harm," I told them.

"We think you're a cruel mother to keep her away from other kids," they said and they ran off.

I questioned whether I was over-protective. I knew if I let down the gate I would be torn with worry. I realized I didn't have any guidelines.

My sister wrote that John arrived in England safely and she couldn't get over what a fine young fellow he had become. Peggy was looking after my other brothers because it was still hard times in England.

Brenda was doing fine with her cream-of-wheat formula and Barbara wasn't jealous of her anymore. She made Brenda coo and laugh.

When I was packing and throwing some things out, I came across my maternity corset. Those crazy laces! I wore the thing after Barbara was born and was shopping when a lady came up to me and tapped me on the shoulder. "Maybe you don't know that you're trailing this long piece of lacing behind you!" she said.

I made arrangements for the movers and got tickets for the train to Sudbury with a stop-over in Ottawa. The cousins wanted to see us again and they would put us on the Sudbury train the following morning.

Loretta, Anne and some other people I had gotten to know came for a farewell tea. I had never felt that Cornwall was my true home but when it was time to leave, I remembered the good times I had there and thought there never would be a place where I would undergo such dramatic changes.

And in spite of the tug of war with Loretta, I would miss her. Anne and I had become close, and Helen was a sweet sister-in-law. Everyone wished us luck and off we went to be with Ted and to see what Sudbury was like.

The cousins met us at the Ottawa station, chattering all the time, with all attention on my two girls. Aunt May and Uncle Fred were waiting at the house. Aunt May had seven children herself but took on the responsibility of loving Loretta and her sister Daisy as well. If there was ever a good example of Christianity, it was Aunt May and Uncle Fred.

The cousins studied the cream of wheat in Brenda's bottle and were not pleased because she didn't have the usual formula. Barbara went from one cousin to the other accepting lollipops and small toys. We sat down for a meal and there were sixteen people at the table. Aunt May made sure everyone was looked after. She had such grace, so it was nice to hear Uncle Fred say, "Doris reminds me of Aunt May when she was young." I wondered if everyone she came in contact with felt her kinship like I did.

But I was tired — so much talking and leaving Cornwall took its toll. Aunt May led us to a bedroom. I settled Brenda in a crib and Barbara in a cot and thankfully sank into a feather mattress.

The next day the cousins drove us to the train and made sure we had the right compartment.

"All Aboard! Embarké!" the train men shouted. The hisses of steam and the massive wheels started to move, I leaned out of the window to wave goodbye to the cousins. I was thankful for their kindness and their figures got smaller and smaller as we pulled away from Ottawa.

I hoped the cream of wheat I had with me wouldn't go sour on the trip. I took another look at the lovely make-up case Ted had bought me and I smiled. We slept well to the rhythm of the wheels and when we had the warning that we would soon come to Sudbury, I gathered everything together to have an organized exit at Sudbury station.

The train squeaked and braked for the stop and there it was, Sudbury. Ted saw us before we saw him. Once again, the smell and warmth of him made me feel good. I wondered why he felt so warm and realized I was shivering with cold.

"You're not dressed for the cold Dody," Ted said. "It's twenty below zero."

I wondered if I'd heard right. Twenty below zero? We left Ottawa when it was thirty ABOVE zero. We'd freeze if we stood there much longer. Twenty below zero!

Can people exist in that temperature I wondered? The cars that waited for passengers were running their motors full tilt, exhaust steam belched from their rears. Everyone was bundled up like mummies, eyes and noses red as cherries. Our breath sent out small clouds of steam as we talked. It felt as though we were standing in an isolated world of steam.

The train took off and I checked we had all our stuff but I couldn't find my make-up case. I remembered someone bumping into me; it was probably a ruse to steal the case. My insides got all mixed up and I was cross with Ted because he didn't tell us we were going to go to Siberia!

Ted got a taxi and we drove on roads that wove around what resembled the moon's surface. The few trees that were there were stunted and gnarled. The houses looked like they were in a movie set for the Wild West and there was a heavy black smoke over everything. The town had a deserted feeling.

We came to our house and it was nice to have Ted to share the carrying of the children as we were to live upstairs. The kitchen area, which was large, looked out at a granite rock which was six inches away from the house. There was an over-powering smell of the oil paint that Ted had used to paint the place. I guessed I'd get used to it.

The furniture man came and wanted his money. Ted argued with him, telling him he'd pay him later. Did that mean we didn't have enough to cover it, I wondered. At last, the man agreed to wait a week and together they hauled the furniture up the stairs. If we didn't have enough money, what happened to the money from the sale of the house and all his pension, was it all gone?

The lady downstairs said we could use her phone in an emergency. The washing machine which was there, was broken and I would have to do the washing in the bath tub and hang it on lines put up in the kitchen.

At last we put the girls to bed and climbed into our own. It didn't matter if we lived on a moonscape and that it rivaled the north pole; we were together again and that was the main thing. The next day I would walk downtown and see what there was and I slept and dreamed of the little house on Vimy street, of Loretta and Aunt May. I could clearly see the cousins waving to us and my make-up case sprouting wings and sailing off. I woke up and knew that was the past and this was the present and let's get on with it.

I was anxious to see the store so the next morning I wrapped the girls up well, put Brenda in one end of the carriage and Barbara facing her and took off to find where all our hopes and finances were housed.

Somehow I lost my way. The landlady had told me her husband owned an electrical store on the street where I had found myself. Their name was

Poule and I saw his store and went in to ask where our shop would be.

"Mon Dieu Madame Paterson," he said, "what are you DOING on this street? No respectable lady and certainly not one with children would dare walk here." I surmised it was a red-light district. I was told where I'd find our place and headed there. Not many ladies-wear stores, but many mens clothing and jewelry shops. Pubs and more pubs. I heard that a lot of transient men came to work in the mines. It was the men who spent the money. Chances of Sudbury needing women's elite clothing were practically nil. I found our place but it was far away from the town's main drag. It was small but I had to admit it was elegant. I had a lump in my throat because I thought it couldn't succeed being so far from the other stores. Oh! Why hadn't they let me have some input — from a woman's point of view? All our money gone. They should have kept some back so they'd have something to draw from while they were getting known. Wasn't it partly my money too? Did Ted ever pay the moving company? Why didn't he discuss it with me? He knew I had heard him argue with the mover so why hadn't he said something to me? I couldn't help but feel put-out about it.

However, once inside I felt the dove grey walls, the carpet, the soft lighting and plush sofa would make women feel pampered. Ted showed me the latest fashions. I would have defied anyone to tell him they had concerns for his future in the face of his pride and his hopefulness. If he hadn't gone into that business, he would never have found another with a partner who would train him in every aspect.

When we got home from the walk I was horrified to find Barbara's hands were almost frozen. The sun was bright, so it had seemed warm, but the landlady told me it was now twenty-five below zero.

I tried to warm my girls, but it was difficult as we kept the heat low in the house – Ted barely brought in enough money to pay for groceries, let alone heating – and to make matters worse, that awful granite rock outside the kitchen window left a cold feeling inside me.

Some days, Ted would only sell a pair of stockings. He was finding it hard. And he was missing contact with other men, quite apart from missing his beloved sports.

His partner came from Cornwall and instructed me in how to be an advertizement for the shop. I was to wear the latest fashions, plus gloves and a hat. And he wanted to know what was the matter with one of my shoulders — the right one was lower than the left. He discussed that with Ted!

Six weeks went by and things weren't any better. Ted hired a Mrs.Perdue who would take charge of the shop while he got a job as a lab assistant in the mines. Inco was trying to cut down the noxious fumes from the stacks in Sudbury. Health officials were concerned that if the mines were having such a bad effect on vegetation – the countryside around the town was like a moonscape – that perhaps it was also affecting the people who worked in the mine and lived in the town.

We heard that Frank, Ted's brother, had secured a job as a disc jockey and announcer in the Sudbury radio station and would be coming with Marcie to live here.

We had been in Sudbury for six months and if Ted had not been employed by the mine we would have gone under with the business. Ted worked from seven to three and then worked in the shop till closing time.

Soon after Frank arrived, he and Ted decided to help out with the local air force cadets. Perhaps part of the enticement was the bar in the nearby officers' mess that just happened to have a "happy hour" about the time they were finished with the cadets.

The brothers also decided to buy a wreck of a car. I presumed that Frank knew how to drive and would teach Ted. Marcie presumed Ted knew how to drive and would teach Frank. Neither of them had a clue. But somehow they muddled through and both got their licences.

The house where we lived was to be sold. Housing was tight and there was nothing available for rent.

But there was a one-bedroom apartment above the shop available. Ted asked me if I thought we could manage, living like that. I'd found out I was pregnant again and I just couldn't imagine three children and two adults living in such a confined space so I refused. I felt I had let Ted down because of course a lot of families do manage in a small space.

So for the time being, life went on as usual. Brenda was crawling and Ted loved to watch her challenge herself. She'd throw a toy from the play pen and lay on her tummy and reach and reach until she retrieved it. "She's made of good stuff," he said "She doesn't give up easily."

One night we had a couple over to play bridge. He had known them in Cornwall. I thought of playing cards as a way of passing time, Ted regarded the game as all-out war. We were partners and my mind wandered as I talked to Clara about a recipe and completely forgot what was trump, at which point I thought Ted would burst with rage. After the couple left I asked him why he'd been so angry.

"Only a fool would have played like you did," he told me.

Well! I just couldn't help it. I let fly and smacked him in the face — hard. Shock, dismay and hurt was on his face. He recoiled, grabbed his coat and left.

I nursed my anger and then as it always was with me, I started to cry, and realized I shouldn't have slapped him. I looked around me. I hated Sudbury. I hated the cold and I hated the store and Ted's partner. What did we have? Nothing. It was all useless and if they had consulted me, a woman, I would have told them people just wouldn't shop away from main street and they wanted cheaper dresses that they could change every season. But no, I was not even slightly involved other than to wear clothes as an example and cry about losing his pension and any financial safety net we had.

I phoned the store in the chance he was there and Thank God he was.

"Oh Dody! How could we have let that happen? Does it mean you don't love me? I couldn't bear it if that were so."

Ted and my children were my reason for being. It was my fault.

And I told him it was a reflex action and of course I loved him and to please come home.

So we made up but it had left a wound. Instead of being renewed in the morning I felt depressed. I was putting shoes on little Barbara while she was sitting on the counter and I found myself crying again. Tears splashed down on her and she reached over to pat my head. Dear little girl. A good mother wouldn't have shown her feelings in front of one so small.

I knew sometimes it was memories of my homeland and my family that I was still grieving for, especially for the mother and sister left behind — so very long ago it seemed to me.

Looking for another place to live, Ted was often met with "We don't take children!" Finally he handed one lady fifty cents and told her the next time she put an ad in the paper, the money would pay for extra words saying "No children wanted."

So we had to go to further out of town and found what looked like a warehouse. The owner lived downstairs and had a painting business. The apartment itself was okay but it was stuck in the middle of a field which caught every bit of wind. It whistled around the place as if it would root out the whole building if it had a mind to do so. Absolutely nothing was in walking distance. But that was where we ended up living.

We got a letter from John. He was working on Dad's farm and was resentful once again.

I also got news that my two English friends in Cornwall had died. It seemed too much of a coincidence, could it be that the town's paper mills were dangerous to health?

Measles

Both Barbara and Brenda had high fevers. Then red spots appeared. Barbara got over it but I had to call the doctor fro Brenda. It took him ages to get to our place and the wind was howling again. Everything seemed worse with the steady whining of that ruddy wind. He said her measles were in-grown which was a serious state and I spent the night trying to bring her temperature down. The doctor said if she didn't get better she would have to go to the hospital. Her will to fight saved her. Loretta had lost her hearing from the afteraffects of the measles.

The girls were finally over the measles so I loaded them on the toboggan and went for a run in the field over light snow. It was good to have fresh air on our faces and worries of measles gone from us.

Ted eventually found us a place in town which seemed too good to be true. It was upstairs in a large house and close to the store. Ted would be able to come home for lunch, something he had missed doing.

Ted had another season's dresses coming in and new styles to buy but the old ones still hung there and stared him in the face, not sold. Bills were piling up. But Ted wouldn't give up, we had too much at stake, We could only hope there would be a break somewhere. More women were finding the store and they liked dealing with Ted.

I went downstairs to tell the landlord we'd be moving. Three small children were around a bare table. They had a gigantic tin of corn syrup in the middle and were dipping pieces of bread into it. Syrup was running down their chins and onto the table. The wife looked on helplessly. Maybe they were having trouble with their business like us.

We moved into the new apartment and my soul felt content. The people downstairs came from Syria and they also owned the apartment block across the road. Zakia was thin with chiseled features, giving her a look of strength.

We took to each other right away. She told me I was the spitting image of her sister who died. Entering that place was like a soothing balm.

I was pregnant again and Ted didn't complain even though the business was now in very bad shape. We were often invited downstairs to share an evening with the family to play cards and we enjoyed the comradeship.

Brenda now drank plain milk from a cup which solved the vomiting problem. No more cream of wheat! She started to walk at nine months old and at eleven months, toilet trained herself.

I found out the local theatre group were calling for auditions and I asked Ted if I could apply and he agreed.

There was a long line of applicants stretching right around the block, but the wait was worth it: I was given one of the leading parts. I was exhilarated. The young girl downstairs would look after the children. Theatre was in my blood.

Ted must have had second thoughts and didn't like the idea. "How can you want to be part of that world? They live in a dream land and it makes me nervous that you will be with them" he said. But he didn't say "No."

Life became more interesting and I didn't mind doing housework or even if Ted was late getting home because I had my lines to learn, and rehearsals to attend.

Ted brooded more and more about the theatre project and guilt prodded at me. He had so much to worry about and I was rocking the boat. On the other hand, acting was part of me and surely it couldn't do any harm.

Two weeks before the show was to go on, the play was going well but Ted blurted out, "I can't stand it. You'll have to give it up."

"But what will the cast and the director do at this late stage?"

"I've told you, I have all I can stand."

With a heavy heart and a red face I told the director I had to quit. And they managed all right. The play was performed and the sky didn't fall, but my reputation was tarnished.

Ted had been right. Our lives were more important than the stage. He'd had to give up the job in the mine to spend more time in the store.

Frank was doing commercial spots on the radio for an eccentric fellow who was wealthy. This man had formed some kind of religion based on the number seven. He was so fond of Frank that he insisted Frank was to voice the commercials. It was funny because Frank, forever the clown, would imitate a heavy-duty, old-time minister saying "Now hear ye, my brethren," and so on. It was all a big laugh but he got a massive response. The old fellow was so well pleased that he told Frank he'd set him up with any kind of business he wanted to get into.

Frank came into Ted's business with some finances and became a partner, hoping that the business could survive with the extra money put in the pot.

Scott's birthday *(19th March 1951)*

I was due to have our third child. This was the first pregnancy that I didn't have a hemorrhage. And it was heaven to have Zakia stand by to look after things while I went into hospital.

We were playing cards downstairs when Zakia saw I was uncomfortable. She told Ted to take me upstairs and my waters broke. Ted panicked but Zakia came upstairs and told him not to worry, her husband would drive me to the hospital and she would look after the girls.

The pains weren't as harsh as with the other two births and the doctor announced, "It's a boy." The baby was cute and well-rounded and I knew Ted was glad he now had a son. Men tease each other when there are only girls in the family: It was pretty stupid, but they said it was because the man wasn't man enough!

I had a feeling of tremendous peace when the baby was in my arms.

I surely wasn't ready for the excitement in Ted as he burst through the door, "Oh Dody, how wonderful," he said, "we have a boy! Isn't it great? I phoned Mother to get some BLUE baby things. Oh! Dody! A boy!" Ted couldn't wait to go to the nursery to have a look at him and I was actually relieved when it was time for him to go home because I was exhausted with all the excitement.

Nothing had prepared me for so much enthusiasm but I was glad. We were to name the baby Scott. His first name would be Joseph for the saint's name but he would be called Scott. Ted's father came from Scotland so Ted thought Scott was an appropriate name for this baby.

Another lady was wheeled into my room. She had given birth to a girl and had named her Colleen because her mother had come from Ireland. It was such a coincidence.

I thought all boys were to have circumcision but our doctor thought it wasn't necessary. Bringing Scott home was different to dealing with the girls. I wasn't used to diaper changing needing to be a matter of fleetness of hand, worthy of a magician. As soon as I uncovered his diaper, a geyser of urine would hit the wall or whatever stood in the way. The business of cleaning his penis was not as simple as it was made out to be. Even his sucking from the bottle was different. Strong sucking and massive burps when he'd finish. He slept through the night early on and I suspected it was because he drank so much milk.

He was completely bald and even though he was too young to hold his head up, he did it regardless and wobbled about. He would focus on something so hard that you could almost see his brain working to figure it out. We had to laugh.

The girls thought he was a real live doll, and they were good with him, even sometimes holding his bottle so I could get dinner on the table. Frank and Marcie came to see the new baby and Frank picked Scott up in his arms, cooing and playing with him. Ted couldn't seem to enjoy that closeness with babies, but then he never experienced it from his father.

Bills at the store were getting further and further behind, but somehow Ted juggled them. He'd been trying to collect outstanding debts. One wealthy lady owed him a lot of money. Her son phoned Ted and told him he'd shoot our whole family if he persisted in asking for the money. His partner in the Cornwall store was demanding payment for dresses sent previously since his store was not doing well either. The suppliers were threatening not to send any more shipments. Ted was juggling everything.

We heard from John in Australia that he was going to leave my father's farm and would try to live on his own. He hoped to work on another man's farm and was a bit nervous because the farmer was a very hard Australian and demanded a lot from everyone.

When Scott was four months old, his penis became swollen and he wasn't urinating. I had to take him to the hospital so they could circumcise him. It wasn't pleasant for either him or for me to deal with. It was a worry because there was always a danger of infection.

So we reached yet another winter in Sudbury and the days were full of cold and pollution. It was difficult to take three little ones shopping with their snow-suits, boots, scarves and mitts. We would go into a large department store and one of them would want to go to the bathroom. If I took one inside the stall, the ones outside would be scared and cry so we'd all land up scrunched in the stall with me trying to undo all the outer clothing so they wouldn't wet themselves. If they did wet their clothes, they would be a living icicle by the time we got home!

Marcie was pregnant. Frank was so happy about it. I heard from the mother of Colleen, the lady who was with me when Scott was born. She was bathing the baby in the kitchen sink when some rowdy teenagers came into her yard hitting at everything. She left the baby on the counter and rushed out to chase them away. When she returned, she found her little one had slipped into the bathwater and drowned. Nothing could console the mother. How horrible!

I ran into Scott's room and held him tight. How could a mother live with herself when something like that happened? What a responsibility mothers bear I thought, poor little Colleen.

Ted had organized a massive sale for the store and went down early to the shop. Women were lined up for a block to get in first. He was happy to see the advertising had worked and went to open the door. A man appeared in front of him, took a large lock and bolt and fastened it to the door, took out a Bailiff's notice from his case and stuck it on the window. Ted walked up the waiting queue of women and told them the sale couldn't take place. Some reached out and touched his arm in sympathy. He couldn't bring himself to tell me it was over.

I was doing household chores when Ted came in with Frank.

"What are you doing coming home at this time?" I asked.

It was Frank who told me as Ted was clutching at his stomach. "The Bailiff came Doris. We can't even get the personal stuff from the store. It's all gone, finished!"

At least Frank had a job to go to. We had no money and three little ones. My brain seemed to go into "park." Ted turned from me, mumbling "Got to see what we can do." And they left.

I couldn't get my brain to work.

The girls were blissfully playing with their dolls unaware of the calamity falling on us. The sun was shining and there was a good smell of cookies baking as if everything was normal. What would we do?

It got to be evening and Ted wasn't home. Didn't he know we should be sharing that situation? Did I know him really?

The door opened and a ghost of my husband walked in. His lovely, intelligent eyes were glazed with despair. "Dody I've failed you and the children and I don't know where to turn."

We held on to each other and somehow the night passed.

Morning light arrived and Scott was bellowing for his breakfast.

Zakia came up with a tray of Syrian cookies and I told her what had happened. I told her that maybe I could sell the clothes that I had hardly worn. I had only worn them once as advertizing for the store.

She spread the word and her friends came and went through my wardrobe, they took the best things and left me with a few hundred dollars.

At last. At last, Ted sat down with me and we talked about what we should do. There was a department store in town, similar to Eatons. They had ladies and children's clothing on one floor and needed a manager for it. He would apply. I happened to pass Birks jewelry store and I went in to ask for a job. I filled out their form but didn't have the qualifications they asked for. However, when I reached home, I got a phone call. They asked if I could start right away.

Ted said "What do you think you're doing?"

I told him I could make a contribution and asked him to let me try. But he was angry and he was clutching his stomach again. "It would be proof that I can't look after you. You'll have to refuse."

They phoned again and I had to tell them my husband wouldn't let me work. Ted applied for the job as manager for the other firm and they assured him he'd get a big bonus at Christmas and, if things worked out, he'd be a partner in their business.

We felt obliged to pay off our debts, and had to find five hundred dollars to pay the fees for going into bankruptcy: Ted sold his beater of a car and I sold anything of value I had, and we eventually scraped together the required money. I told my family in England. My father still owned the orchard with the cottage. He wondered if he could sell it and send me the money but I told him no, because we could manage till Ted got his first paycheque.

So we went on, a bit older and a lot wiser, hoping the new job would turn out to be a good experience.

Ted worked long and hard for the Jewish brothers in their store. He came home at night exhausted and his feet hurt so much he could hardly walk. But he had a carrot in front of his nose — the bonus at Christmas — and he pushed through the days, weeks and months.

Finally Christmas came and the brothers gave a party and presented Ted with a gift. He brought it home so we could open it together. And inside the box was a silver muffin dish. He opened the envelope that went with it and a card said "Merry Christmas!" Absolutely no bonus cheque. We were both devastated. After all the anticipation we had received a muffin dish!

Ted went to the brothers and reminded them of their promise. They told him he hadn't been there long enough and besides their nephew was to join them and they would train him to be a partner.

Isolation in North Bay *(December 1953)*

Ted knew if the nephew was joining them, he'd never be a partner so he went to the recruiting office of the forces to see what was available.

They told him they were setting up a new organization called the Ground Observer Corps.

Radar could track aircraft flying at normal heights, but newer aircraft could fly much lower, under the radar beams, and thus they avoided being detected. The airforce was in the process of setting up a manned network across the country, including the arctic, to report sightings of such low-flying aircraft. He was accepted for the job and he gave notice to the Jewish brothers and readied himself to go into the forces again.

Loretta appeared on the street in Sudbury and Ted was shocked to see her when no one had said she would be coming. She was there to help Marcie with the baby and made them swear to secrecy and not let me know. I would never understand her.

Ted went to North Bay and lived on his own until married quarters were ready for us. Our medical would be covered and housing deducted from his salary. Heating was free so we would have a chance to get on our feet again.

We survived until we left for North Bay and went to the base which was five miles from town. The house was large, four bedrooms, big kitchen and a dining room and hardwood floors throughout.

I promised Zakia I would write often and I was sorry to leave her.

The base was surrounded by bush and there were bears around. I worried about the children and kept my eyes glued to the window whenever they were playing outside.

My neighbour was good and had a car. She told me to come with her to shop for groceries and her daughter would babysit.

Scott didn't talk. He tugged at my skirt when he wanted something and pointed to a cookie or whatever. It was worrying but we were sure he would be all right later.

The isolation of the base was hard to take. Ted set off every morning in an airforce van and I didn't see him till six or seven at night. They trained volunteers for a vast area. When they received word of sightings, it was traced and the unidentified aircraft was checked. When the downtown office was underway, he would travel to further-out places for ten days at a time. Ted enjoyed going to the mess but I resented it.

When it was late Summer I took the children with their little baskets to pick wild strawberries in the bush. We had wandered far and I realized we were lost. I was frightened but didn't want the children to know it and I got them to sit on a rocky outcropping. I got out snacks I'd brought for them and when I looked up, the three of them had their eyes glued to just behind me and their mouths were opened as if they were surprised.

I froze to the spot, thinking it must be a bear behind me and frantically tried to think what someone had told me about bears. Nothing. I couldn't think of a thing. Three little ones; a bear could run faster than them. With a herculean effort I turned my head so I could see the animal, and there was nothing there! Such relief I felt. I laughed but ended up crying. I'd felt so vulnerable and lost in more ways than one. I never did find out what the children had been looking at, but perhaps it was just my nervous apprehension at our predicament. Anyhow, after we had rested, we soon found some recognizable landmarks and arrived home tired.

I'd always been looked after in my life and now I had this responsibility to carry. I knew I would have to manage alone because Ted was away so much. I was no longer the fluffy young damsel that I used to be. One thing I learned about the non-existent bear was that we weren't in England where the largest wild animal was a little fox, we were living amongst monster wildlife and going to pick strawberries was something to think about two or three times before venturing out with the youngsters.

Ted tried to do the right thing. He helped bathe the kids at night and read them stories when he was home. He couldn't help being the restless person he was. He hated being confined to the house and liked to socialize. I tried drinking at cocktail parties but it wasn't the world I wanted for my family. Everything seemed unsteady. I thought it might be the reaction to the previous few years.

Frank phoned one night in a panic. Marcie had a recurrence of TB and had to go into the sanatorium. As Frank had to work, he asked if we could look after Brian and we said we would.

Frank and Marcie arrived not only with Brian but with nine-month-old Rickie as well and told us there wasn't anyone to look after the baby either.

My heart sank. I didn't know if I could do it. Frank gave me twenty jars of baby food and some diapers for Rickie while poor little Brian stood holding a small suitcase. He was only four years old and my heart melted. "I'll see if I can manage," I said.

When we went to church I prayed God would give me strength to take on this burden. I asked forgiveness to think it was a burden but it weighed heavy on my soul. The thing was, inside, I was still the girl who was a star on stage, one who was loved and protected. I'd never been required to take on a job of looking after and disciplining extra children.

Six weeks later I talked to Ted and told him it was too much for me. I'd look after Brian but they would have to find somewhere else for the baby. Brian was buddies with Scott and I went to register him for kindergarten.

My sewing machine had gone with the store, our radio was broken, and I didn't even have access to a library.

But I had made friends with the wife of Ted's boss. Her name was Wilda and she suggested she drive me to the arts and letters club downtown once a week. Sounded like a miracle.

I was pregnant again. I had miscarried earlier and it took a long time before I got over it. The little fetus I was carrying was expelled while I was on the toilet. I flushed the toilet without thinking and stared with horror as I realized what was happening. Miscarriages are hard enough to deal with and I grieved just as much as if one of the living children had died. And to have flushed it down the toilet!

We only had the army doctor on the base and when I went to him he prescribed some pills that he said would help prevent another miscarriage.

I reacted badly to the medication — and I'll be eternally grateful I did — so I threw them away.

The doctor had given me thalidomide, known to be effective for morning sickness, but it was also an effective tranquilizer so I can only surmize my doctor was thinking it might also work for preventing miscarriages.

And as everyone knows, thalidomide babies were born with deformed, missing, or stunted arms and legs.

The volunteers that Ted and the other officers recruited downtown, were the best looking young women.

There were get-togethers after the evening sessions and he came home later and later smelling of drink. He joined the softball team and we would go to sit on the rafters to watch him play. He loved talking sports and even envisioned having a sport restaurant. He said I could cook and he'd look after the business and talk to the sportsmen who came in. My heart sank lower and lower.

Marcie and Frank dropped in on their way to a vacation in Florida! I told them I was pregnant and on their way home they were to pick up Brian and take him home. He'd been with us for a year.

I didn't know what had happened to my dream of a perfect married life. When we dressed up to go for a dance at the mess, we regained a small aspect of how we used to be.

The officers looked dashing in their evening dress uniform. The trousers were slim-fitting with a line of gold braid running down the outside of the legs. The jackets were short with vest-like points. The collars and facings were a darker-blue satin. White, formal shirts were finished with black bow ties, and red satin cumberbunds were worn around the waist. Epaulets with gold fringes complemented smaller editions of their medals across the left breast. The evening gear was expensive but Ted looked like a prince in his.

But for the most part we were drifting in different ways.

Wilda — who was married to Ted's boss — took me to the first session for oil painting at the arts and letters club. I enjoyed myself so much and everyone ooh'd and aah'd when they saw my work. I wondered why on earth I hadn't thought of painting before. And memories came back of the pastel paintings I used to do.

There was a stirring in my soul and I knew that no matter how I felt about our lives drifting apart, I could forget about my troubles when I painted.

I had a kidney stone stuck in the tube which went to the bladder. Nothing would dislodge it, so the doctor said I had to go to Toronto for an operation. He told me they would have to cut my back from one side to the other and that it would take six weeks before I was on my feet again.

Every time I did any work, I felt pain there so I thought I'd try aggravating the stone: I went on my hands and knees, got the scrub brush and scrubbed the kitchen and bathroom floors while I yelled with pain, but the large stone was dislodged!

Ted later told me he would have rented an apartment outside the hospital and lived there with the children until I could come home. Heavens!

Patrick's birthday (14th November 1954)

Ted was away when I went into labour with Patrick, our next son. Ted was giving a speech at a conference in Toronto. My good neighbours came to my aid as if it was all pre-arranged. One took care of the children, and two of the husbands drove me to hospital. Not only drove me to hospital but paced back and forth in the waiting room as if they were going to be the fathers. When the doctor told them I'd given birth, they cheered and were so happy for me that I found it hard not to cry, because I was so touched by their caring. They phoned Ted to tell him we'd had a boy. He was in the middle of his speech when someone hollered that he had a baby boy and the whole audience stood up and said, "Way to go, Ted." And his boss told him to get on the next train home.

I was surprised when Ted came into the hospital room because I thought he was still in Toronto.

"How did you find out?" I asked him.

He reached out to kiss me and hold me and to examine our little newcomer. A parcel fell on the bed.

"It's for you" he said.

I opened it and started to cry. It was a beautiful powder blue, silk nightgown. I couldn't believe it. A personal gift from Ted. It made me aware that I was still young enough to be loved.

He even stayed quite a while which was unusual for him as he was always en route somewhere else. We talked like old times while little Pat lay between us with a smile on his lips.

The reason I had cried was because our anniversary had been on the 10th November and Ted had presented me with two large boxes richly decorated with ribbons and special anniversary paper.

I had torn off the paper saying "Surely it wasn't you who decorated these boxes." And he said "No, Janice at the office did it for me."

To my dismay, one held a Dutch oven and the other a saucepan.

I didn't know what it was with Ted but he seemed to have a fixation

148

with saucepans. I was sure he didn't give his mother presents of saucepans. I felt like acting like she had done — flinging them at the wall. The boxes had been so lovingly decorated I felt for sure there would have to be something really special for me in them.

Well, all was forgiven when I saw that lovely nightgown.

I got excited to bring little Pat home to show Barbara, Brenda and Scott. Scott had been dying to have a baby brother. All was well in the world.

Pat was a most contented baby. He looked like a little elf and so sweet looking, he could have been an advertisement for baby cereal or something. He never cried, drank all his milk in the bottle, and waited patiently if I didn't have it ready right on time. He never fussed and his eyes always seemed to have a smile in them. He was always like that. When he was about three years old, he went outside to play in the back yard and when I checked on him, he was nowhere to be seen. Oh what a feeling that was, I ran to the neighbours and all of us searched around. We knew he couldn't have gone far because I'd seen him a short while previously. When we spied him, he was in the far end of our back yard where there was a large hole and he had lowered himself into it and was happily playing with his toy cars, making roads for them on the sides of the hole!

It was cold in North Bay and I told Ted I had to have a new coat. He gave me a cheque to pay for whatever amount it came to. I saw this lovely black Borgana coat. Borgana was a classy fake fur. I tried it on and with its stand-up collar, full cut, and silvery black colour I actually looked glamourous. I made out the cheque and got ready for fireworks at home. And there were fireworks! Ted never, ever splurged on clothes for himself. But that coat became an icon for the family. The children cuddled up to it in church and stroked it and felt warm next to it. It could become a makeshift bed for babies when we visited. It became synonymous with me and the coat lasted for nineteen winters.

During that time we went to get Barbara a pair of shoes and the salesman noted that one foot was smaller than the other and from that time on, we had to buy two pair every size update to accommodate the difference. The doctor wondered if she had polio when she was tiny and Ted took her to the children's hospital in Toronto to be tested. She was diagnosed with spina bifida that had affected one leg and her pelvis.

It didn't hold her up much but she found it hard to ride a bike. I told the school about her condition and asked that she not be required to jump over those wooden "horses" they use in the gym. They thought I was being over-protective and shamed and coerced her into participating, telling her, "You can do it if you try!"

Loretta couldn't stand Barbara having straight hair, so one day, when Barbara and Brenda were visiting her, Loretta gave her a Toni home permanent. The next morning all the curls were gone again, but Loretta bought another one and this time it stayed.

Loretta had been a fairy godmother to the girls. They loved her jokes, her stories, her clowning around, and the special treats she would give them. But there was a limit to Loretta's patience and by the end of a two-week stay, Loretta lost her temper. The girls were so frightened they started planning to run away. But luckily, their Aunt Connie (Ted's sister) was visiting from Toronto and calmed them down.

Scott still wasn't talking but the neighbour's mother knocked on our door one day and told me he was just getting everything he wanted without talking. If I stopped accommodating him, she was sure he would soon speak. Sure enough, I ignored him long enough and he reeled off long sentences as if he was ten years old!

Ted came home drunk sometimes and the whole of me was disgusted. I hated him next to me in bed after these occurences and I'd cry quietly until morning. I was tired out from trying to find a way out of that way of living, but I couldn't find any answer. I had nowhere to go and no support system. I knew many other women had it worse that I did and Ted never hit me, so people would say to me, "You're lucky it isn't worse than that."

I prayed to God to take one of my legs or anything if He would change him from drink. But it was the let-down of all my romantic dreams. I wasn't on the stage now: It was for real. Back then, there were no support systems or places for women to go.

My heart sank lower.

Wilda called for me every week to go to the arts and letters club. The other students thought I was a genius the way I mixed my oil paints and painted. But to me, my work looked ordinary. However, I had such a wonderful time and knew this was what I was meant to do. It gave me a life raft and I could hang on to it no matter what else was happening in my life.

An art teacher came to the base to give lessons on painting. She would set up a still life and talk about shading and composition. I was amused by one of the students, a group-captain who painted — on a tiny canvas — the whole room, including all the students. By the time he got to the apples in a bowl on the table, the apples were barely the size of a pinhead! I found it hard to connect that larger-than-life war hero with the tiny still life. During the war, he had piloted a Spitfire shooting down German bombers. He not only did that but when the enemy sent over pilotless buzz bombs, he went up after them to shoot them down over the empty fields of Kent before they could reach their target in London.

It was about this time that I was trying to learn to drive. Ted just couldn't stand to teach me so when it was dark at night, I got in the car and drove around the base. One time, when I returned to our shared driveway, someone had parked on my next-door neighbour's side, but had left very little room.

"Don't be scared I told myself," and drove right into the side of that brand-new car.

I went to ask Ted to help me out but he said, "You got yourself into it, so get yourself out of it."

Trembling I rang the bell next door knowing they must have heard that awful scraping noise of metal on metal. Who should open the door but the same group-captain hero. "I'm so sorry, what can I do?" I asked him.

He smiled at me and said, "Doris let me tell you how much I admire your painting. And as for the car, I'll have a friend see to it and we won't talk about it any more!" He was not only a hero but a true gentleman.

I told Ted and he just raised his eyes to the ceiling in disbelief and said, "I give up!"

I was determined to get my license to drive but had trouble with the gearshift. The lady next door said, "Heavens Doris, we women should never let our husbands teach us to drive! You need another woman. So she took me out. When the gears made an awful noise, she was calm and said, "Don't take any notice of a little noise, just try again. There now, you're doing wonderfully, men are so intolerant of music in the gears!"

And bless her, I learned to drive.

Ted found out that the cartilages in both his knees were shot. He went to the veteran's hospital in Toronto and was gone for six weeks. I thought I'd surprise him with a visit while he was there because I'd got my driver's license — leaving the driving inspector shattered — and so I made arrangements for a babysitter then took off on my own for the four-hundred-mile drive.

Ted had casts on both legs and was using crutches. And yes, he was surprised to see me. But he just wanted to be with me after such a long absence and couldn't wait to get out to a motel room. The hospital had several rooms nearby that they provided to visiting wives but there were notices pinned up everywhere saying in large letters, "No men allowed."

And to make sure that rule wasn't broken, a fierce-looking woman was at the desk guarding the entrance to the rooms.

"I just want to see what kind of room it is," said Ted as he cased the joint. Horrors! He sneaked around to my door without the dragon noticing and we went into the room.

I don't know if my reader has ever had sex with a man when he had his legs bound in plaster casts, but I can assure anyone, it can be done, difficult as it may be.

Later, there was a knock on the door.

"I've been told you have a man in there Mrs.Paterson," the fierce-looking woman stated. "Get him out right now!"

Ted didn't seem the least bit bothered, and left.

While recuperating, he kept himself busy making woven scarfs for the children and he even embroidered and decorated a Christmas felt stocking for each child.

Five weeks later Ted phoned from the train station in North Bay to say he was home and to come and get him. It was November so I started the car and left it running to warm up while I dressed all the kids in their warm clothes. As we went out to the car there was a loud C R A C K! I got in the driver's seat but the car was dead. I called to a man walking by for help.

"You've cracked the block, lady, and the engine's ruined."

I asked my neighbour if he'd go to get Ted from the station. When he arrived home he was furious. Six weeks he'd been away and he hadn't even asked us how we were.

Instead, he just lectured me angrily: "You know nothing about cars and now you've got us into this fix."

The children were silent as he unloaded his traveling case.

I was so humiliated that I walked out of the house and closed the front door behind me.

How could he be like that? Couldn't he sympathize with me first and then find out what happened? I felt he was wrong to do that and my heart hardened towards him.

He discovered our new car was guaranteed to have anti-freeze in it but the dealership had forgotten to put it in. It hadn't been my fault after all. He apologized, but why don't men realize that the words have been spoken and they don't quickly go away? I returned home of course, because I had to.

The dealership replaced the engine but it took a while.

8:

Moving to Quebec

From North Bay Ted was posted to Trois Rivieres, Quebec, in 1957. We were led to believe that it would be advantageous for Scott to attend French schooling. But the first year he just sat at his desk and refused to do anything. The second year was much better as he made friends with the French students. At one point he asked me if he could put shoe black on his head because he was the only one with blond hair! He soon turned into a true French Canadian, thinking, writing and dreaming in French.

The girls attended an English-speaking Protestant school. It was during this time that Brenda, at nine years of age, was diagnosed with diabetes. She had a visit from a fellow diabetic who told her she was lucky to have been born since Banting and Best had discovered insulin, an effective treatment for diabetes. He said that when he was first diagnosed — before insulin — he was told he'd be dead within a few months. I suppose he thought he was giving Brenda good news when he said she could maybe live long enough to see her thirtieth birthday! Luckily, she's still going strong at sixty-two!

Nobody knew the symptoms to look for in child diabetics. She'd been sent home from school often but there was never any fever or vomiting. However, the doctor diagnosed her after I told him she was always parched for a drink, especially at night, and her skin was always dry.

We were able to send her to a diabetic camp for children and it was there she learned to give her own needle. While there, she met many other childhood diabetics with similar problems and so she came to terms with her disease.

Housing was scarce in Trois Rivieres so Ted thought the family should wait in North Bay until something was available for us. But after a few weeks of waiting I thought the sooner we moved the better I'd be able to get on with what lay in store for us.

I looked into booking the movers and arranged to make all the necessary cancellations. When Ted arrived for his first weekend leave, he was taken aback, to put it mildly.

"There's absolutely no accommodation," he said.

"Then we'll stay in a cottage until we find something," I retaliated. "If we can't find anything for a while the furniture can go in storage."

So we loaded the necessities and the four children into the car and, with high hopes and innocence in what we would find, took off for Trois Rivieres.

These postings created mixed feelings for me. Sadness on leaving the familiar terrain, house, clubs and friends. But I was used to moving, having done it all my life, and felt a certain excitement for new experiences. Some wives, however, just gave up striving to start new friendships or trying to get fond of a new place: They behaved as robots to make it easier.

We arrived and found a cottage quite far from the centre of town. The cottages were clapboard buildings situated in a field with some bush around and a quick-flowing river close by and nothing else.

I prayed that the children would be able to amuse themselves as Ted took off for work in the mornings and I wasn't feeling well. Dampness penetrated the cottage, the place was in a low lying area and the darkness and smell of rotting wood pulled my spirits down.

After mass on the following Sunday, we took the children to explore the area around the cottage. There was a rickety bridge crossing the stream and it looked interesting so we started to go over on it. Brenda started screaming as she looked down, her eyes riveted to the swollen turbulence beneath her. We all — except Brenda — found there wasn't much on the other side, so retraced our steps. Brenda could not be persuaded to budge from the middle of the bridge and was hysterical. I tried to help her but Ted stopped me and said, "Wait a minute Dody, she will do it." And she did. I always wanted to help but children would learn if you would let them get through these things on their own. Hard for me to do.

Ted was having a difficult time adjusting to his new job. The boss was French-Canadian and there were problems for Ted with the language. And at the same time, we were turned down for renting an apartment because we were "The Anglais."

I was really responsible for Ted not going ahead with learning the French language. He had just been on a three month course in New York and on his return, head-quarters said he should go on a two-month course in Ottawa.

I hate to say this but I must: I rebelled. Told him I wasn't prepared to have him go again. It was too hard with the children and to be isolated on a station with nothing on the base for wives but a grocery store and a hair dressing place. Without a car, with buses running only once an hour, and with the town twenty miles away, it was like being on a desert island. So Ted didn't take the course with the consequence that he was by-passed for promotion because men in the forces were required to be bilingual.

I experienced bleeding again so we went to a doctor who ran a pharmacy on the side. He told Ted to get a prescription filled in his pharmacy. Ted said it might not be necessary for me to take the medicine. The doctor's face went livid and berated Ted for a full five minutes.

"You're telling me you don't care if she dies!" he yelled. But Ted stood his ground.

We found out later that it was the norm for doctors in Quebec to have a side business in drugs and most people came away with a hefty bill for medicines. We didn't have the extra money. The bleeding subsided anyway

Ted's birthday *(30th October 1957)*

Young Ted was born in a French-Canadian hospital where the nurses couldn't understand me and I couldn't understand them. I begged the nurses for a hot water bottle but they brought me a bottle of hot water. We called the baby Ted, but Ted Sr. wasn't too happy about it because he knew there would be difficulties with it later.

Ted brought the children to stand outside of the hospital as they weren't allowed inside and they waved to me as I stood at the window. He had to take a few days off from work again.

Ted Sr. had put clean sheets on our bed and had everything nice and clean for me to come home. When I got there, I laid the baby on the bed to change him. Off came his diaper and with delight he let go a stream of urine into the air. Ted Sr, had to change everything all over again. But what could one expect? he was a boy!

Young Ted was such a lovely looking child with large eyes and eyelashes to die for, but I couldn't understand why he was often unhappy. Mostly at night he'd cry and finally I was so tired of being up so long, big Ted took it on himself to try to soothe him so I could get some rest. I was grateful for that help. I took young Ted to the hospital so they could check him over. When I visited he was smiling and happy and all the nurses were in love with him. What was I doing wrong, I asked myself over and over. Like everything in life, his crying eventually stopped and he became a jolly little fellow and so advanced with his walking and running at eight months of age that I was ever watchful of him. He would gaily walk off the top steps from our back door like the cartoons of Donald Duck walking on air. He played hockey with a ball and a lavatory brush and he splashed and ducked under the water when he was bathed. Of course being so young to walk meant he fell often and careened into walls and his bruises were many. It was a good job we didn't have a visit from a social worker as they would think he was being abused. But he just loved being active even though he wasn't old enough to understand his limits.

The next baby was due a few weeks before Christmas. As usual, I had the scare of bleeding at three months pregnancy and thought for sure I would lose the little one, but no, everything had been good since then. We were all hoping for a little girl because we'd had three boys in a row.

I was pretty well up to date for Christmas. I'd been processing a crock full of relish which is a favourite of all. Christmas cake was made and the turkey was in the fridge — Ted had found a twenty-six pound bird. The men were having a competition on who would have the biggest turkey!

I was checking that we had enough small toys for the children's stockings when my waters broke!

"Teddy, now don't panic but I have to go to the hospital," I said.

His face read panic regardless and he said, "You can't mean it".

"Yes. I mean it. You phone the doctor and I'll throw things in a case."

He walked back and forth and didn't pick up the phone, saying, "The relish! the relish! what will happen to the relish?"

"It's simple I'll write it down. But quickly, phone the doctor."

I'm usually organized but it was very early for the baby to come now. I grabbed my case and said goodbye to the children and tried to act calm. When we left the house Ted still had a comb stuck in his hair and his hair was standing on end. I had to laugh and after a minute, he did too.

"Brenda's needle. What will I do about Brenda's needle?"

"Don't worry, she's good and knows what to do. It will be all right."

We had learned by practicing with an orange but it sure didn't resemble your child's arm. Anyhow, there was nothing I could do about it and I had mentally handed over the responsibility.

Laura's birthday *(22nd December 1958)*

Laura was born on the 22nd December, 1958, in a different hospital where they spoke English. Actually it was the only time someone stayed with me during labour. A nurse named Mary undertook to see me through the delivery. She coaxed me to breathe shallowly and deliberately. She talked to me. Her voice acted as a balm, soothing, healing. And she was there with me. She told me the baby was coming and the doctor was there as I went into the delivery room. All the time Mary talked to me. I couldn't believe it was such a peaceful birth.

"It's a girl Mrs. Paterson!"

Mary cleaned the thin little arms while the baby's legs were pummelling the air as she let out a few yells. As she was put on my breast it never failed, love poured out of me for this baby. I blessed Mary for her help and caring.

Ted came and visited the nursery and said the baby looked red. "And," he said, "the relish looks okay but what about the turkey?"

It was Christmas day when Ted brought in the family to visit. The only day that youngsters were allowed. The hospital was thronging with people.

Ted came loaded with parcels and the children all wanted to talk at once but Ted had to tell me the calamity. The insulin needle had broken in Brenda's arm. He had to get the pliers to get the other piece out and didn't have enough insulin for another injection for her. He'd been knocking on every pharmacy door trying to find one that would open up.

The children first complained about having to eat mashed potatoes and scrambled eggs all the time and then they went to see the baby in the nursery. Barbara and Brenda were ecstatic that she was a little girl.

Ted gave me a present as usual, something for the kitchen, a kitchen canister set. I tried to beat down disappointment as I unwrapped each one.

Glory be! The last one had in it a rhinestone brooch and earrings. Lovely!

There was so much noise in the room but it was great to see them all. It was so quiet after they left I fell to sleep for hours.

The doctor suggested that I conform to the regular practice of most Quebec mothers who, for the first two or three weeks, placed their babies in a *pouponnière*, a nursery for new-borns. The mothers can then rest and regain their stamina and, by the time the little ones come home, they are pretty much on regular feeding and sleeping schedules.

It struck me as a great idea. But then I heard these nurseries had been known to give the babies sips of brandy or aspirin so they wouldn't disturb the managers. I visited one, and found it eerie that not one baby was crying out of the twenty there. Anyhow, I like my babies to come home with me, and I would be bereft without them, even for two weeks.

Barbara and Brenda loved dressing Laura up and looking after her after she came home. They really helped.

It was in Trois Rivieres that Barbara turned twelve years old and for the first time I let her babysit when I went for a walk. I couldn't believe how fast the years had gone by. Barbara was no longer a little girl. She was proud to have some extra money. Just the same, it was a long time before I felt at ease about leaving her alone to look after the younger ones.

Our landlord was a burly French-Canadian and had a repair business for boats and cars. We were situated right on the St. Lawrence River and could watch all the nationalities of ships going by. We had a large map on the wall so the children could recognize the flags and tell us where that country was on the map. The place we lived in was what they called the *banlieue* (the outskirts) of Trois Rivieres. Young Pat soon knew all the countries and when he recognized the flag on a ship, he would stick pins into the country of their origin on the map.

While we were living in that apartment, I was sewing a dress for Brenda in our large Quebec country kitchen. There was a knock on the door and I heard the voices of a couple we knew; they had come for a visit. This kitchen had in the corner a cold storage locker with a heavy insulated door. Brenda was semi-undressed while I was fitting her new dress and she didn't want the visitors to see her semi-nude so I put her in this locker, thinking the people wouldn't stay very long. But we got talking and I completely forgot about her. Poor girl was calling and calling and couldn't open the door from inside. The visitor said she thought she heard a noise coming from that door and mercy me! I got a small blanket to wrap her in and got her out of there.

We bought bunk beds for the boys and the girls. Ted said we must get an automatic washing machine. When it was delivered, I couldn't fathom how a machine could do so many things by itself. When I turned it on, I sat on the bathtub in case it would do something it shouldn't do. After a while, I got used to it and blessed it for saving me time and energy. However, we didn't get a drier until after we had ten children.

The girls were driven to school by Ted. It was a Catholic school but it was English speaking.

We were two years in that city. Ted tried to get the language but somehow his tongue couldn't get around the pronunciation.

Brenda and Scott had their tonsils out while in Trois Rivieres. It was a shock to both of them.

Forever looking to further my knowledge in art, I took up sculpture, using acrylic medium and asbestos! Well, we didn't know any better then.

Now we're off to Rimouski (October 1959)

We were posted to Rimouski, Quebec. Life in the services was like that — continual moving and having to come to grips with ever-changing residences, schools, doctors and friends. And there was a feeling we never really belonged to any of the towns where we were posted. Women rarely had cars and the social activities were geared for the men and their drinking.

Rimouski was ninety-nine percent French and there was only a one-room school for the English-speaking children. Scott and Patrick went to the convent in the next street and were adored by the nuns.

I asked a lady who couldn't speak English to meet with me once a week so we could both learn each other's language. I thought it would come easy because of taking French at the convent but I could only understand Parisian French.

I was feeling everything was too much for me to deal with and told my doctor about it. He said the best prescription would be for me to go for a walk after supper. He said to tell my husband that that was his prescription and for him to make sure I went on that walk if I was to regain my stamina. It worked for a while as it cleared my mind to be outside and it brought me some peace.

Ted talked to a lady, encouraging her to rent us her father's house. It was a big old house that had been boarded up for years. To this day, my children remember me saying that I didn't have to sweep the floor after meals because the mice would come running out to eat all the crumbs! I loved being in that house because it had a large yard with fruit trees that reminded me of our orchard in England.

One day I was digging the earth for a small garden when I came across what I thought for sure was a dinosaur bone. It looked like the head of a massive animal. I told the children to run to the newspaper and tell them about the find. They came to see what it looked like and killed themselves laughing: It was the skull of a cow!

Rimouski people were not welcoming to us, the English. Fortunately our landlady was well known and would not allow any mistreatment if she heard of it.

We were told we had to pay for a privileged pew in church: Ted's rank meant he was deemed to be of the upper class and it was therefore expected that he live up to expectations — and pay a ten-per-cent tithe from his wages to the church.

Our driveway was also the access to the apartment block behind our house. Once, while I was pregnant, I was stuck in the snow in that driveway; all the window curtains in the apartment block moved to the side as the residents looked down on my predicament but not one person came to my aid. I told the landlady I had never experienced anything like it and she repremanded the people who lived in that block.

Ted and I went to a maple sugaring camp and the French-Canadian culture is a rich one. Everyone there knew all their folk songs and they danced in the snow and had lots of fun. We were just beginning to find a few new friends when we were posted once more.

Ted and I took a few days off and drove around the Gaspé peninsular. We were struck by the wonderful scenery and the contrast between the luxury mansions — American vacation homes — and the extreme poverty of the local fishermen who lived in nothing more than huts.

When we got home, the children cried and pleaded with us not to leave them with a babysitter again. She had been drinking with a boyfriend and frightened them. The children had huddled together upstairs crying. And I'd been so careful to get a recommended older lady.

I was pregnant again but it was always the same when I was initially pregnant; if I worked too hard in the house I would start bleeding. I went once again in an ambulance, Scott having collected a bevy of youngsters to observe me leaving, proud to have something to show off. The nuns in the hospital wouldn't just let me rest and poked and prodded until I hemorrhaged more and it was all over.

I left the hospital angry at the nuns who hadn't listened to me, resentful towards Ted and how he didn't understand what I was going through, and tired of the church and its rules which were nothing but rules made by men.

Just when we were getting acclimatized to Rimouski we were to leave for another part of Canada, Prince Edward Island.

The government had now phased out the Ground Observer Corps and let all staff go. Some of the men were offered other jobs and luckily Ted was one of them — a position in nuclear defense.

And now to Prince Edward Island (1960)

We headed off for PEI — us and our six children piled into the car — with Barbara holding her goldfish in a bowl. As we crossed over the Northumberland Strait in a large ice-breaker ferry, we were tossed about in our car, sploshing the fishbowl water, but the goldfish survived.

When we arrived in Prince Edward Island I was amazed to see whole apple orchards with all the fruit lying on the ground rotting. We stopped to ask a man why that was and he said it wasn't worth the price of pesticide to keep them free of pests because the price of carting them over on the ferries was too great and they couldn't make any money from it.

There weren't any available houses for us on the base in Summerside, so once again Ted used his powers of persuasion to talk an owner into renting us his house in Kensington, a small town ten miles from Summerside—this house was also boarded up. The owner, a former mayor, lived next door and was unable to use it.

The town was laid back and peaceful. The school was an old-timer with creaky wooden floors. The town library was small but the librarian knew her stuff. Barbara got a job as her assistant and learned a lot. One day, Barbara told us the librarian's corset squeaked — just like the school floorboards —

whenever she bent down to examine the dusty books.

Scott learned a poem called *The Lion and the Crocodile* and was to recite it on stage for the school. We waited in the audience until he appeared. He looked around at us all and started the poem. But then he paused and said, "I'm not going to say it!" and walked off the stage. The audience just broke up with laughing.

Contrary to what people had told us — that Prince Edward Island was always warm and didn't get any snow — we found it the worst place to live with tremendous snow accumulations. We were snowed in twice, for a week each time, during our stay there. Electricity went down and, as both the water and the furnace depended on electricity, we had to huddle in the living room with blankets and use wood in the fireplace for heating and cooking.

PEI had many true characters and the priest of the Catholic church ruled our whole area. He knew the gossip of the town and wasn't backward in naming names from the pulpit if someone had not gone to church or had been seen at a dance in an inebriated state. The parishioners would enjoy going to church because they wanted to hear his booming voice condemn the latest scandal.

Then there was the large and strict looking night nurse who demanded respect and was a little feared by the community. She always enquired as to my health and knew everybody else's health too.

I was asked to fill in for a second table of bridge every week. After a year of doing this and thinking they should be more organized — listing the name of the next house they'd be playing in, instead of spending half an hour wrangling about it every time they were ready to go home — I said I had written down the order on a list.

They looked at me as if they didn't even know me and one said, "You can't decide what to do, you're only a fill-in player!"

I don't know if they ever used my suggestion: I moved to Summerside!

If one came to PEI from the mainland, you were never a certified member of the clan. You could live there for twenty years but they would still say your were not an "Islander."

Beaches there were lovely and the rocks were red-coloured. But we could only swim a few times a year because of strong currents or hoards of jelly-fish which stung like Billy-oh! The sand was pure white and the wind brought the salty taste of the sea. We picnicked and built sand-castles or buried each other in that great, white sand.

The building kitty-corner from us caught fire one night and there was a real danger of the sparks of fire getting to us. We spent the night watching the big building go down and keeping alert in case we needed to evacuate as well. In the morning we breathed a sigh of relief as the danger had passed.

The arts people held a painting competition and I entered a small watercolour of the red rocks at the beach. It won honorable mention. I was stunned. Did it mean that even though I didn't have much training I could be with the good painters?

Ted came home one day to say there was a house on the base in Summerside for us. Houses on the bases were very good and we felt more at home with other members of the forces. I was pregnant again. After some time of living there, Ted asked to be released from his department of nuclear defense and to go into public relations — his true calling. When he had gone to train in the nuclear defense business, he came home an altered man. A lot of it was secret but I surmised that he had seen some terrible sights to be so changed. A lot of fun was knocked out of him.

I lived in fear of having the baby in a snow storm. The birth was expected in mid-February. Prince Edward Island had snow and wind the like of which I'd never encountered. So I made a make-shift incubator in case we had to get to the hospital by horse and sled!

Pearce's birthday (24th February 1962)

Young Ted was booked to have his tonsils out when Ted Sr. arrived for a few days leave. I went into labour and as there was no snow, off I went to the hospital.

I recognized the night nurse in the maternity ward — she was the one who had been in Kensington and knew I had a large family.

She told all the staff, "This woman needs rest, she's to have a private room and given special care and don't bother her after she's had the baby."

Pearce's birth was not too bad and there was no point in me worrying about what was going on at home. I did what the night nurse had ordered, I slept and held my chubby baby and regained my strength.

Ted had to take young Ted to have his tonsils out and when he got back to the house the sewer had backed up and flooded the basement! What could

I do but let Ted cope with bailing out the basement, getting young Ted after his operation and seeing to the rest of the family. (More mashed potatoes for the family, like it or not.)

Moving to Edmonton (spring 1963)

He told me that after his course was through in another six weeks, we were to go to Edmonton where he had been posted. He left, I'm sure thankfully, to go back to Ottawa while I returned home quite refreshed thanks to the night nurse.

But that lasted only a short while because the whole eight of us came down with German measles!

I had to get the packing and arrangements done even though we were all sick, but we pulled through. Ted came back finally and made a wooden crate to sit on top of the Plymouth with all our essentials in it. The movers were going take quite a while to bring the furniture. Meanwhile, we were to drive across Canada from PEI to Edmonton — in an ordinary car — with all nine of us; seven children plus Ted and myself.

You can believe it or not, but it was a good trip. The baby was six weeks old and we were organized to give him his bottles with no trouble. The only hitch was when we crossed the US border into Detroit. Ted's grandfather — Loretta's father — was supposed to have built the first highrise in Detroit and Ted was intent on seeing if he could find it. He turned his head this way and that, searching for the building and completely ignored the border guard. The guard grew suspicious with our hand-made crate on top of the car and Ted not answering him. He ordered us all out of the car, even though it was ninety degrees outside, and examined everything in the car and the inside of that crazy crate.

It may have been a crazy crate, but it was a saviour for us when we arrived in Edmonton a month before the rest of our stuff arrived.

Regardless, it was a good experience for the children. The prairies lasted forever. I told them the first one to see a hill would get a dollar. It was hopeless and at last I conceded that a molehill sort of hump could be called a hill and gave up the dollar.

We stopped over in Chicago, where I met with my friend Letty, whom I lived with in Leamington Spa. She had left England to reside in Chicago. We were supposed to go to her apartment for lunch but when she saw how many we were she took us to a restaurant instead. We visited the museum and it was absolutely stunning for the children to see the science part and new technology; Barbara was intrigued with fetuses in bottles during different months of development; there were phones connected to a persons face so that people could talk and see each other at the same time — just like it is today with Skype where you can communicate over the Internet.

We tried to get tickets to see Julie Andrews in the *Sound of Music* on stage, but it was sold out.

The soil in the fields around Edmonton, was dead black. Of course we know now they were oil fields. The city looked very civilized with large buildings and good roads but once again there wasn't room for us at the base. We rented a house which wasn't easy to do as it had to accommodate seven children.

Warren's birthday *(mid-summer 1963)*

I was not feeling well and, at five months pregnant, I went into labour and was taken to hospital.

It was the middle of the night and the baby was born. A little boy. I knew if he wasn't christened, by laws of the church, he would go in the trash, so I called the nurse and told her to take him to the sink, dab some water on his forehead and say, "I baptize thee in the name of the Father and of the Son and of the Holy Ghost, Amen." And I called to her to say his name, Warren. She was shaking but she did it and then the doctor came to see to the afterbirth and it wouldn't come away and it wouldn't come away. He gave me one injection to encourage it to come but it didn't work, he prepared to give me another shot and I stopped him

"I'm liable to hemorrhage," I told him, but he ignored me like the nuns had done, and gave me another shot. The doctor pulled back the sheet and there was nothing but blood. They took my blood pressure and went into code blue or whatever, everyone panicked and I was wheeled into the operating room. I found myself rising above the table looking down on what was left of me and then a beautiful light appeared and seduced me to go

167

towards it. But my children's faces came to me. Who would look after seven children? No one, so I pulled back from that wonderful peace and the light and came back to the operating room.

It was a near-death experience and the doctor was lucky he wasn't sued because I told him not to further induce the placenta and there were three nurses with us at the time. Little Warren lived for two hours and was then buried with an unknown adult but registered as a child.

Mark's birthday (1st July 1964)

The older children found it hard to change provinces, especially as each school system across Canada was different. This was compounded for Scott because he had spent three years in French-Canadian schools. He was almost fourteen and was giving Ted and me a terrible time, fighting authority at every turn.

We moved into married quarters at the Edmonton base which was actually in Namao, about fifteen miles north of the city. School was closed for the summer holidays and Ted had taken Scott, Pat and some other boys to Jasper Park for a scout gathering. It was hot and I was irritable. I shouted at the children to be quiet; Teddy and Laura were running around the house and the girls were laughing and giggling. I felt very uncomfortable from my pregnancy and wanted so much to sleep. My nights had been spent trying to find a good position to be able to sleep.

My waters broke. Ted wouldn't be back for ages. Had I got enough food prepared? The washing! I shouldn't have put off the washing!

The hospital was twenty miles away, and after having so many pregnancies, I thought I'd better not delay.

I called in Barbara and Brenda and told them I needed them.

I didn't realize how much I'd frightened them. They were standing wide-eyed and white faced.

I wiped up the floor and grabbed the things I'd put by to take to the hospital and told them to go next door and ask the neighbours to take me to the hospital. While Barbara left to do that, I gave Brenda instructions on what to do until their father came home. They were good with little Pearce so I thought it was okay to leave them.

The neighbours, thank God for neighbours, bundled me into the car and whizzed down the highway. I could see that Jerry's knuckles were white as he clutched the steering wheel.

University Hospital was the same place that my premature baby Warren had been born, but this time I didn't dread the delivery room.

The pains were regular. Whatever will be will be. The doctor arrived and to my great joy, a little boy was born. I looked over as the nurse cleaned him and what a perfect specimen of a baby he was.

Barbara and the neighbours had been phoning for news at the hospital and they told them that Mrs. Paterson had a baby girl. So it was a surprise for Ted when he came to see me, and they told him he had a baby boy. There had been another Mrs. Paterson in the hospital at the same time who had a girl!

We decided to call him Mark, although that changed to Markie or Marcus when we got him home.

Pearce had wanted a brother so much and he wanted to mother him because he was so cute.

Mark was a cherub of a baby and a contented child. Never fussed. If I put him in the crib to have a nap, he didn't sleep but would be quiet until I came to fetch him. He was a sensitive child and could sense if there was trouble with people around him.

I was able to drive to an art teacher to study pastel painting portraits and also to the university art courses. It was on the base that I realized that wives of the servicemen needed a voice. I found out there was a council on the base as in a town, so I went around to the women and asked them to vote me in. Well it was so interesting: They'd never had a woman on the council before and I saw some good ways to improve our isolation. The phone was constantly ringing for me and Ted fumed.

A Catholic priest came to see me and asked what was more important, to be on the council or to be a good wife and mother. Well of course I said my family.

"Then you will resign from your position and what's more you will not tell anyone why you would do so. Ted has enough to worry about without you diverting your attention away from your home. He cannot stand it."

The end, as they say.

Barbara was now sixteen and had finished high school. She wanted to go into medicine so she boarded at the university, there being no transportation feasible for her. She found out it was a ball to be away from home discipline and had such a rare old time she did not make her year. This devastated her so much that forever after she would never relax with her studies.

Scott's rebelling had started when we were in Prince Edward Island: He lit fires behind some sheds, then stole Christmas gifts at a big store. Patrick and he thought they had tricked everyone until they felt the hands of a policeman on their shoulders. Scott ran away to escape his father's wrath and it just got worse from there on.

A move to Winnipeg *(August 1965)*

Ted was sent to Winnipeg and there was a chance we'd be there for a long time. Once again, there was no housing available at the base, so we had to stay in a motel – the Flamingo – until we found a place to live.

I was brought up to believe it was a good policy to own your own home, and as we now had eight children, I asked Ted to buy a house.

But Ted's parents had never bought, so he had lived in rental accommodation all his life and any talk of buying was not easy for him to accept.

In married quarters we were not allowed to bang any nails in the walls, the places were always painted a dull cream colour inside, the hardwood floors would stain easily and had to be polished with hard wax every week, and we were not allowed to plant any flowers or vegetables. Rent was deducted from income, although fuel for heating was free. The men were close to their work (and the mess). Women and children felt a kinship with others on the base.

So we clocked in to the Flamingo Motel which had kitchen facilities and a nice couple, the Yakimews, managed and owned it.

I wasn't feeling well with my current pregnancy. Scott was worrying us as he had done for a long time. We hoped a new environment would change things. Barbara applied to register in the nursing program.

When Ted got off from work in the evenings, we went house hunting. We had five hundred dollars for a down payment. We came across the house I felt should belong to us. My heart flew into its corners and came to rest. I felt the children would be happy in it. The real estate agent said he would come to the motel that night with the forms. My excitement knew no bounds.

He came all right but wanted another five hundred dollars down. Ted did the arithmetic and said, "No."

The agent said he knew how much officers in the forces made and saw no reason why he couldn't afford it. That made Ted furious and he told the man goodbye.

I cried and I cried and nothing could stop me. We went to bed and still I cried. I understood that Ted was right but it didn't help me in my despondency. I yearned for some kind of roots. I was tired of moving and that house shone like the Golden Fleece — a haven for us in that artificial world of the forces. Ted got tired of trying to comfort me. He had the new job and he was fed up with facing problems at home as well. He had to support nine children after this coming one was born and he knew we would have too-hard-a time if we spent more money on a house. Exhausted, he fell asleep but I sobbed the whole night through.

Next morning I looked in my purse for money to buy milk. I knew I had a two dollar bill because I had counted the money the night before: I called the children.

"Who took my money?" I asked. Young Ted spoke up and told me that Scott had forced him to take it for him.

I was absolutely heart-sick and searched Scott's face for the truth. He turned around and ran out of the door. My despair overwhelmed me and I felt weak. I felt the familiar hot sticky liquid between my legs and had to lay down on the floor while my poor children looked down at me horrified. Me, who was supposed to be the pillar of strength. And they had heard me cry so bitterly and had seen me thrown for a loop because one of my own had taken money from me. I was stretched out before them, a mess of a woman who could not help herself, let alone them. And the blood kept gushing.

Barbara ran for Mrs. Yakimew. Bless her, she didn't wait, she phoned for an ambulance. She came over right away and told me, "Don't worry about the children. I'll take full responsibility for them. I'll see they get their meals and I'll call Ted. DON'T WORRY."

But I was beyond worrying anyhow. My head felt lighter and lighter as the siren screamed through the streets.

Dr.Paul came into the stuffy room of the hospital, saw the amount of blood, nodded to the nurse and told her to prepare for a D&C. In other words, abort the baby so it would save the mother's life.

Weak as I was, I knew there was a chance as long as they left me alone.

"I plead with you," I said, "I beg you. I have experience with this. Just let me lie quiet for a while."

The doctor believed me.

They hooked me up to an intravenous drip and left me in absolute quiet. The doctor checked if the flow was slowing and it was. I heard him in the corridor saying, "I would never have believed she could survive losing that much blood."

I DID survive and returned to the Flamingo Motel where everyone had coped with Mrs.Yakimew. Scott, fifteen years old, had disappeared. We notified the police but there were many runaways and I hardly expected him back until he needed us.

Ted bought a sweet little house in Westwood, a suburb of Winnipeg and the estate agent accepted our five hundred dollars down.

At long last we had TWO bathrooms, and I hoped we could have a more settled life in our new home.

Barbara and Brenda were saving their money, wanting to buy a bassinet for the baby and hoping for a little girl again.

Joy's birthday (28th February 1966)

Once again labour pains started two weeks early and I called Ted to leave work and drive me to the hospital. And I asked him to stay with me.

After prepping, I lay on the bed and we could watch my stomach jerk with contractions.

The nurse came in and examined me saying, "Looks like false labour: you're psychologically making the contractions. Women often do that."

Ted looked awkward and I felt like five cents and tried to stop the contractions. "She hasn't even started to open yet," the nurse said in a disgusted voice. So Ted left to go home.

Naturally, he was hardly out of the door when my waters broke and the pains came surely and truly and in only an hour I'm wheeled into the delivery room and Dr.Paul came and we had a little girl. She was so cute. Large eyes and cuddly. They put her on my breast and she nuzzled there. I felt so good and asked if I could phone Ted. I dialed the number and Ted answered. "Hello Ted," I said "We have a lovely baby girl."

"Ha Ha!" he laughed, it being only a little over an hour since he left with the nurse telling us there was nothing happening.

"What's the matter with you? We have our little Joy." I told him.

"Why are you joking with me, I've only just left you and you weren't even in labour."

The nurse took the phone and said, "Mr.Paterson, I guess we don't always know. It's true. Your wife went into labour and you have a baby daughter."

So Ted blew me a kiss through the phone and said he'd be right there and I felt peaceful and thought the girls would be glad.

Dr. Paul came in the room and told the nurses how it had been a similar situation six months previously.

But after two days, Joy was losing weight and had a bad case of jaundice. She could tolerate only a small amount of milk. I asked to have her to feed every two hours instead of the standard four. I loved the extra time with her as I checked her fingers and toes and laughed at her gassy smiles.

Then came the snow! Not ordinary snow but Winnipeg snow in a blustery, howling Winnipeg snow storm. Everything outside shut down, roads were impassable. The hospital had its own generator so we kept warm. The staff had to stay because no one could venture out and no one could come to relieve them.

We couldn't get home either and, of course, there were no visitors. A nurse came to talk with me. I guess she was about fifty and was bitter about life. She'd just been divorced.

"I want to live with a man," she said, "but they have the advantage. They can be silly old goats but can still get young girls. We women have to be content to live the rest of our lives without a mate. Women my age are bypassed. You'd better stick to the man you have my dear because you're just about that time of life too."

I was forty-two.

The storm slowly eased, having broken all kinds of records. The main street was open but not the outlying ones.

I phoned Ted and he was going berserk, trapped in the house with so many children.

So he set about to shovel the width of his car, the snow being three feet high, all the way to the ploughed highway and he actually made it. He was that desperate. He was then ready to fetch me home, and Joy, having gained enough weight but still jaundiced, came home with us.

Everyone loved her and she loved the bassinet which rocked to and fro.

Everyone pitched in to help bringing diapers and giving her a bottle. Ted let out a huge sigh and settled back in his chair to catch up with reading.

Paul's birthday *(8th June 1967)*

Of course I had gone through excessive bleeding at three months pregnancy as was true with most of my birthings. I had to go to hospital until it stopped but then the rest of the time was good.

Nine babies and still Ted didn't know what went on after the doors had closed behind me at the hospitals. It was now the "in" thing for fathers to experience the birth of their child.

Surely after so many children, it shouldn't be a hard birth so I asked Ted to stay with me this coming time. It was wonderful when the nurse had coached me at Laura's birth and maybe Ted could massage my back which always felt as if it would break.

Mark was three years old and Joy was fourteen months old; I would have three children under three years of age and I was forty-three-years old. Sometimes I wondered if I could manage. At the end of pregnancies the weight of the child pushed out varicose veins until they were just purple pipelines and I could hardly walk.

The other children were very good with their chores which they had to do before they got their allowances.

Baby bottles were easier to manage now they had electric warmers and the new sleepers were easy to launder and kept baby warm.

In the past, we had made flannelet nighties for them, but they would bunch up around their necks.

We used to knit baby booties and I remember when a bootie ribbon caught around Patrick's toe and cut into his foot. We couldn't figure out why he was crying. We'd given him a bottle and changed his diaper but still he cried. We couldn't see the ribbon. Poor little guy.

We had to hand wash sweaters and booties in cold water because otherwise the wool would shrink. Aunts and grammas would knit sweaters for each child and it was like a bond between the baby and them.

I was impatient with little Mark. He'd been wetting his pants and I got cross and one day he was shaking as I was changing him because he knew I was fed up with it all. I felt guilty about that but it was the thought of all the diapers I'd have to wash as well as having Ted, myself, two babies and eight other children.

Barbara only came home for weekends.

I received a telegram from Australia. My father had died. He was sixty-four years old. It seemed awful I would never see him again or receive a letter from him which at least kept up the bond between us. I cried for the finality of it all and regretted that he was half around the world from me. And it brought back the ache of losing my mother and I wished they had known their grandchildren.

We decided to sell the house and move onto the base. It would save us money if we didn't have a mortgage and the upkeep of owning a home.

Scott was still running away and coming back home, it didn't matter what we did or said he was bound to live a more exciting life, as he thought. Two policemen brought him home at two in the morning after they caught him stealing a motorbike. I told them I couldn't do anything with him and suggested that they took him with them.

"No. No," they said "we just want to scare him."

But nothing scared Scott. It was a game to see how far he could push things. He was so suave, good looking and intelligent that absolutely no one would believe he was conning them. But it had to end sometime, so I said, "I repeat, take him with you. He's incorrigible."

It tore my insides to do it but it had to be done.

Barbara and Brenda were home, wanting to put up the Christmas decorations and I told them they had to clean the living room first and they were not happy about it. I was feeling weak and again I fell to the floor and red blood oozed around me. Barbara called the ambulance as the red spread further and further. The paramedics came and they tried to move me. Barbara at this time in a panic screamed at them, "You can't move her while she's bleeding like that. STOP! STOP!" She was more upset than I was. To me it was either I'll make it or I won't.

I got to the hospital and Dr.Paul once more let me stay still and quiet with my legs elevated.

It was a time to think of my new art classes which were nothing like I had before. The professor was a friend of Fitzgerald (Winnipeg's favourite artist) and had gleaned all he could from that good artist. He showed us to look at things in an abstract way and I loved every minute of experimenting.

Another six months pregnancy, and I was prepped and in the labour room with the strangeness of having Ted with me in the delivery room for the first time. I tried to show him how he could help by massaging my back but he was in agony with indigestion and completely in left field (a pun because he played left field in softball). There was no let up of the pain.

An hour passed. Two hours passed and as the third hour came around he could bear listening to my crying no longer. I told him to go to the waiting room. The doctor checked and said I hadn't dilated much. The Phillipine nurses thought that gave them permission to have lunch in the next room and put me out of their mind.

Four hours, five hours, six hours. I was moaning and screaming constantly. A new expectant mother came into the room. At least she brought me a glass of water and a washcloth for my forehead.

I called the nurse to tell her the baby was coming but she just smiled and walked away. Seven hours. I could hear Ted talking to the doctor, probably about sport, as they were sitting outside the room on a bench.

My head banged from side to side to numb the world and with the slightest push the baby was born between the sheets.

I turned to the kind woman in the room and told her in a voice that seemed far away, "My baby is born."

She leapt out of bed to get the nurses and they panicked and got the doctor but they didn't need to, because having a baby that way instead of feet in stirrups and everyone examining you, was as if I'd gone to paradise with the peace of it. Another boy. I told the doctor we were naming the baby Paul, after him.

Ted came in now it was safe, and I hoped this would be the last time I would give birth because I was afraid if there was another, it would probably be ME who didn't survive.

When it was time to go home, it was Barbara the nurse who carried little Paul in the elevator of the hospital. A visitor thought it was the nicest thing to see this tableau. Our eldest and our youngest.

Paul was a contented child and he got a lot of attention from the other children. He didn't have colic and that was a relief.

The social service people took Scott to a boy's reform school in Portage la Prairie. A man on staff told him about behaviour modification and let him read books on it. He let him go to his office and do some work there. Scott did try to escape but it was forty degrees below zero and he froze his ears so had to return. The man helped him understand that running away wasn't any kind of answer and, finally, Scott was able to return home. He told me some awful stories later about being in that home. The boys had ganged up on this frail boy and had beaten him so hard he was almost dead. They had covered the noise he made with a blanket so no one came to his aid.

Scott learned to play an instrument and was in the marching band there. He loved that part of it. We visited him every Sunday, even one time in white-out conditions from the blowing snow. You absolutely could not determine where the road started and where it ended — everything was white. I had given up hope that Scott would ever see the light and change his ways. Just before he was let out, I started getting phone calls enquiring when he would be home. My antennae twitched — some young men were waiting for their leader so they could all fall back into their bad old ways. Danger!

I phoned my brother John in Australia and asked if he could use a helper with his business of putting up windmills for bringing water to the surface. John said, "Sure." With the money we had from the recent sale of our house we sent Scott to Australia.

Winnipeg has ungodly weather — so terribly cold in winter — and it lasts until May before the snow is gone and the freezing leaves the ground. Then during the short summer — which is blazing hot — you can never sit outside without being devoured by mosquitoes.

Barbara married a Ukrainian lad who was ten years her senior. I was late for the wedding because the Ukrainian church was at the north end of Winnipeg and my driver got lost. The first baby they had was deformed, a great catastrophe because Barbara loved children so much. He died and the couple went on to adopt Karen and Stephen.

Montreal Expo 1967 — and then to Ottawa

Ted wanted us to go to Expo. We needed to see what the future of our world would be like so Ted rented a tent trailer and off we went — eight of us — on an adventure. We had left the three youngest — Joy, Mark and Paul — with Barbara to look after while we were away.

Habitat 67 — a grand, new approach to housing that was the centrepiece of Montreal's Expo — was designed by Moshe Safdie as a balance between single-family dwellings and the economies of modern apartment construction. And there was a big globe-like structure — made from triangular pieces — designed by Buckminster Fuller called the Biosphere which created an enclosed living space.

We stood on a moving platform which went slowly past the wonderful Michelangelo masterpiece *Pieta*, brought in from Rome. It was enough to bring me to tears it was so beautiful. Everywhere you turned there was something new and remarkable and a monorail train went around above us.

On the way back from Montreal, we stopped in Ottawa and Ted talked the reverend mother at the Catholic hospital to take Brenda on as a trainee nurse. No diabetic had been accepted there as a nurse before.

Brenda graduated as a registered nurse in Ottawa and Barbara worked towards her masters' degree in nurse education.

Brenda met a young man and they wanted to get married. Keeping to tradition, they came to us to ask Ted for permission. The young man had nothing to live on and Ted said as far as he was concerned it was a bad idea. It didn't stop them and they got married anyway.

It was a sad story as they broke up and then came together again, broke up and came together again. Later, Brenda and her son Jason came to live with us for a while in Winnipeg but eventually she and her husband divorced.

Ted was given another posting, this time to Ottawa.

As I was unpacking the boxes, I heard a man on CBC radio ask us women listeners what we were doing right then: And had we stopped thinking about our dreams? And did we think we were only good at being housewives?

I felt I should make some goals. I decided on the art world and realized I fit in best doing portraits. I went to a good portrait artist who worked in oils and talked him into doing my portrait for half price — he charged so much normally. I observed him carefully and the steps he took while working: that way I thought I could become more professional myself.

The result of his portrayal of me wasn't like me at all.

I have a chubby neck and he gave me a long one.

He eliminated anything that wasn't perfect.

I knew then that if I wanted to be a professional portrait painter, I'd have to flatter the sitter.

I rebelled at that.

Ted was offered the opportunity to take over ten clients in Toronto if he wanted to take early retirement and start his own public relations firm.

It would mean he would have to find more clients in order to survive but he jumped at the chance.

He bought a house for us in Mississauga.

Patrick, then seventeen, said he would refuse to move any more after we went to Mississauga as he'd had a different school for every year of his schooling. And he was heart-broken because he'd worked so hard on his Austin car and we had to leave it behind.

I promised him that when we moved next, he could stay behind if he wished and if we could find a suitable place for him to stay.

Back to Winnipeg *(fall 1972)*

Well of course we did have to move again, because Ted couldn't swing enough clients to make the job worthwhile.

He had a tremendous offer from the USA from a firm which more or less said he could name his price to work for them. But he discovered they were known for shady practices and wanted nothing to do with them

Instead, he accepted a position as executive director of the United Way in Winnipeg, a role that enabled him to help people. The previous executive director had just killed his wife and then himself. I wondered what that meant for us.

Meanwhile Scott had some sort of nervous breakdown while in Australia so we insisted he return home, hoping his bad days would be behind him. He was due to fly home for free in a forces' aircraft but we sent him $500 just in case that flight was cancelled.

It wasn't cancelled, but he arrived home having spent all the money we sent him. He had bought, among other things, a "fertility" necklace for me that he got in Hawaii! Me! With a fertility necklace! I put it out of sight.

Ted took him to Winnipeg with him and began his work while I was left to sell the house.

There was a new development right next door to our place which had the same type of house as ours. They were offering no down payment and no interest for a year! We didn't have a chance of selling ours.

However, one day a real estate agent came to look at our place — but he chose the worst time possible.

I was sitting on a lawn chair outside, trying to recover from a fright over young Ted: He had fallen off his bike going down a hill and had scraped the flesh off his leg. The doctor had to take out the gravel while Ted screamed and hollered. In the meantime, the dishes hadn't been done and the house was in a mess. I had to tell the children to sit on the curb outside while the people looked through the house. They sat on the curb looking like discarded waifs and kept asking, "Can we go in now?"

The people said they'd take the house if I could be gone in forty-eight hours! I phoned Ted about the offer but he said he wanted five hundred dollars more! I burst into tears and couldn't stop crying because Ted knew nothing of the stress I was going through and here was a chance to get out of it and I felt he didn't care.

The real estate agent couldn't stand my crying and said he'd just tell the prospective buyers I'd agree to move quickly if they agreed to an extra five hundred dollars.

And they did!

I phoned the moving companies but they were all busy. I kept on phoning until, by chance, the vice-president of one picked up the phone. "How big a move is it," he wanted to know. After a slight pause, he told me the packers would be over right away. The children were wonderful and helped pack and clean up.

Patrick, as he had previously told us, was not going to move with us. We gave him three-months rent for a hotel room and the family car. He said the hotel was awful because it had a dirty sink, and he crashed the car right after we had left.

Ted and I were now down to just six children: Teddy, Laura, Pearce, Mark, Joy and Paul. Scott was sometimes home and sometimes not.

I thought I'd give the children an education in what trains were like and booked our tickets to join Ted in Winnipeg. A friend let us stay for the night in her house. It had off-white walls and carpets and art objects all over the place. I warned the children to be careful and no sliding down the banister. We went out to Dairy Queen to have hamburgers and a birthday cake for little Mark. We came home, I tucked them in and we went to sleep.

In the middle of the night I was awoken by a noise — one by one, the children were running to the bathroom and vomiting. And not necessarily in that order. I was exhausted cleaning up and then trying to find something to put on them to keep them warm. Finally, morning light came through the window and my dear friend Wilda came to the front door, ready to take us to the commuter train that would take us to downtown Ottawa.

The Ottawa cousins came to see us off at the main station and there was much waving and calling out goodbyes.

I had paid for sleeping compartments on the train and had arranged for Pearce to be with young Ted on the bottom bunk just ahead of mine because Pearce sometimes walked in his sleep. There was a priest on the same seat as them and he was supposed to be on the upper bunk at night but he sent the boys to me to ask that they use his upper bunk as it was hard for him to climb up. I explained to the priest in a stern voice what the situation was and I had paid more for the bottom bunk because I worried about Pearce. The boys had to boost the priest up by his bottom when night came, but I didn't care.

Laura and Joy were above me and I slept with little Paul and Mark. I didn't get much sleep and was dying for a smoke. Joy and Laura parted their curtain at night and asked passers-by for candies!

But it was wonderful really, and I was never sorry that we went to Winnipeg that way.

I thought the reunion with Ted would be romantic and happy but something went wrong with the purchase of our new house, something about the lawyer not letting go of our money. We had to stay in a motel outside of town for two weeks. Scott joined us there.

When we got into the house on Garriock Avenue, I had to congratulate Ted because it had five bedrooms, three bathrooms, a recreation room, a nice yard and a great kitchen with a dishwasher.

Ted couldn't take time off when the movers arrived and I was still yearning to take up smoking again. But we managed, and the children registered for schools, and I found we had good neighbours — although one of them told me when he heard that a couple with ten children would be moving in, he almost put his house up for sale.

I loved the living room with its heavy, powder-blue silk drapes and powder-blue carpet, and Ted said I could go to a furniture store and buy some furniture.

I remembered the time my father had asked me to choose furniture for the living room.

This time, I bought two love seats with a tasteful floral design, and then a small barrel chair in burnt orange which offset so much blue. Ted was proud of the look of it and, for me, it was a peaceful refuge to escape to. The kitchen had a desk for the woman of the house and I spent quite a bit of time there, using it as an office.

A knife-sharpener man knocked on the door saying he'd do any kind of work for money. I got him to saw off the end of a jutting-out part of the kitchen countertop — with cupboards underneath it — to make more room to accommodate our large family.

I was a bit scared of the way this man had sweat pouring from his forehead as he worked. I remembered hearing that alcoholics would sweat a lot and feared I might be inviting future problems — he could come back and bother me for more work. However, the kitchen was made more open and I never saw the man again.

One of the first things I did was to enrol in art classes, joining the Winnipeg Sketch Club — one of the longest-running sketch clubs in the country — but it was run by a severe woman. When I was being evaluated for membership, she stood behind me with her arms crossed and I trembled. However, she was the reason the club kept going so you had to admire her for that.

I went to the malls with the club to do pastel portraits and made a lot of money. I was now able to complete a pastel in very short time, especially children. People paid in advance so no one could say, "Put a smile on the face," or, "Make her hair curly." What they got was what I came up with.

There were five hundred thousand people in Winnipeg when we were there. Ted worked hard, nights and weekends too. He was one of the first to employ housewives who proved to be good at organizing volunteers. I also tried to be a volunteer fund-raiser, but no one gave me the training that others got — I assume everyone thought I wouldn't need it as I was Ted's wife.

But the first door I went to, a crippled man answered and I couldn't ask him for money.

The children helped out at Ted's office when they could.

Scott was at loose ends and was thinking of traveling across Canada. I paid for him to have a bar-tending course because it was the only one offered that was short and concise. At the end of it he knew how to make cocktails but little else. He was still interested in behaviour modification so he enrolled in psychology at the university and there he met Kathy, a lovely girl.

They lived together while he went to university. They had a little baby boy who died in Scott's arms and he went to pieces over it. I went to hold the little soul as he was dying. I told Scott it would bring some comfort if he would christen the baby. The minister came and tried to console both Kathy and Scott. But Scott never forgave God for taking the child who hadn't done anything sinful. It racked his heart. They later had a girl named Jenny.

Scott got his degree and planned a five-hundred-mile canoe trip through Manitoba like the mapmakers had done in Canada's history. He has ended up doing the trip twice and loved every minute of it.

Ted Sr. started to play volleyball once a week at night. My antennae were twitching and I began thinking there was more than volleyball going on. He was suffering from ulcers and despite his pain he took off to play one night. He wasn't home by two in the morning so I thought he must have been taken ill. I woke Laura to keep an eye on the children and I woke young Ted to come with me. At this point I had bought an old car for a hundred dollars. It leaked transmission fuel all over but it got me to places. We took off to the site where they played volleyball but no one was there but two cars parked close to each other on the street. One of them belonged to Ted. While young Ted and I waited, parked opposite those cars, Ted and a young woman came from the other direction and talked for a while as she got in hers. I was going to go over but young Ted stopped me.

"You go home Mother," he said. "I'll go over and drive home with Dad."

I didn't know if that was what I should do or not — maybe I should have confronted them there and then but maybe it was better if I waited to get my thoughts in order and not rush into accusations. I'd had lots of hints that he was seeing someone else; his new underwear, his "getting in trim," his refusal to let Mark help him on the weekends at the office, his impatience with my learning about abstract art. And I had the feeling he was tired of coping with the worries of both his job and his family.

He told me there was nothing to him being with this woman. He said they wanted to talk about a problem at work which needed working out. He was training her to take some of the load off his shoulders.

He still attended church, whereas the rest of the family was drifting away. Patrick would ask questions about the Catholic church that neither Ted nor I could answer. I requested a meeting with the head of the church in Manitoba and he came to sit with the family and me, although Ted absented himself: it was Ted's way of dealing with what were, for him, stressfull situations. Well, the priest couldn't answer the questions either, even though I'd told him it was important.

"I'm the mother of ten children and what I do will affect them, plus their spouses, plus their children," I said.

But all he could reply was, "You must have faith."

How could one have faith if you don't believe some of the rules and think they're just plain silly.

For instance, Loretta would pay money to the priest and they would give her what was called "dispensation:" With that payment here on earth, she would have fewer days to wait up in Purgatory before she got to Heaven.

Oh! For Pete's sake! Who in his right mind could believe that?

And French-Canadian mothers believed they'd have a special place in heaven if their sons went into the priesthood.

And babies who died without having been Christened were not allowed to be buried in hallowed ground.

And if your husband or wife divorced you, you were not allowed to take the sacraments, even if it was your spouse who cheated on you!

From that day on, the children and I did not attend church.

This was hard for Ted to take.

There was a clinic in Winnipeg which did much to relieve poverty. They provided many services, particularly for the children of poor, single mothers. They provided medical and health care, and would look after the children to give their mothers a chance to look for work. They helped the mothers through their pregnancies and, if it was their wish to abort the baby, they helped them with that too.

Much of the clinic's funding came from the United Way.

To the Catholics, abortion is a mortal sin and so the priests in all the Catholic churches started announcing from their pulpits that their congregations were to stop giving to the United Way. And that led to reduced funding for all of United Way's projects.

That wonderful clinic struggled desperately without those funds. Ted did a lot of soul-searching and decided it was hurting everybody for the church to promote this thinking and I don't think he's been to church since.

Getting more serious about painting

Meanwhile my painting had taken on much more importance for me.

After all the courses I had taken were done with, I was told "For goodness sake you don't need any more education in art, sure enough you haven't gone to university for your degree but you've got everything you need to go on your own."

I rented a studio at Portage and Main Street in a large building which used to hold offices. My first day in my studio, I opened a large, heavy cupboard door and hundreds of false teeth casts came tumbling out!

So, what I would paint?

At first I thought I'd invite to my studio some of the native street people I could see through the window to do their portraits. But I got a bit scared of that idea and instead ordered large canvases and started experimenting with more modernistic approaches.

I was loving my new work. I was feeling my oats and liking the fact that I was now a "real" painter as well as a wife and mother. However, although Ted had agreed to the studio, it wasn't his idea of a loving wife waiting for him to come home at night — never mind that I was only in my studio while the children were in school.

My friend Ann joined me and paid half the rent. She painted on days that I didn't go in. It was a good time.

Laura left home for Winnipeg University to fulfill her lifetime dream of teaching English. I asked her what it was like to go to university so she asked her professor if I could sit in on a class.

I did, and I was enjoying it when the professor started talking about a class he had attended where he knew the lecturer was lying. I asked, "Why didn't you call him on it?" but he fluffed off my enquiry. I put up my hand again — after all, why wasn't he teaching these young pupils what was right and what was wrong?

"You're right," he agreed, "I should have."

When Laura graduated with honours-plus, she told me it was because she was the only one who had brought her mother to class!

I heard about an art retreat which was gathering a good reputation in Emma Lake, Saskatchewan. Every year the art teachers and some of the better artists would invite an important North American artist or critic. One of my peers suggested we get the world-famous critic Clement Greenberg to visit our group of twenty in Winnipeg. They gave me the job of writing to him and setting up arrangements. He came for a week. We rented a room where we could show him our work and discuss art and we all chipped in for his hotel stay.

Greenberg appears in many art history books and his influence was so powerful that many galleries were hesitant to show any artist who hadn't been recognised by him. When he looked through our work, he didn't remark on the composition, colour or any weakness, he just said either yes or no, leaving us to figure out why.

For me — after I pushed him to comment further — he said no matter what I did, I was good: My work was good whether I used a knife or a brush and whether I did landscape or semi-abstract. But if I put a figure in the painting no one could look at anything but that figure — particularly the face — because it was too powerful.

He told me I was looking for the key to art but there wasn't any, and I was to stop wishing there was. It was a matter of just working and striving, and the rewards would come.

He told us we should not feel inferior because we were isolated from the New York scene — in fact it was a benefit because we were not bombarded with the shifting world of fads and superficial work in that city. Because of Winnipeg's long winter, we could nestle down to be ourselves in our burrows. That way we could do honest and meaningful stuff.

After that visit, he came up one more time to be on the jury of our country-wide juried show.

He said he was fascinated by my monoprint and when he came to my home one evening the others persuaded me to bring out a large canvas I'd painted of a black man sitting on a bench in New York, with pigeons at his feet. The face of the man gave Clem (as we called him) a jolt and he said it was wonderful and asked why I didn't put it in the show. I reminded him that he had told me my faces were too powerful and distracting, that the viewer wouldn't look at anything else and so I shouldn't show them!

I guess he had changed his mind.

He invited all of us to visit him in his apartment in New York. We went for a week. He told us which shows to see.

One night, he slid open one door to his knee-high, wall-to-wall cabinet: It was full of dozens and dozens of bottles of Vodka. Above the cabinet, and on all the other walls were paintings by all the leading minimalist abstractionists of the day — all the famous names we had read about, including Jules Olitski and Jackson Pollock. Most of the paintings had been given to Clem as thanks for his critical recommendations.

And he showed us a landscape that he had done himself in his youth.

"To be a visual artist is too tough a life, and the competition impossible," he said. "I used to earn my living as a literature critic but could see that the world needed an art critic, and I gave up painting."

Unfortunately, he eventually lost his reputation: One of the reasons was as a result of his being executor of the will of David Smith the sculptor. Smith made large, stainless-steel sculptures and often painted over his lovely surfaces — Clem always thought it was wrong of him. So when Smith died, Clem ordered all the paint removed from those pieces. Such tampering is sacrilege to an artist and many accused him of being unethical: In his later years, his lectures would often attract boos from the audiences.

Still, he was a humungous figure in our art world and for us, it was a spur to go on and not think we were of no account because we lived so far from the major happenings in the art world.

9:

Becoming a divorced mother

Ted had to work harder to regain the donations for United Way, lost after the Catholics refrained from sending money. He went out on Christmas Eve, calling on doors, working on the spirit of Christmas to get money. It was during this time that I went to find a cheque to pay someone, and I came across an account that I thought we had cancelled. But it wasn't cancelled. And I saw a list of cheques from the account dated regularly every week — and for an amount suspiciously like a night at a motel!

I confronted Ted with it but still he wouldn't admit he was playing around. I had no more proof.

He told me he had been in unbelievable stress and wanted to go away on his own, maybe attend his beloved ball games in a nearby city. I said it might be a good thing for both of us for him to go, and he set off in a happy way and with my blessing. But then nagging suspicions started in my head.

The kids had wanted to take up skiing, and, since I had previously talked to this woman about skiing, it gave me an excuse to phone the United Way office. But the secretary answered by telling me she was sorry but that woman wasn't at the office as she had gone on a vacation TO THE SAME CITY where Ted was headed.

I felt the ceiling was falling down on me. I picked up the phone book to look for her husband's number.

By jingo! I was going to have it out with him, and tell him what was going on — if he didn't already know.

But before I could find the number, the phone rang. It was Ted. He asked me what was happening and I told him I was in the process of clearing the air with the woman's husband.

"Don't do it! Don't do it!," he said in a desperate voice. "You've got the wrong idea, I promise you."

"You think I'm a fool?" I asked.

"Wait till I come back and we'll sort it out. I'm pleading with you just to wait a short while."

I gave in. After all, this would erase all those years of marriage and the children would be without their father. So I waited for him to come home and insisted we go to see a marriage councillor. I knew a Lutheran minister who gave help to couples in trouble.

We went for about six weeks: The minister was interested in what Ted did and in his work. They talked about sports.

He didn't spend much time with my concerns. I thought it was a waste of time for me.

But at the last session, the minister demanded Ted give him an answer: Yes or no that he had a lover.

Ted refused to utter a sound.

The minister turned towards me and agreed it was obvious that it was so. From that moment he took no further notice of Ted, even when he had an ulcer attack.

"He's not worth it," he said to me. He then gave me a list of things I was to make sure I had enough money for, and said he'd come to our home to talk to the children. In the car going home, I felt like we had a big placard over the car which read, "This marriage is over."

The minister came and talked to the children individually.

He asked Joy what she thought.

"It won't make any difference, he was never here anyway," she said.

Pearce wondered what was going to happen to him, and young Ted had always had a hard time with big Ted.

Mark didn't say anything, and Paul was only eight years old.

I was grateful to the minister and proceeded to go to my friend, the lawyer. I had to encase my heart with an iron cage while I went about selling the house and buying a smaller one.

To give Ted his due, he never fought me over our finances. However, he was always saying he had worked all his life and still he had nothing, so I gave him ten thousand dollars from the sale of our house — most of what was left over from the purchase of the smaller house I had bought. In return, he gave me the family car and paid alimony to keep the family going. But he drew the line at sharing any of his pension.

Before we moved, I gave him one more chance to try to work things out but it was hopeless.

It was one in the morning and summer heat filled the bedroom, the scent of wallflowers in the garden came through the open window and I heard him say, "I don't love you as I used to."

I told myself to keep calm and I said, "Could you explain? Do you mean you love me only as you would a maiden aunt?"

He laughed a dry laugh in spite of the seriousness of the situation.

"It's just not the way it was." he said.

I told myself that this was the crunch. I must be rational. I must deal with it properly and not get hysterical.

And before I knew what I was doing, I reached for a dress and a jacket from the closet. I put them on a body that felt like wood. I fumbled under the carpet for emergency money I'd stashed there. I grabbed my purse and left the room. I went downstairs and out the front door, and closed it firmly behind me.

I told myself to think of the children but could only think of myself right then. How would it be possible to absorb anything else? I always thought that no matter what happened to us, our love would be there. With that taken away, what would remain?

A bus was coming and stopped just ahead of me. My fare clanked into the metal box. There were no other passengers. We rode through the night like ghosts on a never-ending journey. It was all half dark and still around me, all half-dark and still inside me.

We stopped at the train station and I told myself I should get out here and catch a train. Once on a train I wouldn't be able to turn back. I clanged the bell to get off and I saw the driver's face in his mirror and he looked concerned.

Inside the train station I read the departure tables. There was only one leaving in an hour for Sioux Lookout. Tired native families were sitting on luggage, waiting for time to pass.

I tried to get my brain to work. Would I get on the train? Or not? I went to the ladies' room and paced up and down. When I looked in the mirror I couldn't believe it was really me. My face was ashen, dark rims around my eyes though no tears had come. No makeup, but who would care? Decisions wouldn't come as I left the room to get a ticket.

I looked in my purse for the price of the ticket and out of nowhere, I felt a stab of pain. At least it was some form of feeling. The children. I mustn't let them think it had anything to do with them.

I went to the phone and dialed Barbara's number. I hoped I wouldn't wake her husband. It was two-thirty in the morning.

She answered, sleepy and frightened. "What is it Mother?" she said.

Poor girl has had to take my crying jags over the phone for the past few weeks. I told her I was going to Sioux Lookout and when I got back I'd try to sort things out.

She talked and talked persuading me not to go but I felt cold, like one of the marble pillars in that old-time railway station.

"Stay where you are, I'm coming right down," she said.

And all of a sudden, blood returned to my drained body and feeling came back to me. For me and my children.

"It's all right," I told myself, as blessed tears soothed my burning eyes, "I'll go home and somehow we'll deal with things."

I looked around the station and knew some in this group of waiting passengers had problems too. Everyone has some cross to bear.

As I walked outside for a taxi. I was aware once again of sights and sounds. I gave the taxi driver our address and paid the fare when we arrived. Leaving the taxi, I looked up at our house and it had changed. No longer the fortress of safety it once was, it now had an element of strangeness about it. I looked for the key in my pocket but it wasn't there. I went into the garage and, feeling hopeless, tried to find a comfortable way to sleep in the back seat of the car.

Morning came and Ted opened the garage door and laughed when he saw me all mussed up. My son was close behind him, shock and disbelief on his face. All my hours of struggle and Ted had just rolled over and gone back to sleep.

Well, what had I wanted? For him to go running after me? That wouldn't have solved anything, I told myself. I would have to deal with everything myself. But life would be completely different from that moment on.

The lawyer tried to tell me not to accept that I would not have access to Ted's pension. But I wasn't going to do what so many wives do and fight over money. If he didn't want to give me any money from his pension, then so be it. I wouldn't have the children know we were fighting over money. I might not go to church any more, but I believed if I had done the best I could over the years, then there would be no Hell for me.

Ted suggested he live in the basement of our house, have his meals with us, and, I guess, have me do his laundry too. I scotched that idea!

He went to live with young Ted who had moved into his own place, and I gradually adapted to being a single mother and made plans to move into the small house I had bought — it was in the same area, so the children didn't have to change schools.

We were legally separated for a year or so, and one night we met for dinner and I told him it was time to divorce each other. As we sat at the restaurant table, it was as if someone had taken out my lungs and my heart and there remained just an empty shell of a woman who had truly believed in the man who sat opposite her.

There was a gift shop adjoining the restaurant and he bought me a clay mobile with five angels that would clink in a breeze.

He had met a woman sixteen years younger, I knew it always had to be a younger woman.

It wasn't the one he had the affair with. I was glad of that. It would have been hard to be civil to her, knowing she went with my husband while he was still married to me. His new lady was Janet and I had heard she was a potter – a fellow artist who's medium was clay. And she sounded fine.

I had changed from the romantic, pretty girl of long ago. I could see that Ted was changed now as well. From the time he was a boy, he had helped with the finances of the family and then, with the extra strains of work and caring for a large family of his own, he was prevented from ever experiencing a carefree life like those men around him. He was obviously envious of them being able to take off for holidays abroad, go on skiing trips, or immerse themselves in sports. All of their children had already left home.

As for me, my painting had gone beyond the realistic stage and to a place where hardly anyone else understood them, let alone wanted to buy them. But I found it exhilarating to know that painting could grow in stature and yet have feeling as well. It was always a challenge, and I felt I was accomplishing a maturity in my work.

I had resented his devotion to his job and his extra playtime. Where was my satisfaction with a partner? I won't go into our sex life, but there was a rift there too: I was weary of the routine of it while Ted wanted more.

I had to go to the courthouse and have the judge say that our divorce was legal. My lawyer was there but Ted was not. The judge called me up to his desk, looked at the papers, and said, "This is ridiculous! Thirty two years of marriage and ten children and then cut out of pension money. Why don't you get that changed?" I told him as long as I had the alimony I would manage and I didn't want things delayed. He banged his gavel down and we were officially divorced.

Scott and Ted Jr. helped get our new house into shape and set up two bedrooms in the basement. Scott also blocked out the dining room so it could accommodate my art things and a printing press. I was doing some teaching at the local art club. I also entered three paintings and a print in the large juried show and asked my children to come to the opening.

I won for the most innovative, the best oil painting, the best watercolour, and the best print.

The juror waited for me to come up to him and took a step backwards. "But I thought this was the work of a man!" he said.

That's why I only signed my work D.J.Paterson, so they wouldn't know I was a woman. After all these years, it hasn't changed: Male artists have an advantage. I must say though, women have not made their mark for strong work, they rely too much on flowers and pretty colours.

I proved to my family that I really could stand up in the painting world, even in competition with the best. I told them it was necessary for me to have a part of my life that was just for me.

Now Joy was a problem.

She got to a point where she'd leave her bedroom at two in the morning and skedaddle to her boyfriend's place. She wasn't going to school at all, even though I saw her off in the morning — when she was at home — never dreaming she wasn't in class.

The principal 'phoned and said he'd send the truant officer to me and I could go to jail.

I just laughed.

"And what good would that do? Are you going to tie her to the bedpost and have a policeman escort her to school? As for me going to jail, bring it on, because I'll make sure it'll make the newspaper headlines!"

Ted came over with Scott who was working in a school for incorrigible girls. They said they'd take Joy to the girls' school. But I told them she was in my care and I wouldn't have it.

Then Joy had signs of being pregnant and I took her to the doctor who confirmed it. I'm sure everyone in the waiting room heard her sad wailing through the flimsy partition and I felt like wailing with her. When she calmed down, the doctor said, "It is my duty to say that Joy may lose her life if she has the baby. Her kidney condition is such that it's a risk, and at fourteen, her outh is all against a healthy birth. She should have an abortion."

The father of the would-be baby and I went with Joy to have the procedure done. It was a very unhappy time in our family's life.

Brenda gave birth to a boy named Jason. It was a life-threatening birth and it was a terrible trial for Brenda and the baby to go through because of her diabetes. She divorced and married Rex. Rex's mother went to live in Vancouver and Brenda and Rex joined them there. Brenda kept phoning to tell me what a wonderful place it was, with the mountains and the English-like weather. She told me she'd help move out if I wished. So I put the house up for sale but it didn't sell. Anyhow, I wanted Mark to complete his grade twelve, so I spruced up the place and figured I'd try again the following year.

Mark finished his grade twelve and I sold the house. I was ready to move to British Columbia.

It was necessary to get rid of all I could, because I only wanted a small amount to send by the movers. I had a garage sale and one of the items I put on a table was Ted's dress uniform. He'd looked so elegant in it but I had to be hard about getting rid of all non-essentials. To my surprise, Ted came over and saw it was for sale. He was very upset, but I had offered it to him and he hadn't wanted it. It was no time to be sentimental.

I had kept his letters to me from the war years. I'd kept them for thirty two years and they were historic really. I asked the children if they wanted them but none did, saying it would hurt to see what had been a loving relationship.

Ted had been coming over every Saturday to take the children downtown to dinner at a restaurant. He mostly included me but sometimes I was working at the gallery.

There was a young Ukrainian man who worked at the gallery too, and we'd often go out for dinner after work. On one of these occasions, the restaurant was very dark and I lighted a cigarette and drew in the tobacco before I realized that I had sucked through the wrong end of the cigarette! My chest burned and hurt so much and I couldn't get my breath. I thought I would die. I recovered somewhat and he drove me home but from that night on I never smoked another cigarette.

I had organized classes in Japanese woodcuts with artist Noboru Sawai who was living and working in Vancouver. He arrived carrying a bigger load than a donkey could handle. He had wood blocks and brushes and knives and Japanese paper. Twenty of us loved every second of our time, chipping and pasting our blocks.

Noboru came back for another session and told us that Calgary University was to subsidize a student trip to Japan to study under Noboru's former master, Toshi Yoshida, at Toshi's boarding school. If I could get ten more people for a three-week trip, who each had three thousand dollars, we could go with him.

Ted said he'd mind the children and Laura, who was twenty-one, could help out as she was at home waiting for her wedding day. I went to the bank and borrowed three thousand dollars and signed up.

There was funny incident while we were going through customs in Japan. they asked what we were going to do and we said, "woodcuts." The customs men keeled over laughing and they told others and they laughed till they had tears in their eyes. Noboru discovered they had thought, "you little old ladies were going to cut down trees!"

Toshi's boarding school was set up so people from other countries could stay there while learning about Japan's art and culture. We had screen painters and potters and kendo sword fighters who put on two shows while we were there. They had a famous pianist – whose name I forget – and the even more-famous synthesizer musician Kitaro who is well known in Canada for his *Silk Road* and *Caravansaray* CDs.

Kitaro was practicing in the gym and I just about swooned with his music. He told me that my prints had the same spirit — the same spirituality — as his music. On our last night I was still chipping away on one of my wood blocks when it was time for the farewell party. I didn't go because I had to finish my print. Kitaro led the other artists down the corridor playing a guitar, came to my work room, hopped up on my work table and played his music as one dedicated artist to another.

It was absolute heaven, and I learned so much and worked hard to make up for leaving my children. I had joined a co-op gallery in Winnipeg and when we returned home we had a show of the prints we'd made in Japan. The show was a knockout. And I made over three thousand dollars in sales so I was able to proudly return my loan.

Janet became Ted's wife.

All my children were at their wedding while I spent a lonely and sad day at home, remembering all the times Ted and I had shared. I also felt sad that none of my English family was nearby to comfort me.

10:

A new life on the West Coast

I sent boxes of items ahead and Brenda stored them until we arrived. I destroyed as many paintings and prints as I could bear, and of course the furniture was given away. It was to be as clean a cut as necessary because we didn't have an address to go to and moving vans were expensive.

My friends gave me farewell parties and I thought I'd tied up all the loose ends. Only Joy and Paul were to come with me but that was their choice. Joy was then fourteen and Paul was thirteen. I expected we'd be telling the rest of the family how good everything was on the coast and they would want to move out later.

I checked in with the doctor for the last time. He took some tests and I told him goodbye.

Then Barbara and Laura got word from the doctor that I was to stop everything and get to the hospital because my blood sugar reading was going through the roof. But I refused and was given some metformin — an anti-diabetic medication — to tide me over till I got to BC.

We registered at a hotel for a night and word came through from the real estate agent that I had to sign a form saying I didn't have any banned insulation in the house I had recently sold. I signed the form: What else could I do?

The new owners had already moved in and I had our tickets to fly the next day.

That last night in Winnipeg, Barbara treated us to a wonderful dinner.

But Joy and Paul were getting nervous and I spent the night on the bathroom floor hanging on to the toilet where I couldn't stop vomiting.

YIKES! It must have been either something I ate or just nerves — or perhaps my blood-sugar problems.

But we made the flight all right and Brenda was waiting in Vancouver for us. By the time we arrived, I felt awful, but, thank goodness, she knew about diabetes and how to monitor me. Regardless, the scenery was stunning and the flowers everywhere made me think I was in England again.

I had a good friend, Yvonne, from Winnipeg who had moved to Nanaimo, on Vancouver Island. She had said she would pay me to live with her for a while and teach her Nanaimo group about art. She said they were "stuck" and needed a new spurt.

At first we lived in Mission with Brenda and Rex. I had bid on a house there but I didn't get it. And then, out of the blue, Yvonne phoned me from Nanaimo and said, "Come now. Don't buy anything in Mission until you see Nanaimo!" So Joy, Paul, and I took off on the ferry to Vancouver Island.

I loved the modern design of Nanaimo's Malaspina College (that was before it became a universtiy) which looked over the Strait of Georgia. Yvonne said she would drive me to classes there if I wanted to enrol in any — and she said she'd even go with me. She took me around to see houses for sale and I fell in love with the cutest little house in the world. It was tiny, but it seemed perfect. Mortgages were high at seventeen and three quarters per cent and there was much to be done to bring the house to order but I was hooked and bought it.

Brenda was not pleased that I had made the decision so quickly and that we wouldn't be close to them. Nevertheless I will always be grateful for how she helped us come to BC because I don't think I could have done it without her help

When Ted heard I was leaving Manitoba he said, "And what am I supposed to do?"

I just said I was going to where I could have a better climate than Winnipeg's. And I told him it wasn't me who broke up the family.

Friends had warned me he might not send alimony if I was in another province, but I said I knew he was basically a good man and would not let us down that way. And he didn't.

Rex and Brenda helped us get to the Island and when they left, a storm blew wind right through the walls. Insulation was the first thing to get done. Then basement cobwebs had to be swept away — the older lady who had owned the house before had never been down there.

There was what looked like a small garage door into the basement which I swapped for glass patio doors to let lots of light into what became my painting studio. Hooray!

Paul and Joy went to their new schools but Joy, forever the rebel, acted up and was told to leave.

We had bought her a cat named Buttons, which became a rebel like her. Joy discovered she was allergic, so the cat became mine (thank you very much!), giving me a harder time than all of my ten children. He would play hockey with the bath soap in the bathroom at early hours of the morning and he got his head caught in the door of the fridge as I closed it and nearly died, I did too when I got the vet's bill. When he got outside he would take leaping charges at my next door neighbour when she tried to put up clothes on her washing line and when the kids were playing horseshoes in the back yard, he would leap up to try and catch the horse shoe. Naturally, one hit him on the head and knocked him out. It was a competition to see if I could get in the bedroom at night without him squeezing in between my feet and then hiding under the bed where no amount of coaxing would get him out. Then at three in the morning he'd meow and wouldn't stop till I got out of bed and let him go to play and do damage outside.

It reminded me of when Scott brought home a husky dog that was still part wild. It was fine when Scott was with him but when he left, I had to tug it to go outside in the yard and he would snarl at me. Young Ted teased him and I didn't blame the dog, but it bit Ted. After that – and because I was scared of it — I said that was enough. I took him, with all the children in the car weeping and accusing me, to the SPCA.

Joy returned to Winnipeg, got pregnant there, then came back home to attend college and become a care aid. I took care of the baby for the first six months. Her name was Camellia. Joy passed the course, which qualified her for a job to care for seniors. Hooray again.

I taught the Nanaimo art group and made some wonderful friends. I tried my hand at pottery. I won first prize in art when there was a competition for ALL of British Columbia's artists.

We started *Art 10 Gallery* in a mall because there wasn't any gallery downtown. Wonders! It's still going as I write this today, twenty eight years later. I took courses on sculpture, lithography and drawing. We had ten artists in an advanced art group at the college. We put on a tremendous show in the nearby town of Duncan, using a "four foot by four foot" format where each painting was that size. I fixed two boards together to make an eight foot by four foot canvas to work on.

We found it incredible that so many people poured in to see our show which we titled *Four by Four*. But then we found out that there was a church called Four by Four, and everyone that belonged to that church thought our show was connected to it!

I took lessons on the potter's wheel but it was a flop for me, so I tried hand building clay, which I found more satisfying. Nanaimo Arts Council gave me an award for my contribution to the arts of Nanaimo.

It was a happy time for me, except for trying to meet my mortgage payments on the house. When I tried to get a credit card, everyone, including Simpson Sears, refused me. They said they didn't know if my former husband would continue paying my alimony. Finally, the Bank of Montreal relented and I was able to manage okay.

Someone had once accused me of running from success: Whenever I became known and admired in a community, I moved to somewhere else. And then, as if to prove them right, my youngest son Paul left home and I got the itch to move again. I felt that everything of any importance was happening on the Lower Mainland. Brenda was then living in Abbotsford and I landed up in the nearby town of Clearbrook.

And I came to be a writer.

Once when Brenda visited me on the Island, I told her that I wanted to write but didn't know how to go about it. The only background I'd had was writing all those letters home when I first came to Canada and then I remembered the sisters in the convent liked my essays so much they kept some. Brenda suggested I do what one author she had heard about did — make a typewritten copy of all her letters. In the end, mine added up to a story. Barbara said she would rent an electric typewriter for me every month.

So I started by writing about my life since I came to Canada.

An art tour to remember

I had to pack for the move to the mainland. Brenda's mother-in-law had just bought my dear Nanaimo home when I received a letter from Wilda, asking me if I'd go with her to Europe for three weeks. Her father had died and left her money. She wanted to use the money in a way that would be memorable. She had been to Europe before, but wanted to see the places where artists had painted.

At first I thought no, I couldn't manage it, what with my move to BC's Lower Mainland coming up. But Wilda said she'd already bought the tickets and had everything planned. She would pay for everything. And she asked was there something specific I wanted to see?

So I said okay and yes, I'd like to see what Matisse considered his masterpiece, the chapel he designed in Vence, a small town high up in the mountains west of Nice, in the south of France. Matisse was considered a modern painter who often used a female model but used a decorative way of combining her with the background. His work went further and was more creative than the impressionists. And he was considered to be a master who showed a new path in painting

He had been ill and the nuns of Vence nursed him back to health. He asked them what he could do to repay their kindness. They asked him to design them a small chapel. Not only the chapel but the stations of the cross and the priest's robes.

We managed to find the site but an iron gate stopped us from entering until the nuns decided to open it.

Talk about stripping everything down to its most simple form! The chapel's walls were white, the floor tiles were white and black. The stations of the cross were just outlines of black iron. The altar cloth was all white. One whole wall had magnificent leaded glass panels of brilliant red, green and blue. The sun outside was not too bright but the colours streamed across all that was white inside, making us suck in our breath with wonder.

The thing that made it great was that each sector taken individually was not ornamental but the colossal colours of the window brought everything to life. We stayed there a while and felt the holiness of it and we were there long enough, sitting on the simple chairs, that my insides KNEW that was what I wanted to aim for in my work. I mean the simplicity .

We visited all the museums connected to the famous artists, like Van Gogh and Cezanne. But once again Matisse triumphed because his designs were there for the priest's robes and were shown either on paper or on the robes themselves. I got the biggest thrill when the plant he used as a design motif in a lot of his work was sitting right there. He never stopped working even when he was too ill to stand. He had a long pole which was affixed with a paint brush. The assistant put this into a pot of paint and Matisse would outline a pattern on large canvases hung onto the wall.

Later he found even this tiring so the assistant coloured pieces of paper so he could sit in bed cutting out his arabesques and leaves with scissors. He then told the assistant how to combine them to make a painting. He called them cutouts. Today in Paris these cutout designs are copied and sold, fitting in with today's art. His designs became so well known that Americans ordered some large original pieces to grace their homes.

When we first arrived in our small hotel in Munich, in sourthern Germany, the manager freaked out about us having so much luggage. Wilda had brought peanut butter and jam and breakfast cereal and I was so keen to teach Wilda about painting that I'd brought a whole stack of books on art! I had taken some classes on watercolours before we left and I got Wilda interested in the medium and we both enjoyed the companionship of painting the oodles of castles and chateaux in those countries.

However, when we got to Switzerland, I packaged up all the art books and and sent them home.

We walked and walked and walked and at one point my back gave way and we had to take a taxi.

I thought the art museum in Zurich was one of the best.

In Paris, the Museum of Modern Art was showing Montreal artists Jean-Paul Riopelle and Paul-Emile Borduas.

In Monaco, I gambled five dollars just to say I did, and we loved the famous sculptures all around the ocean-front promenade. I think they must have a rule that all buildings must give a percentage of their cost for an art piece on the site. I wish it was a Canadian practice too.

We stayed in a small town near Lyons, but we didn't seem at all welcome. Whenever we walked on the street, many residents would draw their curtains across the windows and take their children indoors. It wasn't a nice feeling to be treated like that, but Wilda had rented a car and we were away most days. It turned out the townsfolk were jealous of our landlady, not fearful of us. She owned the chateau we had rented and also owned the house where she lived. She had us over for a real French meal and told us the townsfolks' reaction was nothing to do with us. She explained she was in their bad books for several reasons, one being the fact she was Catholic but had divorced her husband — a no-no in their eyes. They also complained about her owning two residences, while they themselves had to rent their homes and had to struggle to meet their rent payments. I'm sure another reason was the fact our landlady had a great figure and long wavy hair that the townspeople would have considered not right for a married woman.

Well, regardless, I sat on the side of a hill in the town to paint a lovely scene of an old-fashioned doorway with pots of geraniums outside and creeping honeysuckle climbing the wall. A truck drove up and parked outside of the doorway, seemingly to spoil my view and prevent me from finishing my painting. The driver came across to me in a threatening way and, what I understood him to say was, "Get out of here." I showed him my small watercolour and in my hesitating French told him I admired this scene very much. He took one look at the painting and was shocked yet pleased at the same time. He went to move his truck, went in the house and came out with a woman I assumed was his sister. She spoke English.

"May I see what you have done," she said and, after chatting with her brother, asked if she could buy it, and how much was it?

"You can have it as a gift," I said, thinking I'd take a photo of it the next day and work on it at home.

"You are very kind," she said. "I see you have a little more to do, but my mother will love it."

She disappeared into the house and reappeared with an old lady in black who had to be at least ninety years old. She opened the shuttered windows, moved the pots of gerainiams and took away the brooms and spades that had been leaning against the brick wall, all of which had made my tableau so interesting! I just remembered how it was and gave her the painting. She chattered away in French so fast I couldn't understand a word. But I did much smiling and nodding.

I had to return down the street where the townsfolk had previously shuttered their windows. Now curtains were left open. The children were allowed to stay out in the street, and I talked to them in my strangled French, making them curl up with laughter.

Another day, I sat on the roadside, wanting to paint another house that looked elegant but neglected.

Someone from one of the nearby houses brought me a chair and a cup of tea with much smiling. Then a gardener came over and started telling how the house belonged to the village squire — at least the French equivalent of an English squire.

He said it was the squire's job to look after the town and the people, making sure everyone's welfare was secure, and the village kept functioning for everyone's benefit. However, his wife had died and the squire had lost all interest in his duties and no longer cared about them. Since caring for the town's fok was a centuries-old tradition, it was a terrible thing for them to bear. He smiled when I told him how my little watercolour had made a small difference to the old lady up the road.

I finished my sketch and could hardly wait to tell Wilda about the turnaround with the people who had been so rude before. It was our last night there and in the twilight we walked to the bridges covering the many small canals near an old church.

"Wilda, this place feels like home to me. Look how great the scenery is wherever you look. I could paint non-stop here." I said.

We leaned over the side of one of the bridges and as we watched, thousands upon hundreds of thousands of rats came out from the side banks and crept towards the church and the houses nearby.

It showed us there isn't a perfect place in the whole world and the place at that moment looked ready for the Pied Piper to come around the corner and I think even he could not have charmed that many rats.

However it had been a wonderful trip with my wonderful friend Wilda — another one of my angels who look out for me.

Back in BC, when I had moved to the small town of Clearbrook, Brenda asked me to join her writer's group, so every week I would write a couple of pages on my life. We would read aloud what we had been writing the previous week and I could tell the others were interested in my pieces. And, compared to their writing, it wasn't too bad.

I joined the graphic arts group in Abbotsford and quickly made friends again. Ruth, my new friend, drove me to meetings and shows.

The only trouble in Clearbrook was my apartment block. It was a nice-enough complex, but my one-bedroom unit was on the main floor,making it impossible to escape the frivolities of life: There were the goings-on in the bedroom above me, and I was sure the husband was beating his wife and throwing her against the wall next to me. The only person who was talking to me turned out to be a thief who held up a drugstore with a sawed off shotgun, and every Friday night I could hear outside noises of clanking beer bottles and fights.

But the owner was a great person and seemed really proud of me as a tenant. He wanted to promote my paintings and hung several down the ground-floor hallway. Then lit two enormous gas torches by the front door and stood outside trying to attract people into the show. He couldn't believe they weren't all sold out!

Once, his wife — a darling of a woman — drove me out to the country where they owned a ranch. On the way, she told me about an accident when she was driving in winter and flipped her car into a ditch. She hung upside down in the seat belt for six hours before someone rescued her. I prayed it wouldn't happen again while I was in the car with her.

Just down the end of my street, I could catch the express bus into Vancouver and be there in fifty five minutes. I loved doing this and could visit Joy who lived there. She was married to Dan and had a new baby, Cody.

Her daughter Camellia and I had a bond. On one visit I took her for a walk and I was surprised to hear her telling me the names of bushes and trees as we came across them. We got to a camellia bush and she was excited that she had been named after the lovely flower that blooms in early spring in British Columbia.

Brenda moved back to Mission, across the Fraser River from Clearbrook. And when I went to visit her new place I saw a banner across the main street advertising an art show. I said, "Hey, this place must be involved in the arts," and decided then and there to find an apartment in Mission.

At first I had trouble finding a decent looking place to rent. I put a down payment and first month's rent at one place but then discovered it was loaded with Hells Angels. Needless to say, I never moved into that place and I never did get my money back. I eventually put another down payment on an apartment that looked promising.

It seemed excellent. Except instead of upstairs frolicking and beating of wives and sawed-off shotguns, there was a TV downstairs, blaring away from sunrise to sunset. It belonged to a lonely lady who was completely deaf and wouldn't admit it. I had to go down and complain. She also put out food in an aluminum plate for racoons. They got to her apartment by passing over my balcony and they'd move this ruddy plate around on the concrete enough to wake me every night. Pretty soon the racoons had babies and they'd go in marching order across my balcony ledge as if they were being featured on a TV nature show. Complaining didn't work and I was just about to give up apartment living entirely. But then an apartment on the south side of the same complex came up for sale. It looked out on Mount Baker instead of a forest of blackberry bushes, there was no one underneath that apartment, and only a gentle lady above it who was already a friend.

When I sold my Nanaimo house, I ended up with only five thousand dollars to spare. I had put this into what I thought was a secure bank plan. But when I went to withdraw my savings to use as a down payment on the new acquisition, I was told, "You can't have the full amount because twenty percent goes to the government for income tax." I was flummoxed but someone suggested I get a loan for the rest.

The loan lady was Shirley. She sat unfrazzled and put me at ease with a smile and she actually believed that Ted would continue giving me alimony.

And so it was that I bought the apartment on the south side of the building and it was good. No sounds from other people, no racoons, no rattling beer bottles. I sat near the patio window on the day I moved in — when the most vicious storm of the year was raging — and I said a prayer of thanks. The rooms were large and there were plenty of cupboards to store everything and most important, I felt at home.

I went to a meeting called to discuss who would be on the strata committee and found they needed someone to fill in as secretary while the current secretary was away.

"I could do that," I said.

I was reminded I was not the REAL secretary and I was told not to put that in the minutes, and so I didn't.

Willy comes into my life (1989)

There was a bit of a ruckus because no one wanted to be president of the strata. Eventually, one lady offered to fill the position but she was told in no uncertain terms that it would have to be a man!

Well, I saw a shy-looking fellow in the corner who hadn't said a word, so I pointed at him and said, "What about him?"

Someone else said, "Would you take it on Willy?" and he said "Yes."

I had set up my painting area in the bedroom, which was large, but there wasn't enough light. I was so glad to be quiet and thought I'd get something done about the lighting later. Not having a car made it difficult to get around town but I bought a walker, like older folk had, that had a basket attached to the front. That allowed me to cart books from the library or carry my groceries

208

home. It was easy to walk down to the town or to Brenda's house. It also helped my back which was giving me a lot of pain. There was no way I could think of a car because I didn't have money to spare. I had returned some of the alimony to Ted when the children were no longer with me and, on my sixty-fifth birthday, I started receiving my old age pension so I accepted even less from him. Ted had told me, "Whether you like it or not, you are attached to me for your money for the rest of your life."

I wanted to see if I could do something so I wouldn't be attached — maybe win the lottery? But no, I didn't believe you got anything without working for it.

Willy had asked to see the layout of my apartment to compare it with his. He saw my paintings on the walls and asked if he could buy one. I took out some of my best ones and started to show him.

"Don't worry about all those," he said, "I'll take that one from the wall."

It was a good painting of Azaleas, pinks and mauves and strong for a watercolour.

I told him it was two hundred dollars and he didn't flinch while he took out a wad of notes and counted off ten, twenty-dollar bills. I was surprised because I had thought he was poor.

I gradually got to know him and found him strange. He never turned on his fridge and hardly ever used his truck, preferring instead to cycle everywhere. However, his Nissan truck was new and he did use it to go across the river to his dentist, even taking me with him once because my dentist had just moved there as well.

Later, he asked me to go for a drive. And then to dinner.

Along the way, he'd slip notes under my door, trying to get me to agree to have a solo show of my work in New Westminster's library. I told him I couldn't participate in art shows any more because I didn't have transportation. He said he'd be happy to take me. I said, "Okay," and I had a show in New Westminster with him doing all the carrying and packing.

One day in December, I paid for his lunch at the local Greek restaurant because he had done so much for me. Very quietly, he told me it was his sixty ninth birthday. He was three and a half years older than I was.

He was always available to help me in any way, particularly when it involved driving. I got used to him as you might get used to having a sibling. The children teased me about him but I said, "Don't be ridiculous, he's just a good friend."

Then all of a sudden he wasn't there anymore. His truck was gone from the parking area and the phone wasn't being picked up. After four days I couldn't stand it any longer and woke one night tossing and turning and wondering why I was so upset. I realized not only was I lonely without him, but heavens to Betsy, I loved him.

The next morning I put a note under his door inviting him to my apartment for dinner.

He phoned shortly after.

"I got your invitation. And the answer is yes! Yes! Yes!"

I was nervous getting the dinner ready but it all turned out fine. He had been away visiting a friend and had just come back that morning.

After dinner he wanted to walk down to the library so I went with him. On the way home the winds chilled us through. I had some left-over Christmas brandy so I invited him for a drink.

"I've missed you these past few days," I told him.

He smiled.

"Coming from such a lovely woman, that is a nice thing to hear," he said, "I thought it would take another few months to break the ice."

I stumbled on. "I care for you but I want you to know that there's a whole iceberg in here," I said, pointing to myself. "I'm not interested in having a sexual relationship."

Like a torrent of rain, his words poured forth:

"I'm going to tell you that I love you . . . I'm going to get you ringed-up . . . I'll buy you a gold necklace . . . And I'll buy you a stereo for your music . . . And I'm going to pay off your mortgage."

Then, with barely a puase he said, "Give me another glass of that brandy."

The colour in his face was blooming, but his voice was steady.

"Don't think I'm saying this because of the liquor; I always know what I'm saying and doing."

We both laughed, but in the back of my mind I'm allowing doubts to crowd in. What about those men who take older women for a ride, wooing them with romantic love and then wiping their bank accounts clean and taking off?

Only trouble was, I didn't have a cent in my bank account.

I looked across at this man who was grinning from ear to ear, his face becoming a maze of laugh lines and I decided it was worth a risk to let him do exactly what he said he'd do.

He came to sit next to me and God, it felt good to rest my face against his shoulder. I looked up and slowly, tentatively, he kissed me. His eyes were the colour of brown beer bottles.

Next day he took me shopping for a lovely stereo and I walked around holding two dozen peach-coloured roses and a card that said, "It's your day."

Back at my apartment, we lay down on the bed, "just to hold each other," he said.

The radio was on and the CBC announcer said, "We interrupt this program to tell you a most strange thing has happened in the town of Mission, BC. The Fraser River has flooded and scientists can't explain how a large iceberg has melted in that spot."

A visit to Australia (January 1990)

My brother John paid for me to go to visit him in Australia. I had just started to sleep with Willy, but he was quite happy for me to go.

John took me to the hills to take photographs of the wild flowers that bloom in abundance during their Spring. He took me to see the last whaling station which had been preserved as a museum. He had been on a whaling trip and was able to explain everything to me. I was fascinated by the wonderful patterns of rust on the old metal buildings and the harpoons and ropes on the deck of an old whaling ship moored at the dock. I took some wonderful photographs of everything. They had a skeleton of the largest whale and no one would believe the scale of the thing unless you could stand beside it.

He showed me paper-bark paintings and there was a society of Australian paper-bark painters.

John's wife, Coral — the daughter of the farmer he went to work for and who I loved dearly — took me for a walk in the meadow (watching out for snakes) and gathered a bouquet of Australian wild flowers for me, then took me to see a paper-bark tree. The bark came off the trunk easily and consisted of twenty or so layers of fine, different-hued bark.

As they had a cottage attached to their house, they allowed me to make a mess and make paper-bark paintings, which I sold when I came home.

I met my father's daughter by his second marriage and she told me anecdotes from my father's life.

She was the one who had owned the doll that I broke so many years ago. My father's second wife died and he married a third. He found her by visiting the woman's ward of the local hospital! She was a concert pianist and gave him some really happy years and spoilt him rotten.

John took me on a trip on a sailboat. The wind was gentle at first but then turned into a raging blast. I spent the time clinging on for dear life. At one point I slipped and the sea came up to meet me. John saved me by grabbing my coat. John told me not to worry because the sharks were quite tame if I fell over!

We all went to the seashore and had a picnic on the so-white sand and later, I met my niece and nephews.

I told John I wanted to visit our father's grave. He didn't usually go — he didn't like cemeteries — and besides, he was still angry with my father and he never felt close to him. Nevertheless Coral and I put the flowers which she had cut on the grave and John and I cried and cried. I was glad Dad was on that lovely hill overlooking the water.

We went up an extraordinarily high hill where we could see where Captain Vancouver had sailed into port. John had rented a movie camera and tried to voice a narrative while he was filming. He then drove around town leaning out the window, continuing his narrative and swaying the camera around to take pictures of houses without holding on to the steering wheel. I sat a prisoner in my seat thinking I would never get out alive! When we later played the movie, all we heard was the crying and moaning of the wind.

At the end of my visit, John and his wife drove me half-way to my brother Stanley's place in Perth and Stanley drove down to meet us.

One day, Stanley and I went for a walk along a stream and he told me he lived in dread that maybe he had brought his wife to a place that didn't suit her. He owned a parcel of land and they had lived in a shack until they could finish building their real house.

His wife had a terrible fear of snakes. One day he returned from town and opened the door to see her frozen stiff with her hands on the baby carriage handle inside the shack with thousands of migrating snakes coming through a crack in one wall and slithering over her feet to get to the other side in their race to get to a nesting area. It was a good job she didn't move and it probably saved her because they were very poisonous snakes.

But as in all our lives, we manage to go on and now they are both in a retirement home and enjoying it.

I started to write about how Willy and I managed to live together when everything about us was opposite. He'd never been married and I had ten children. He was frugal and I couldn't give a hoot about money. Ah! But he was very witty and made me laugh and laugh. He was a smart man, had good taste in clothes — although he refused to buy any new ones — and he could work as no one else worked, never stopping once he started, even when someone would try to claim his attention.

About this time, Willy gave me money to go to England to visit my sister Peggy and to have a grand dinner out together. It happened to be Peggy's anniversary and she wanted to go to a cheap place and invite the whole village with the money but I said, "No, Willy wanted it to be special."

We had a glorious dinner in a tudor restaurant in Stratford on Avon and how happy I am that we did because she died not long afterwards. She had lung cancer, no doubt from her smoking. I would have gone back to see her and actually put aside the money but she begged Denys not to let me come because she had deteriorated so badly and she wanted me to remember her as she was when we had so much fun at that dinner.

She died when she was seventy one and my brother Gordon, who I loved, also died young of a heart attack. Stanley lives near Perth in Australia and is fragile. John, my youngest brother, had by-pass surgery and continues to live as if he's fifteen years old. He lives in Albany, Western Australia, and has come to visit us here. He also, unbelievably, tracked down the house where my mother had lived in Germany. The house had an attached workshop where my German grandfather made shoes. The names of the family are in the church records but John couldn't find anything more about my mother's brother. Perhaps he died in WWII.

Publishing my first books

My Willy stories were well received and so I self-published a collection of them and called it *The Willy Stories*. I sold two hundred copies right away, printed another hundred and sold those.

After that, Mary Dixon of *Portage and Main Press* in Winnipeg published the book professionally but changed the title to *Willy & Me*. She also took it on herself to publish *The Life Series,* a book about my paintings which included thirty-two, full-colour reproductions of works depicting some of my more memorable life's experiences.

I would be remiss if I didn't tell how *The Life Series* came about.

I had become restless with the limitations of watercolour painting. A friend and I went down to Whitby Island, an island just north of Seattle, to take a course on acrylics. What I hadn't realized was that the course was not only on acrylics but also an introduction to "unconscious" painting.

Using the full sheets of paper, we were to flood light washes of shapes on the paper. We had to close our brains and not enquire of these washes what they were going to add up to. We added another layer of shapes, and then another layer: Transparent washes over others, making different textures and colours. Along the way, after being patient, some subject showed itself and that is what was to be your painting. You could erase some and define others until you had a semi-abstract thing going on.

The first one that appeared as if by itself was a bride with her legs apart with the Virgin Mary at the side and the husband leaving the scene. One has to go along with what appears, otherwise the Muse will not stay with you.

Driving home at the end of the course, I told my friend, "I will lose all my customers if I continue with this and yet I feel a strong pull to do it."

When I arrived home I got a phone call from a couple from Germany who were here on holiday. They asked to see what I had done at the course and bought three of the works — including the bride. The husband pointed to the legs-apart bride and said he'd like something to cover that area.

But his wife said, "No way."

I had to be brave and follow this way of working because it had a powerful pull on me.

I had a show already booked for Richmond gallery in three months time and I wanted to show this unusual work but could not include my older work with it — it just didn't fit.

So I worked like a mad woman against that deadline to create enough work for the Richmond show. I'd finish one piece, put it under my bed, take up another sheet of paper, paint furiously until it felt finished, put it under my bed, and start yet again. I didn't stop to examine the paintings, or think about what I had made until I had completed twenty.

Some time later, I fished the work from under the bed and placed them on the floor around me. As I knelt on the floor and looked at each one, tears came to my eyes: These were all images from my past; they were all major episodes of my life!

My painting had gone in an entirely new direction. And despite my fears, the Richmond show generated a great response from everyone who saw it.

Art teachers were even bringing their students in to see the strong, colourful and different work.

I felt a need to add words for each painting and realized that, together, they would make an even more powerful statement. I took a photograph of each and put it in a binder. I wrote a small piece of prose to go opposite each one and these I put in the binder as well. I went through my older work and found some pieces which would fit in with the story of my life and included those. I wrote myself notes saying, "The Life Series," and, "WILL BE SHOWN," and pinned them around my studio walls.

Afterwards, Mary Dixon from Winnipeg — whom I knew because she had bought my work in the past — came for a visit to Vancouver and asked if she could come out to see what I had been doing.

She was affected by these powerful images and asked to show my binder to her publishing firm. She did me proud by publishing a lovely, full-colour publication, *The Life Series*.

Mary framed and crated works that were featured in the "Life Series" and put them in a show with my prose and that show traveled for a year throughout BC, Manitoba and Alberta. It was my top achievement to have all this happen.

As I now had two books published by a publisher, I had to admit I was a writer. I attended most of the openings and in all the years that I have gone to shows I've never seen the kind of emotional reaction as at these openings. People were unable to talk as they were choked with emotion. They would react to paintings which reminded them of their lives. Men as well as women cried with me.

I wanted to save their tears so if I wasn't sure that my paintings were meaningful, I could look at the tears and know that my art mattered. Our glassblower in Mission, John Phillips, blew me some glass tears. I made a small clay shrine and they stand in a glass bottle, shaped like the figure of a woman. It stands always on the window ledge of my studio and is a testament to my inner spirit.

That was in 1996, but the book remains relevant today and women especially are moved by it.

When the show traveled, most of the paintings were sold. They will stand the test of time.

Mary has retired from her business now but told me publishing my book was a labour of love — she knew women, especially, should know about it.

Mission's Fine Arts Five

In Mission, I asked four of the best local artists to join me and we formed *Fine arts five*. Every other year we rented a big hall, rented boards to hold our work, rented lighting and a musician, and invited two other artists to join us. We put on a New-York-style show. People of Mission responded in droves to our three-day shows. They had never encountered anything like it in Mission and someone told me I had raised the culture of Mission.

The *Fine Arts Five* worked well for me because I was told I was too professional for the Mission Artists Association shows and I had nowhere else to show my work.

As a group, we always had to have new work and we met once a month to pay dues and discuss art. We each sold enough to pay for the following year's show.

Unfortunately, our group ended when our large venue quadrupled the rent and introduced new rules about insurance. One of our members left Mission and another was in bad health.

Now Mission has an art centre in a hertitage house at the east end of town, thanks to the hard work of three brave women who took a chance to make an art centre work – and it has been successful. My work has been shown in solo shows every other year in that intimate space.

But when it comes to solo art shows I am finding it too big a responsibility, carrying, framing, advertizing and having an opening. It is all getting too onerous for me at eighty-seven. Yes, I have the help of friends for which I'm grateful, but I don't know the future and I must give that question full attention. Right now I've put aside my paints until I know the answer, mostly because Willy is so fragile and is currently living in a care home.

It is 2011 as I write this book. I'm nearly eighty-seven and Willy is ninety years old. We've been together for twenty-two years. I want it known that since we met, he has changed my life. He gave me a Tercel Toyota car and gave up his precious truck. From being the hero of most young people, biking so many miles every day, he had to face the time when the bicycle was no longer his transportation. He then walked and walked and walked and I went with him every afternoon. Because of that, he's given me extra years on my life.

Then his walking was different, he leaned into me for balance. It got worse until we are where we are now where his brain won't tell his legs what to do and his balance is extremely bad. So we went through about two years of getting him to use a walker and it's tough for a strong man to accept such a thing.

At the moment I drive, but apparently I'll have to have a test on my eighty-eighth birthday so that too will be a change in my life. When it happens that I can't drive I think I'd like to go into assisted living where they supply meals and cleaning. I really don't want to think about meals any more. When I had the children, I cooked lunch and dinner, both followed with a dessert.

Inside, I'm really still the girl who lived with servants or lived in an hotel with no need to get my hands dirty. And I feel that was the life I was made for. Housework has never rated high in my mind. I watched my mother boil clothes in a large boiler on the stove Yes, it was lovely to sleep in brilliant white sheets, smelling of the outdoors, but she had to lug them out of the boiler and into rinse water then carry them to hang on the washing line. And I remember her cooking up feed for the chickens and hobbling down to the end of the garden, holding this large pan, taking it to where the chicken coop was. I saw her tired out of polishing floors and doing the ironing.

I used to hear the wives in the forces bases talk over their morning coffee about nothing but how they cleaned the walls and the floors and my brain longed to talk about writers and countries and current issues but no, conversation always reverted to how to get out stains or how to shine silver with a new polish. Housework shrinks my brain. Now I have Kim to come to clean the apartment for me — thank you Kim.

I read a lot now, making up for lost time. I love a good book, right now I'm reading Isabel Allende's *Daughter of Fortune*. I enjoy East Indian writers; they have such a rich culture to draw from.

In May of this year I had my last solo show at Place des Arts in Coquitlam, BC. Someone brought a watercolour to show me what I had done years ago. I was shocked because the darn thing looked like Renoir had done it. I never thought I was any good with watercolour and here was a little gem. I wanted to show it in my last show but everything had to be for sale. The owner told me to put a high price on it and if it sold she'd buy one of my new ones (the prices of which have shot up). So that's what I did.

I have very, very few older works left. At the time, everyone loved them and they were angry when I veered away from that realistic work.

But I had to do what I had to do and my Muse smiles as she sits at my shoulder and believes that I know what I'm doing.

In 2002 I was elated when the Business and Professional Club of Abbotsford named me "Woman of the Year for Mission." And just recently, Mission held a talent competition for seniors, with competitors doing everything from singing to dancing: I read from my book *The Artist & the Bicycle Man*, a collection of stories about Willy. And what a surprise! I won!

I'm almost eighty seven and have just been awarded Golden Idol of Mission, 2011.

I think it's marvelous.

And so ends my story up to now.

11:

Guided by my Muse, helped by my angels

I have kept away from religion for many years now. But I believe in the spiritual. I know there's a spirit and if you're open to receive it, it will be with you on your journey.

I call it my Muse.

And I think my Muse has always looked out for me and brought to me many wonderful people that have helped me through my life: I like to call these people my angels.

I'm sure I'm missing some, but here are a few:

Margaret Hellings (nee Kirby)

My best freind from 1941 through 1946 when we lived in the Clarendon Hotel in Leamington Spa, Warwickshire, England.

She believed I would be famous one day. She was always at my side. She could up-stage me when we acted in the same play because she was a natural comic actor and the audiences loved her.

Wilda Scott

She has been my friend, supporter and cheering section to encourage me through the down times.

She drove me to my first art lessons and bought my early paintings. She paid for me to tour Europe with her, using her inheritance from her father. She said it was a way to remember her father. We visited the places where the great artists painted and the museums which held their work. She traveled from Toronto to Mission to see me on stage in Mission's fringe theatre. We communicate often and her loving letters mean a lot to me.

Yvonne Cory

She lived next door to me in Winnipeg, Manitoba. She joined the Winnipeg sketch club with me.

She moved to Nanaimo, Vancouver Island, and wrote me asking if I'd come to live with her and teach the local art group. When I divorced and moved to BC, she encouraged me to live there — which I did with her help.

She drove me to classes in Malaspina College (now Vancouver Island University) where I took sculpture, print-making and hand-built clay pieces.

We started the gallery called *Art 10* — the first art gallery in downtown Nanaimo — and it's still going today, twenty-eight years later. I chose nine members of the Nanaimo art group who were good painters and together we did very well.

She drove me up and down the island and everywhere else and we had lots of fun. However, she smoked a lot and died at an early age.

Gerd Bodin

She came from Norway. We were alike in our thinking, wanting to advance in our painting.

She also drove me to different events and places. Her house had a Norwegian flavour from the lace curtains and treasures she brought over from her family.

It was wonderful when we went out of town to dig in the ditch which had clay in it. As our shovels dug into the red clay, we pulled it up as it made a sucking sound. We fashioned bowls, birds or figures from it after the clay was mixed with sand, then fired them in her garden, using cedar boughs.

One day we went to find sand to mix with the clay and as we put our shovels in the bank of sand, a waterfall of gold came tumbling out! We scooped it up in high excitement, thinking it was the answer to our troubles and we would be millionaires. We went to Victoria to have it assessed and found it was "fools gold."

But I'll always remember that wonderful feeling when the "gold" came falling out and glistening in the sun!

Gerd was one of the members of *Art 10* and still is. I went back to celebrate the twenty-fifth year of the gallery.

I loved the nine other women who started it. Gerd is of the earth — solid and dependable. She promotes me and supports me still.

Robin Field

A wonderful art teacher at the college in Nanaimo who encouraged a small group of us to push beyond where we were in our painting.

We had a great show in Duncan to expose our work with a four-feet by four-feet format. Some put two boards together making eight feet by four feet panels. We surprised ourselves how we could leap ahead when we were brave enough to do it.

He pushed me to understand the difference between commercial and true art.

He told me to take my work down to the mall and write an explanation of how an artist strives to go beyond what she's used to doing. At the time I was aiming to be more contemporary. The ordinary people who populate malls came with tears in their eyes, thanking me for letting them realize what at artist goes through. They had thought an artist just sits down with some paint and has fun! And they thanked me for putting my work in a mall as they were nervous about going into "real" galleries.

I came home so satisfied with that event I felt I could spend my life doing it.

Robin was an important building block in my career. Thank you Robin.

Willy Smith

Such a strange name for a man from Denmark! I was sixty-five when I met him in Mission, BC, and this man completely changed my life.

I wrote books about how we managed to live together when we were exactly opposite to each other.

He was Mission's favourite character because he cycled all day and every day until he was eight-five.

We finally married in 2001 after living in sin twelve years. He gave me a car, giving up his beloved truck and gave me money to buy art supplies even though he thought you should only paint another painting after you had sold the one you had!

If you want to know of our love story, get the book *The artist & the bicycle man* from Trafford Publishing (www.trafford.com). My first book, *The Willy Stories* (or *Willy & Me,* depending on the version — my self-published version or Mary's version from Portage & Main Press in Winnipeg) is now out of print: It was the most-loved book in Mission.

Willy now has trouble with his balance and has been diagnosed with Parkinson's disease. He is living in an extended care facility in Mission. He is ninety years old.

Dorothy St.Hilaire

I admired Dorothy's water colours and we became friends.

Once again, she was someone who drove me everywhere because I couldn't drive Willy's manual-gear truck.

She too wanted to stretch her painting skills. We took a week's course in the States with Carole Barnes in unconscious acrylic painting. It was held on Whitby Island not far south of Mission where they have facilities for teaching courses in art. This course changed my work completely.

Dorothy loved nature and drove me to out-of-the-way mountain logging roads and up to the top of Mount Baker where we happily did on-site paintings. I became impatient with landscapes and wanted to create from nothing.

Dorothy left Mission, but while living here she was one of the members of our *Fine Arts Five* group. Dorothy and I were joined by Malonie Kasian, June Pender, and Ruth Adams Booth.

Mary Dixon

Mary arranged to publish both *Willy & Me* and *The Life Series* in Winnipeg. She not only included thirty-two of my paintings in that lovely book — all showing stages of my life — but she also framed and crated them and had them travel for a year in BC, Manitoba and Alberta.

She also bought many of my works and tirelessly promoted me.

Valerie Billingsberger

She keeps Mission's archives going and created "Pathfinders," a way of honouring four Mission women every year who are then named Pathfinders.

The archives are climate controlled and each cupboard or "fonz" has a collection of papers and letters from some of the local people. Much of my publicity and letters are there. Because of Valerie, our histroy is kept alive.

Marianne and Bert Panzer

We have been friends for twenty years and Marianne has a natural ability

222

to appreciate good art. They have been supporters in everything I do as well as being an important part of my life.

Valerie Hundert

She is someone who has an uncanny gift for convincing people that buying a painter's work is what helps them to continue to work with their art. Not only that, but she has been by my side selling my books for me and she works hard to have the general public understand what we're doing.

Valerie works for all manner of community groups and she loves politics. But for me, she is a staunch supporter.

Mady Pechler

How to explain the importance of Mady in my life?

She comes from Holland where the art scene appears to be a bit more up to date than in BC.

When she saw my work she asked to put the paintings in a computer database. Now that I've had my last solo show, she wants to keep all of my work as a "body of work of an artist," and try to interest an organization in keeping it intact.

To enable me to show in the Vancouver gallery of the Federation of Canadian Artists, she comes to photograph my work and sends it digitally to the juries and then arranges to send the original to Vancouver once it's chosen to hang.

For her to preserve my work is so precious to me. I don't know of artists who have had that blessing other than the famous ones. Thank you Mady.

Marilyn Davidson

This is a woman who believes everyone should have a good time.

She loves putting on parties, traveling all over the world with her husband and making people happy.

She was president of the arts council of Mission but most important, she makes dreams come true.

Mission has a professional theatre and I wanted to act my "life series" story on that stage. Marilyn arranged it, and Mady worked with her to make it happen. It was promoted as my "celebraton of life" and I didn't have to die first. The wonderful ladies that volunteer at Mission's art centre decorated and presented refreshments.

And the town's mayor got BC's *Province* newspaper to come to the lobby to photograph us together, even though all the paper wanted was to interview the mayor alone. But what a happy picture!

Afterwards, I gave an afternoon tea out in the art centre's garden to thank everyone, and when someone looked up at the sky, a white cloud had formed the shape of an angel hovering above us! Wonderful.

Barbara Fehrmam

This lady has come into my life and helped me through a tough spot in a way which you only read about in story books. She made me feel that no matter what happened, she would know how to deal with it. Such a kind but tough heart and a pleasure to know.

Adrian Harper

Oh Adrian: How you've enriched my life through making it possible for me to have many of my books. You've worked with me to make sure all my facts are correct and you've made many suggestions to improve the final works, particularly *You do it whichever way you can* and now my autobiography *Confessons of a war bride*. You've looked after all the details of putting a book together and checking, and checking again and then getting it into print — it was all on your shoulders and I could always be sure that I would have a lovely outcome in the end. You have meant so much to me.

12:

Where are my children now?

Barabara has her Phd. in three disciplines and is now married to Rev. George Feenstra, a United Church minister. She is dean of nursing in Kamloops, BC.

They have two children, Stephen who lives in Winnipeg and Karen who lives in Vancouver.

Brenda is married to Rex. She was an RN (Registered Nurse) and for a while the care director of Pleasantview in Mission. They are now both retired and living in Mission.

They have a son, Jason, who resides in Vancouver.

Scott is married to Michelle and they have five children. Scott worked for the Province of Manitoba but is now retired. I am not in touch with him at the moment.

Patrick trained in robotics and works as a trouble shooter for his company. He lives in Ile des Chenes near Winnipeg with his partner Pauline.

Patrick has two children, Melonie who lives in Vancouver, and Evan who also lives in Ile des Chenes.

Ted is marries to Debbie and they live in Winnipeg. He has grown up with printing presses since he was fourteen and was recently trained to work with the very latest printers. Debbie has one son.

Laura married Gregg. They moved into the house Gregg's father built on a lake in Rainy River, Ontario.

Laura is an inspirational teacher of English and drama. Gregg taught at an oboriginal school.

They have two children, Jonathon who is at Stanford University — acquiring his masters degree in art — and Sarah who works in Winnipeg.

Pearce married Nanetter in Lamont, near Chicago. He is a computer whiz and has his pilot's licence.

They have two children, Carlie and Alexie

Mark works on an estate in Syndey, BC. He loves cars and can refurbish any make of vehicle.

He is married to Lorna. They have become serious lovers of nature because they are surrounded by birds and animals of land and sea.

Joy lives in Maple Ridge, BC. She is an extraordinary trauma and emergency nurse.

She has a partner named Dario.

Joy has three children, Camillia, Cody and Chris.

Paul married Jackie and they have two children, Joshua and Ella.

Paul is manager of a sod farm in Victoria, BC. He is constantly inventing new ways of doing things.

Ted Paterson, all my children's father, died in Winnipeg in July this year (2011), mainly from acute lukemia.

I'm told I have twenty-six grandchildren, but because of various divorces and other reasons I'm not in touch with six of them.

All my children are inventive and creative in their thinking and want to make the world a better place.

I am proud of them all.

The Jacket

It's morning and I open the closet.
Your jacket hangs there amongst my dresses.
Warmth floods through me
as I lift the rough-woven sleeve to my breast.
Dear Willy,
it feels good to have part of you here.
How can it stir so many memories
when we've only known each other so short a time?
How can we share so many jokes?
Upstairs, downstairs.
Check mate.
How can you make me laugh so much?
How is it that someone like you really exists?
Did I dream you?
The Harris tweed is two tones of grey,
Harris tweed, my Mother's coat
that she wore for twenty years,
the name of sturdiness and longevity.
Are you like that Willy?
It seems as if it's true
but it doesn't matter if it isn't
for I have known
the excrutiating sweetness of you.
And I stroke the rugged jacket
and silently tell you I love you.

Doris Paterson, 1990

One Door Closes

My shoe caught on the curb
as I got out from the car door.
WOOMP!
The pavement flew up to my face.
I landed face down on the sidewalk.

I'd been on my way to deliver
forms to a store downtown.
Hurrying, because I had so much to do.
Hurrying because I was trying
to get on top of things.

Willy is now living in extended care.
I have his power of attorney
and I was paying bills and getting used
to being in charge of all
Willy used to deal with.

I lay wounded on that pavement in shock.
Not a soul in sight.
I was being doused with
hard pellets of rain and
I couldn't raise myself
from the undignified position
I was in.

A good Samaritan appeared
and carefully picked me up.
I leaned on him and struggled
to the store where
I had been headed for.

Staff circled around me horrifed
at the look of my bleeding face.
They made me lift my banged-up knee
to a low table and swabbed
my hurt hand, face and leg
with a warm, damp cloth.

There was a bump on my head
and they refused to listen to me
about not calling an ambulance.
So it was a visit to the emergency
and a call to my daughter.
She gave me a mirror so I could see
the mess that was my face.
The doctor figured there wasn't
a concussion and
my daughter drove me home.

The next day
Oh! My knee began to hurt
and hurt and hurt.
There was no relief from it.
I suffered for three weeks.
It wasn't broken but
became inflamed and I lay
on the chesterfield,
with it uncoverd
and fed myself Tylenol.

It was a time to think
about being almost eighty seven
and what part of the vortex
my life was in.
I feel I'm different now,
I'm humbled because of the fall
and aware
I'm on the losing end of living,
just thirteen years shy
of being one hundred years old!

Later:
I stood for two hours in a gallery
welcoming an audience
            to the opening

of my last solo painting show,
with my tortured knee
hidden under a long gown
as the scars were forming
skin like a corcodile's
and pulling with pain
because it's healing.

Now that big event is over.
It was a great way to end
years and years of solo shows.
But I feel like a balloon which
had been led with a guiding string
and now is cast adrift.

I'm recovered from the fall
but not recovered from
            the knowledge
that maybe my meaningful years
are done – finished.

Child-rearing is over and
painting seems to have
            shut its door on me.
Willy's in the care facility,
so our togetherness is over.

I wander from room to room
or nap on the chesterfield,
flipping the remote of the TV
in the hopeless hope that I'll catch
a program which doesn't include
trash or guns or murders.

I pick up yet another book to read
which has won a grand award
but it's not only trite
but not good writing.

Where do I belong
after my last solo show and
after that ruddy fall?
Is it like it was,
lying on that pavement
helpless and no use for anything?

But here I am – writing a poem.
Today I'll take a *Willy and Me* book
to give to the nurses who look after Willy.
I'll go with him on the bus
for residents of his facility
to a restaurant. So I guess
I have a role to fill there.

Tomorrow I'll buy some plants
to fill a container at the place
and Willy can fill in some time
looking after them.
So it's being of some help.

I've kept books which tell
how to write novels.
Well – who knows?
My autobiography is getting
put together in book form now
and I look up to see
            mounted on the studio wall,
the angel trophy which I won
            in a senior's talent contest
declaring I'm Mission's
            Golden Idol of 2011.

I'll keep doing whatever
my Muse calls on me to do and
I'll try to catch the string
of another balloon!

Doris Paterson, 2011

230

Other books by the author:

The Willy stories, 1992 (*out of print*)

Willy & Me, 1996 (*out of print*)

The Life Series, 1996 (*out of print*)

Willy & Me 2, 1998 (*out of print*)

You do it whichever way you can, 1999 (*out of print*)

Stories of the Red Rock People, 2000 (*out of print*)

A painter's journey, 2001 (*out of print*)

Willy & Me 3, 2002 (*out of print*)

Mission Arts Council Cookbook, 2003 (*out of print*)

The artist & the bicycle man, 2008 (*available from Trafford Publishing*)*

Confessions of a war bride, 2011 (*available from Trafford Publishing*)*

* www.trafford.com